AMSCO®

ADVANCED PLACEMENT

Macroeconomics

MW00657496

PERFECTION LEARNING®

© 2021 Perfection Learning®

Please visit our websites at:
www.perfectionlearning.com

When ordering the student book, please specify:
ISBN: 978-1-5311-5030-3 or **T053601**
ebook ISBN: 978-1-5311-5031-0 or **T0536D**

2 3 4 5 6 7   DR   26 25 24 23 22 21

Printed in the United States of America

Senior Consultant

Tracy Lowd has taught AP® Macroeconomics at Southwest Miami High School in Miami, Florida, for 12 years. She holds a Bachelor of Science degree in Secondary Social Studies Education from Florida International University and a Master of Education degree in Curriculum and Instruction with a focus on Secondary Literacy from American College of Education. She has been an active member of the Miami-Dade Council for the Social Studies and has participated in the Advanced Placement Mentorship Program in her district. In 2016, she was nominated for her school's Teacher of the Year award.

Reviewers

Woody Hughes, AP® Microeconomics Operational Question Leader, Retired
  Converse College | Spartanburg, South Carolina

Liz Plautz, AP® Macroeconomics Exam Table Leader
  Hun School of Princeton | Princeton, New Jersey

Contents

Introduction

Studying Advanced Placement® Macroeconomics

Welcome to the study of macroeconomics. In this course, you will learn about the "Big Picture" aspects of economics—the elements that impact economies as a whole and how governments respond to challenges and opportunities within individual economies and across borders. You will find out how different economic systems function and how countries with similar governmental structures can respond differently to economic shocks—both positive and negative.

What is the difference between macroeconomics and microeconomics? Microeconomics examines the allocation of resources and economic decision-making on an individual, household, or community level. (Here, the term *community* can mean a business, a neighborhood, a town, or a city.) In contrast, macroeconomics examines resources and power on a national, international, or global level.

What follows is a quick look at how AP® course in general can benefit you, followed by the benefits of the macroeconomics course in particular.

Why Take AP® Courses?

Each Advanced Placement® course is the equivalent of a one-semester course at a college or university. Therefore, an AP® course is more challenging than a typical high school course. It demands more of you in terms of recalling material, understanding sophisticated concepts, and analyzing and synthesizing data. Why, then, do students take these courses?

These are some of the reasons students give for enrolling in AP® courses:

- Evidence that the student has the ability to succeed as an undergraduate
- Increased eligibility for scholarships
- Evidence that taking AP® courses strengthens a college application
- Opportunity to save on college expenses by earning college credit
- Opportunity to test out of introductory college courses
- Evidence that AP® students have better college graduation rates
- Enrichment of the AP® student's high school experience

Because macroeconomics is often taught as part of more general social studies courses rather than as a discrete subject, you might feel you have not had much specific instruction in it. And if AP® Macroeconomics is your first course at the advanced placement level, it can appear very challenging. This introduction will help you understand the structure of the exam and the content of the course. Knowing what you are about to learn can help you focus your mind and get ready to take in new information.

How Is the Exam Structured?

The AP® Macroeconomics Exam is two hours and ten minutes long and contains these sections.

SECTION	QUESTION TYPE	HOW MANY QUESTIONS?	HOW MUCH ARE THEY WORTH?	HOW MUCH TIME WILL I HAVE?
I	Multiple choice	60	67%	70 minutes
II	Free response	including one long question and two short questions	33%	60 minutes, including a 10-minute reading period

What Scores Can I Get on the AP® Exam?

If you have taken an Advanced Placement® exam before, you know that you will receive a number grade rather than a letter grade or a percentage of 100. AP® examinations, including the Macroeconomics exam, score student performance on a five-point scale. Here is how the College Board will describe your performance on the exam:

5 = Extremely well qualified
4 = Well qualified
3 = Qualified
2 = Possibly qualified
1 = No recommendation

Another way to think about exam scores is to compare them to the performance of a college student:

- A score of 5 indicates the equivalent of earning a grade of A in a college macroeconomics course.
- A score of 4 is equivalent to a grade of A-, B+, or B.
- A score of 3 is equivalent to a grade of B-, C+, or C.

Many colleges and universities consider an AP® score of 3 or higher to be evidence that a student has demonstrated proficiency with the material covered in an introductory college course in macroeconomics. But policies in this area vary depending on the school.

How Does the AP® Exam Compare to Classroom Tests?

The College Board prepares AP® exams differently from the way a typical classroom teacher prepares a test. Teachers select questions to assess whether you have learned the materials that they have taught you. A teacher knows what you read, heard, practiced, and experienced in your course of study and creates a test that addresses those things specifically. Although you may not always know the answer on a test in your classroom, you most likely realized that it was something that you and the rest of the class had covered in the reading or classroom activities.

The AP® test is different. A team of college professors and high school teachers from across the country prepare it. Because one single exam cannot assess every aspect of macroeconomics, the team decides what material the test will address and how the test will present it.

Based on the knowledge you acquire and the skills you gain by reading this book and participating in your AP® Macroeconomics course, you should be able to understand and answer materials that are based on those four big ideas just mentioned, even if you did not encounter the specific details of the questions in this book or in class.

Are AP® Exams Difficult?

The AP® exam is designed to be more difficult than the typical tests you might take in classrooms. A teacher is pleased to see all students demonstrate understanding by performing well on a test. In contrast, the AP® test is designed so that it can distinguish students who are better prepared from those who are still attempting to master the material.

You should not be surprised if you find that many of the questions seem more difficult than you expected. But you should not necessarily be worried because of this. Many other well-prepared students will be experiencing the same feeling.

Finally, the AP® exam is scored differently from a classroom test. The cutoffs for the different scores vary a little each year. Why? The scores depend on how well a control group of college students did. These students are enrolled in introductory macroeconomics courses, and they also took the test. You may feel that you performed poorly on the exam and still receive a score of 4 or 5. Much depends on how your performance on the exam compares to that of others who also take it.

How Is This Book Organized?

The makers of this book want to help you succeed on the AP® exam. Therefore, the book is organized so you can find the information you need quickly, gain a thorough understanding of the concepts and examples, and then test yourself to be sure you have understood and retained what you read.

Each unit of this book contains the following elements:

- *Unit Introduction:* Each of the six units in the book begins with a brief explanation of the topic you are about to master. There is also a list of the topics in the unit. This section is designed to get you ready to learn.

- *Long Free-Response Question:* When you have taken other courses, have you ever worried that you learned information only briefly and then forgot it? Answering the Long Free-Response Question at the end of the unit helps you synthesize what you have learned so it stays in your memory. It is also excellent practice for the Long Free-Response Question that is part of the AP® Macroeconomics exam.

Each topic of this book contains the following elements:

- *Topic Narrative:* The 42 topics are organized in a logical sequence as identified by the College Board. Each topic starts with an Essential Question that the entire topic is organized around—a question that you should be able to answer by the time you finish the topic. Within each topic, you will find the basic vocabulary terms and concepts you need to understand and discuss it. Also, you will find real-world examples that illustrate key topics. All of the topics include visuals, such as graphs, tables, or photographs.

- *Answer the Topic Essential Question:* Remember that Essential Question at the beginning of the topic? Now is your chance to answer it in one to three paragraphs. If you have trouble answering the Essential Question, then it makes sense to review the topic until you feel comfortable with it.

- *Key Terms.* At the end of each topic is a list of the vocabulary terms from the topic narrative. Understanding these terms will be an important part of your success on the AP® Macroeconomics exam.

- *Multiple-Choice Questions:* How can you be sure you understood what you read? Each topic has three multiple-choice items that give you a chance to apply what you have learned using the question format that will appear on the exam. Some of these questions may include graphs or tables.

- *Free-Response Questions:* Each topic has a free-response question that you can use to check your understanding and practice your writing skills. This question may include graphs, tables, or brief quotations, and it may ask you to draw a graph.

- *Think as an Economist Features:* The AP® exam asks you to do more than memorize information and repeat it back at test time. Instead, you will need to develop specific skills that economists have and practice those skills by writing, graphing, or calculating. Each Think as an Economist feature focuses on a specific skill that real economists use, such as creating accurate graphs or describing economic concepts.

To help you even more, this book also contains the following elements:

- *Practice Examination:* Following the final unit is a complete practice examination modeled on the AP® exam.

- *Index:* What if you are trying to remember the definition of an important term, but you cannot remember where in the book you learned it? The index helps you find coverage of key terms and topics for review.

A separate Resource Book is also available for teachers and other authorized users of the book. It contains an answer key as well as activities focused on issues of race and justice. The Resource Book is available through the publisher's website.

The Study of AP® Macroeconomics

Economists, like historians, sociologists, geographers, and others, study human behavior and relationships. What makes economists distinct from these other groups is that they study how people and organizations use money, goods, and resources. By studying macroeconomics, you will learn to notice trends, create models, and predict outcomes. This course can be broken down into "big ideas" and a variety of key skills.

The four big ideas were briefly discussed earlier in this introduction, but here is the exact wording of each one as provided by the College Board. Together, they are the basis for this book.

Big Ideas

1. **Economic Measurements (MEA):** Economists construct measurements to monitor the state of an economy and evaluate its performance over time. Governments, firms, and citizens often use these measurements to help inform policy, business, and personal decisions.

2. **Markets (MKT):** Competitive markets bring together buyers and sellers to exchange goods and services for mutual gain. The simple model of supply-demand can be applied in different market contexts.

3. **Macroeconomic Models (MOD):** Macroeconomic models are simplified representations that depict basic economic relationships and can be used to predict and explain how those relationships are affected by economic shocks.

4. **Macroeconomic Policies (POL):** Government taxation and spending policies and central bank monetary policy can affect an economy's output, price level, and level of employment, both in the short run and in the long run.

Source: *AP® Macroeconomics Course and Exam Description*. Effective Fall 2019 (College Board).

Now that you know the key concepts in the course, it is time to get into some of the specifics.

AP Economics Skills

Skill Category 1: Principles and Models—Define economic principles and models.

- 1.A: Describe economic concepts, principles, or models.
- 1.B: Identify an economic concept, principle, or model illustrated by an example.
- 1.C: Identify an economic concept, principle, or model using quantitative data or calculations.
- 1.D: Describe the similarities, differences, and limitations of economic concepts, principles, or models.

Skill Category 2: Interpretation—Explain given economic outcomes.

- 2.A: Using economic concepts, principles, or models, explain how a specific economic outcome occurs or what action should be taken in order to achieve a specific economic outcome.
- 2.B: Using economic concepts, principles, or models, explain how a specific economic outcome occurs when there are multiple contributing variables or what multiple actions should be taken in order to achieve a specific economic outcome.
- 2.C: Interpret a specific economic outcome using quantitative data or calculations.

Skill Category 3: Manipulation—Determine outcomes of specific economic situations.

- 3.A: Determine the outcome of an economic situation using economic concepts, principles, or models.
- 3.B: Determine the effect(s) of one or more changes on other economic markets.
- 3.C: Determine the effect(s) of a change in an economic situation using quantitative data or calculations.

Skill Category 4: Graphing and Visuals—Model economic situations using graphs or visual representations.

- 4.A: Draw an accurately labeled graph or visual to represent an economic model or market.
- 4.B: Demonstrate your understanding of a specific economic situation on an accurately labeled graph or visual.
- 4.C: Demonstrate the effect of a change in an economic situation on an accurately labeled graph or visual.

Source: *AP® Macroeconomics Course and Exam Description.* Effective Fall 2019 (College Board).

It is important for you to have the exact wording of the big ideas and skills so you know exactly what the College Board is asking you to learn. However, the wording of these ideas and skills can be bewildering. What follows is a unit-by-unit outline of the course, so you know what you will be studying in this book.

AP® Macroeconomics Course Content

When you begin this book, you may have only the slightest understanding of what macroeconomics is. By the time you finish, you will understand how economists, government officials, business leaders, and everyday people react to economic opportunities and pressures. Each unit in this book helps you understand another facet of how macroeconomics works.

Unit 1: Basic Economic Concepts

- How do people make the most of the resources they have?
- What are supply and demand, and how do they affect prices?
- How do surpluses or shortages in a market affect prices?

  Big ideas covered: Markets, Macroeconomic Models

Unit 2: Economic Indicators and the Business Cycle

- How can you "take the temperature" of an economy by examining its gross domestic product, inflation rate, and unemployment rate?
- In what ways do gross domestic product, inflation rate, and unemployment rate fail to accurately reflect how an economy is doing?
- How can you calculate an economy's unemployment rate?
- What are business cycles, and how do they affect people?

  Big idea covered: Economic Measurements

Unit 3: National Income and Price Determination

- What is aggregate demand, and what does it say about an economy?
- How do output, employment, and price levels respond to macroeconomic shocks?
- What effects do a government's fiscal and monetary policies have on an economy?

  Big ideas covered: Macroeconomic Models, Macroeconomic Policies

Unit 4: Financial Sector

- How does money allow people to compare the value of goods and services?
- What are interest rates, and what do they say about an economy?
- How does the banking system affect the money supply?
- What is the money market?

  Big ideas covered: Economic Measurements, Macroeconomic Policies, Markets

Unit 5: Long-Run Consequences of Stabilization Policies

- What effects do fiscal and monetary policies have on economies in the short run?
- How are inflation and unemployment related?
- What effects do fiscal and monetary policies have on economies in the long run?
- What does "crowding out" mean to an economist?

  Big ideas covered: Economic Measurements, Macroeconomic Models, Macroeconomic Policies

Unit 6: Open Economy—International Trade and Finance

- How do economists measure the flow of goods, services, and money between countries?
- What are exchange rates?
- Why are some currencies more in demand than others?

  Big ideas covered: Economic Measurements, Markets

AP® Exam Weighting

Some subjects in the macroeconomics exam are worth more than others. Look at how the College Board has weighted the different subject areas.

EXAM WEIGHTING			
Unit	Unit Title	How Much of the Exam Will Cover This Unit?	Typical Number of Class Periods Spent in a One-Semester Course
1	Basic Economic Concepts	5–10%	about 8–10
2	Economic Indicators and the Business Cycle	12–17%	about 9–11
3	National Income and Price Determination	17–27%	about 10–12
4	Financial Sector	18–23%	about 11–13
5	Long-Run Consequences of Stabilization Policies	20–30%	about 8–10
6	Open Economy—International Trade and Finance	10–13%	about 5–7

Source: *AP® Macroeconomics Course and Exam Description.* Effective Fall 2019 (College Board).

Since you know that ideas and concepts from Unit 5 will appear most often on the exam, it makes sense to spend a bit more time studying that unit. That said, however, do not spend any *less* time on other units. Throughout the course, and this book, everything you learn acts as a foundation for the concepts that follow. Having a thorough understanding of basic economic concepts will make the rest of the book much easier to understand.

AP® Macroeconomics Exam Questions

The Course and Exam Description, published by the College Board, describes both the content of AP® Macroeconomics and the basic skills you need to develop. You can practice these skills throughout the school year in all subject areas.

Answering the Multiple-Choice Questions

The AP® Macroeconomics exam includes 60 multiple-choice questions, which you will have 70 minutes to answer. This portion of the exam accounts for 67 percent (two-thirds) of your score. Each question will consist of a stem that can be either a question or statement and five possible choices. One choice is correct and the others are distractors. Distractors are incorrect, but they may seem believable.

Analyzing the Graphic Some of the multiple-choice questions will refer you to a graphic information source, such as a graph or table. Take a moment to read the question, refer to the graphic, and then reread the question. Be careful to look at elements of the graphic that may be important:

- *Graphs:* Check each axis of any graph. Notice where each begins and ends. For example, does the axis go from 0 to 2,000, or did it begin at 1,200 and then end at 2,000? If an axis denotes a time period using years, notice the time period it covers. How big are the intervals or increments between elements on the axes?

- *Tables and Charts:* As with other types of graphics, note carefully titles and any words on the chart. See if you can sum up the meaning of the table or chart in your own words.

Only some multiple-choice questions will have a graphic. Read them carefully. What if, as you are reading the stem, your eyes glance at the choices and you see what you believe is the correct answer? Finish reading the question before you select it. Information at the end of the stem may show you that the correct answer is not what you thought it was.

Tips on Making a Choice You will often know the right answer to a question quickly and with confidence, but sometimes you will not. Here are a few suggestions to help you when you are uncertain about an answer.

HOW TO ANSWER CHALLENGING QUESTIONS	
Advice	**Rationale**
Answer every question.	Your score will be based on how many correct answers you give. Unlike some standardized tests, the AP® Macroeconomics exam does not penalize people for guessing a wrong answer. That means an attempt at an answer is better than a blank space where an answer should be.
Apply what you know.	What if a question asks about a specific place or situation that you have not studied? In that case, focus on the general concept that the question addresses. Use what you know to determine the most reasonable answer.
Move forward.	Since you have 70 minutes to answer 60 questions, you can spend an average of just over 60 seconds on each question. If you find a question difficult, guess the answer, note the question's number, and return to it if you have time at the end.

Recommended Activities Answering multiple-choice questions is a powerful way to review content and practice skills. Each topic in this book presents multiple-choice items to help you check your understanding of important concepts in AP® Macroeconomics. Often, the questions include a graph, table, or other source that you need to analyze in order to determine the best answer to the question.

Answering the Free-Response Questions (FRQ)

There are three free-response questions on Section II of the AP® Macroeconomics exam. Each FRQ will typically include several parts, lettered (a), (b), (c), and so on. There is one long free-response question and two short ones. The long item is worth 10 points, and each of the shorter items is worth 5 points.

You are expected to answer all three in 60 minutes. That means you have an average of 20 minutes per answer. However, you can divide this block of time in any way you would like. Since the long question will have more parts, you may want to spend 30 minutes on the long free-response question and 15 minutes each on the short free-response questions.

You will be scored based solely on the quality of the content of your response. Try to use correct grammar so that you make your ideas clear, but you will not be penalized for grammatical errors.

Composing Your Response The free-response questions used on the AP® Macroeconomics exam are sometimes called constructed response items. This type of question consists of a statement or short introduction followed by a series of related questions or response prompts labeled (a), (b), (c), and so on. Each topic in this book ends with a short free-response question, and each unit ends with a long free-response question.

Your response will often be written as a full sentence, a paragraph, or paragraphs, but be aware that a single word or a phrase will sometimes suffice, depending on the question. The construction of your response should reflect that of the question.

An effective method for answering the questions is to label each part of the question. That is, when you are answering part (a) of the question, label it "A" in your test book. Then label "B," and so on. Within each labeled portion of your response, you may still want to use paragraphing to provide clarity to your writing.

Analyzing the Question The stem of the free-response question is the part that comes before (a), (b), (c), and so on. You can use the stem to help you figure out how to structure your response. You do not need to restate, rephrase, or incorporate the stem in your answer. You do need to pay attention to any limitations it places on you.

Make sure to answer each question fully and completely. Some questions may require you to consider specific concepts, such as "supply and/or demand." In that case, you would look at each part of the question and decide whether to describe effects on supply, demand, or both. Your response should clearly relate to the concepts indicated in the question. Try your best not to stray off topic, as your time is limited.

Task Verbs The key words in the question's prompts that indicate what you are to do are called task verbs. Here are the ones that you will see most often on the exam.

RESPONDING TO VERBS IN FREE-RESPONSE QUESTIONS		
Task Verb	**Definition**	**Expectation**
Identify	To state a clear, concise, specific answer	Often, a single, well-written sentence is enough, but you can add clarifying details. However, do not contradict or add confusion to your original answer.
Explain	To provide information about why a relationship, pattern, position, situation, or outcome occurs	Offer reasons or evidence to make an idea plainly understood, or state how a process occurs. Graphs or symbols may be part of the explanation.
Calculate	To perform mathematical steps to arrive at a final answer	You will need to show your work so the graders can see how you arrived at your answer. When using a formula, write out the formula, plug in the appropriate numbers, and solve the equation.
Draw a correctly labeled . . .	To create a graph or visual representation that illustrates or explains relationships or phenomena	You will need to provide accurate labels for your drawing.
Show, label, plot, or indicate	To point out an economic scenario on a graph or visual representation that you create	You will need to clearly label all axes and curves. Show directional changes where relevant.

If a prompt asks you to identify something or someone, you may need to write only a sentence or two for that part of the question. If a prompt asks you to explain, you will probably need to write anywhere from a sentence to a paragraph for each part of the question. If a prompt asks you to calculate, it will remind you to show your work. For answers involving calculations, drawings, or plots, you may not need to write any sentences for that part of the question.

Questions Requiring Examples Many of the free-response questions on the AP® Macroeconomics exam ask you to supply more than one example or reason to illustrate or explain a concept. For example, the question might require "two factors that can affect the equilibrium price of a product" or "three factors besides price that can affect the supply of a product." To answer these questions, you might want to begin by brainstorming a list of several ideas and selecting the best ones to include in your answer. Provide exactly the number of examples called for in the prompt. You will not get full credit if you provide too few examples. You will be wasting your time if you provide extra examples.

Questions That Test More Than One Skill or Big Idea Some questions require you to demonstrate your knowledge of multiple skills or big ideas. For example, a free-response question might ask you to create a graph, label its parts, and then make predictions or recommendations based on it. Doing all this can seem overwhelming, but do not panic. Instead, take it step by step. Check your work as you go, and keep in mind that even if you do not answer every part of the question perfectly, you can get partial credit on free-response items.

General Writing Advice The principles of good writing that you have learned in school will help you write a good answer to a free-response question:

- *Plan your time.* Take time to plan your answer before you begin writing. It makes sense to take a few minutes to brainstorm your ideas, select good examples, and organize your response.

- *Consider whether to include introductions and conclusions.* You do not need to restate the prompt or write an introduction to your answer. Conclusions are also not necessary. Answer the questions simply and directly.

- *Make changes.* If you think of something you would like to add to part A (or B, or whichever) of your response but you have already moved on to another part, simply add it and indicate which part of your response it belongs in. If you write something that you decide you do not want included in your response, draw a line through it and it will not be scored.

- *Do not let grammar, spelling, and handwriting limit you.* Your answer to a free-response question will not be graded on grammar, spelling, or handwriting. So, think of it as a rough draft. Try to use correct grammar, spell words as best you can, and write legibly so that readers understand what you are saying. But focus on the content, not on these other concerns.

Evaluation of Your Answer You can find scoring guides from previous AP® exams online at apcentral.collegeboard.org. The most important thing to know about how graders evaluate free-response questions is that you can get partial credit for an answer. In other words, the free-response questions are not all-or-nothing endeavors. Depending on how completely and accurately you answer the question, you may receive the maximum number of points, a partial score, or no points.

MAXIMUM NUMBER OF POINTS AVAILABLE FOR FREE-RESPONSE QUESTIONS	
Question 1: Long	10 points
Question 2: Short	5 points
Question 3: Short	5 points

What does this mean to you? If, for instance, you manage your time poorly on Section II of the exam, you could end up with only a couple of minutes to answer question 3. If this happens, do not skip the question. Even if you do not have time to write as full an answer as you would like to, you could still earn a few points by answering part of the question.

Recommended Activities As with the multiple-choice questions, you should practice writing answers to free-response items. Each topic in this book contains a short free-response question that is clearly related to the material contained within the topic. Each unit concludes with a long free-response question that draws on content from that entire unit. The Think as an Economist activities will also help you practice your skills.

Free-response questions from previous AP® exams are available online at apcentral.collegeboard.org. If you choose to practice with these, be aware that many of them are meant to cut across the topics and skill categories in the course. Therefore, you may see parts of questions that you have not studied yet. Using the accompanying online scoring guides as a study and review tool is also very helpful.

What to Do as the Exam Approaches

Set up a review schedule as you prepare for the exam in the weeks before the test date. Studying with a group of fellow students can be helpful. Below is a sample of a six-week review schedule, including information on the topics in this book that cover the content to review. Because AP® tests are given during the first two full weeks of May, this review schedule assumes you begin your review sometime in mid-March.

PROPOSED REVIEW SCHEDULE	
Week	**Content**
1	Unit 1: Basic Economic Concepts
2	Unit 2: Economic Indicators and the Business Cycle
3	Unit 3: National Income and Price Determination
4	Unit 4: Financial Sector
5	Unit 5: Long-Run Consequences of Stabilization Policies
6	Unit 6: Open Economy—International Trade and Finance

If you have seven weeks to review, consider devoting an extra week to one of these sections:

- Unit 3 (because it includes the most topics)
- Unit 5 (because it is the most heavily weighted unit on the AP® exam)
- Whichever unit you found most challenging

You should also plan to review the information in this introduction. The suggestions and ideas about answering multiple-choice questions and free-response items will help you. Good luck to you as you set out to learn all about macroeconomics and ace the AP® exam!

UNIT 1

Basic Economic Concepts

The fundamental issue in economics is choice. For example, individuals make choices about what goods to buy, how much money to save, and what kind of work they do. Similarly, companies make choices about what goods or services to produce, where to operate their factories or stores, and whom to hire. Taken together, the sum of all these choices shapes the economy of a country.

People need to make choices because they lack enough money to obtain all of the products they might want or to hire all the employees they might desire to have. Even if money were unlimited, time is limited. If a person decides to take a three-week trip to Japan, that person can't spend those same three weeks seeing historic sites in India or hiking in the mountains of Peru.

Two ways to expand the range of choices for an individual are through specialization and exchange. People find focusing on one job, such as being a plumber, and exchanging some of the money they earn to purchase food and a car is much more efficient than trying to grow all the food they want and making their own car. Similarly, the businesses in a country often specialize. Canada produces lumber and maple syrup, but it purchases oranges and bananas from countries with warmer climates.

These basic concepts—choice, specialization, and exchange—provide the foundation for studying every other topic in macroeconomics. You will use them throughout this course.

"Naturally, there's a trade-off for its exceptional fuel economy."

Topic Titles and Essential Knowledge

Topic 1.1 Scarcity

- Individuals and societies are forced to make choices because most resources are scarce.

Topic 1.2 Opportunity Cost and the Production Possibilities Curve (PPC)

- The PPC is a model used to show the tradeoffs associated with allocating resources.
- The PPC can be used to illustrate the concepts of scarcity, opportunity cost, efficiency, underutilized resources, and economic growth or contraction.
- The shape of the PPC depends on whether opportunity costs are constant, increasing, or decreasing.
- The PPC can shift because of changes in factors of production as well as changes in productivity/technology.
- Economic growth results in an outward shift of the PPC.

Topic 1.3 Comparative Advantage and Gains from Trade

- Absolute advantage describes a situation in which an individual, business, or country can produce more of a good or service than any other producer with the same quantity of resources.
- Comparative advantage describes a situation in which an individual, business, or country can produce a good or service at a lower opportunity cost than another producer.
- Production specialization according to comparative advantage results in exchange opportunities that lead to consumption opportunities beyond the PPC.
- Comparative advantage and opportunity costs determine the terms of trade for exchange under which

Topic 1.4 Demand

- The law of demand states there is an inverse relationship between price and quantity demanded, leading to a downward-sloping demand curve.
- Factors that influence consumer demand, such as changes in consumer income, cause the market demand curve to shift.

Topic 1.5 Supply

- The law of supply states there is a positive relationship between price and quantity supplied, leading to an upward-sloping supply curve.
- Factors that influence producer supply, such as changes in input prices, cause the market supply curve to shift.

Topic 1.6 Market Equilibrium, Disequilibrium, and Changes in Equilibrium

- Equilibrium is achieved at the price at which quantities demanded and supplied are equal.
- Whenever markets experience imbalances—creating disequlibrium prices, surpluses, and shortages—market forces drive prices toward equilibrium.
- Changes in the determinants of supply and/ or demand result in a new equilibrium price and quantity.

Source: *AP® Macroeconomics Course and Exam Description*. Effective Fall 2019 (College Board).

Topic 1.1

Scarcity

"The first lesson of economics is scarcity: there is never enough of anything to fully satisfy all those who want it."

Thomas Sowell, *Is Reality Optional?* (1993)

Essential Question: What are scarcity and economic resources?

People's **needs**, the absolute necessities of life, are few: air, water, food, clothing, and shelter. But most people want much more than those basic needs. People have learned to put resources to work to produce goods and services that satisfy many of their **wants**, things that are desirable but not necessary for existence. The basic problem of economics is the gap between limited resources and unlimited wants. This gap is referred to as **scarcity**. It requires people to make **choices**, decisions about how to use resources in order to satisfy basic needs and as many additional wants as possible. **Economics** is the study of how people and societies use limited resources to satisfy their unlimited wants. To put it more simply, economics is the study of scarcity and choice.

The Fundamentals of Economics

Since people are unable to have everything they want, they need to pick and choose from among the alternatives in order to get the most out of available resources. This fact holds true for both individuals and society as a whole. Society must try to allocate, or distribute, its resources in such a way as to get the most for its money. Along the way, every society needs to answer some fundamental economic questions:

- WHAT goods and services should be produced?
- HOW should they be produced?
- WHO should receive the goods and services that are produced?

What Do Economists Do? The professionals who study the ways society allocates its resources to satisfy its wants are called **economists**. Broadly speaking, economists are concerned with how the goods and services people want are produced and distributed. They spend much of their time gathering and analyzing data. These activities enable them to identify problems and suggest solutions. Like other professionals, economists often specialize in their work. Some look at the individual elements of the economy, while others focus on the big picture, or the economy as a whole.

Microeconomics vs. Macroeconomics The kinds of problems economists study can be classified as either microeconomic or macroeconomic. **Microeconomics** is the study of the effects of economic forces on individual parts of the economy, such as businesses, workers, or households. When the executives of a firm think about what would happen to sales if the company increased its prices, they are wrestling with a microeconomic problem.

Other economists focus on the big picture. **Macroeconomics** is the study of the impact of changes to the economy as a whole rather than on an individual part. Economists in this field try to answer questions like "What effect will a tax increase have on consumer spending?" and "How will the total demand for elecric cars change if batteries become twice as efficient?"

What Is vs. What Ought to Be Economists deal with two worlds: (1) the world that is (and was) and (2) the world that ought to be. The study of what is focuses on the causes and effects of specific events. For example, federal minimum wage laws set the lowest wage that most workers can be paid. If members of Congress were thinking of increasing the minimum wage, they might ask economists to find answers to questions like "How would a 10 percent increase in the minimum wage affect business profits?" and "What effect would such an increase have on the unemployment rate?" Both questions deal with the world that is.

Like everybody else, though, economists have sets of values that often influence how they view economic problems. For example, some economists support minimum-wage laws because they believe that these laws promote greater economic equality. Other economists, by contrast, oppose such laws, believing that they harm the whole economy. Similarly, economists often disagree about whether government should enact programs to help special groups, such as the homeless, small business owners, or farmworkers. These concerns address questions not necessarily of what is but, rather, what possibly ought to be.

Scarcity and Choice

Economics is about the choices all people must make in their daily lives. Why is it always necessary to make a choice between either this or that? Why can't people have everything they want? Economists try to answer these questions by discussing scarcity.

Most people cannot afford to have everything they want. They may have to decide, for example, whether to buy a new sweatshirt or a pair of jeans. They have to make a choice: which do they want more?

Business firms and governments face the same kinds of decisions. None can afford everything they want all of the time. Instead, they try to satisfy as many of their wants as possible with the resources available. For example, a manufacturer unable to afford both a new advertising campaign and a factory modernization program would have to choose one or the other. In a similar manner, a town might have to choose between building a new high school and expanding public transportation.

Economists refer to the things that individuals and institutions want as either goods or services. **Goods** are tangible items of value, things that one can see or touch, such as cars, medicines, and textbooks. **Services** are intangible things that have value. Intangibles can neither be seen nor touched. Haircuts, medical care, and education are examples of services.

As people use goods and services to satisfy their wants, they consume them. For that reason, people who buy goods and services for personal use are called **consumers**. The act of buying goods and services is called **consumption**.

Economic Resources

Economic resources, or **factors of production**, are the things that go into the making of goods and services. They are natural resources, human resources, and capital resources, sometimes referred to as land, labor, capital, and entrepreneurship. **Producers**, the people and institutions that make and offer goods and services, combine these factors to create their products as efficiently as they can.

Natural Resources As the name implies, **natural resources** are the raw materials that exist on the earth and in the air that humans can use to make goods. Economists sometimes use the term *land* to refer to all natural resources, including soil, minerals, animals, trees, and even sunshine. While some seem plentiful, no country has an unlimited supply of them.

Human Resources Economists use the terms **human resources**, *labor*, and *the workforce* to refer to the people whose efforts and skills go into the production of goods and services. Without human resources, goods and services could not be produced. Human resources influence the production of goods and services through both the size and the productivity of the workforce.

Source: Getty Images

Wind and solar energy are renewable natural resources. These solar panels and wind turbines generate electrical power for energy users in Southern California.

The size of the workforce affects the amount of goods and services produced. If a country has too few workers, it will be unable to make full use of its other resources. It may then encourage its citizens to have larger families, or it may promote immigration. It may also encourage the importation of goods produced abroad.

More important than the number of workers is the productivity of those workers. Worker productivity depends on many things, including how skilled people are. A country of well-educated, highly skilled people is able to produce goods and services more efficiently than a country whose people have little education and few skills.

Capital Resources The machines, tools, and buildings used in the production of goods and services are called **capital resources**, *capital goods*, or just *capital*. A factory that manufactures shirts is a form of capital because it produces those goods. Schools are capital because they house a service industry—education. The term *capital* as it is used here should not be confused with money, which in other contexts is also called capital.

Capital is eventually used up or worn out in much the same way that an automobile or washing machine wears out from use. This process of using up or wearing out machines is a form of deterioration. The term economists use to measure the decline in the value of capital goods is **depreciation**. If new capital is not produced to replace capital that has been used up, or depreciated, fewer goods can be produced. A country's wealth is often measured in terms of the capital it possesses. In order to increase production, a country must produce more or better capital goods than are needed merely to make up for goods that are worn out, used up, or just no longer useful.

Source: Getty Images

Many factories, such as this automobile assembly plant, have made major capital investments in robots to do work formerly done by humans.

Entrepreneurship The process of bringing together the three factors of production (natural, human, and capital resources) is called **entrepreneurship**. An individual who organizes a business and invests time and money in hopes of earning a profit is called an **entrepreneur**. As a group, entrepreneurs often introduce new products and innovative business methods that help the economy grow and become more efficient. Some, such as Henry Ford and Bill Gates, become incredibly wealthy. However, entrepreneurship is risky. In the United States, two out of every three new businesses fail within the first two years of operation.

ANSWER THE TOPIC ESSENTIAL QUESTION

1. In one to three paragraphs, explain the concepts of scarcity and economic resources.

KEY TERMS

needs	macroeconomics	producer
wants	goods	natural resources
scarcity	services	human resources
choice	consumer	capital resources
economics	consumption	depreciation
economist	economic resources	entrepreneurship
microeconomics	factors of production	entrepreneur

MULTIPLE-CHOICE QUESTIONS

1. The term used to describe when a person organizes a business, creating a new product and hoping to make a profit is
   (A) microeconomics
   (B) human resources
   (C) capital resources
   (D) consumption
   (E) entrepreneurship

2. Macroeconomists are more likely than microeconomists to study
   (A) why an individual chooses to buy one computer rather than another
   (B) why a worker decides to leave one job to take another one
   (C) how an increase in oil prices affects the number of jobs in a country
   (D) how a bank evaluates an individual's application for a loan
   (E) how the owners of a chain of restaurants select new locations

3. The fundamental economic problem that exists in any society is the

(A) number of different mineral resources it has

(B) the ratio of goods to services that it produces

(C) amount and condition of its capital

(D) ratio of scarce resources to unlimited wants

(E) ratio of entrepreneurs to consumers

FREE-RESPONSE QUESTIONS

1. Use the passage below to answer all parts of the questions that follow.

"Some commodities [products] are rising in value, from the effects of taxation, from the scarcity of the raw material of which they are made, or from any other cause which increases the difficulty of production. Others again are falling, from improvements in machinery, from the better division of labor, and the improved skill of the workman; from the greater abundance of the raw material, and generally from greater facility of production."

David Ricardo (1772–1823), *Proposals for an Economical and Secure Currency* (1816)

(a) According to Ricardo, what relationship does scarcity have to the value or price of a commodity?

(b) Which types of economic resources does Ricardo mention? Explain.

(c) What effect does labor have on prices? Explain.

(d) In what way does Ricardo refer to capital in this excerpt?

(e) What effect do improvements in technology have on production? How would you expect them to affect prices?

THINK AS AN ECONOMIST: *DESCRIBE ECONOMIC CONCEPTS*

Economics is built on the foundation of a unique set of concepts. Being able to accurately describe these key concepts is an essential part of understanding economic thought. To describe a concept, answer these questions about it:

- What is the definition of the concept?
- How does this concept relate to other concepts?
- What are examples of the concept?
- Why is the concept important in the field of economics?

For example, consider the concept of economic resources. Economic resources can be defined as the ingredients that go into the making of goods and services. Economic resources are related to consumption because they are the factors of production that are combined to make goods and services that can be consumed. Three examples are timber, sawmill workers, and the building and equipment in a sawmill. Economic resources are important because they are required to make the products that consumers need to meet their needs.

Apply the Skill

Another economic concept that you learned in this topic is scarcity.

1. What is the definition of scarcity?
2. How does this concept relate to macroeconomics?
3. What is an example of scarcity?
4. Why is the concept of scarcity important in the field of economics?

Opportunity Cost and the Production Possibilities Curve (PPC)

"Tradeoffs are the central study of the economists. You can't have your cake and eat it, too, is a good candidate for the fundamental theorem of economic analysis."

Arthur Okun, *Equality and Efficiency: The Big Tradeoff* (1975)

Essential Question: What is the purpose of the production possibilities curve (PPC)?

If all of a society's resources are being fully utilized, production in one area can be increased only by decreasing production in another. The same thing can be said for businesses. If a shopping mall is built on land that had previously been farmland, that land can no longer be used to raise food. Workers building a sports complex cannot be employed at the same time building a hospital. Equipment needed to produce SUVs and pickup trucks can produce more SUVs only by taking some of the machines away from the production of pickups, resulting in fewer pickups.

Since individuals and institutions are unable to have everything they want, it is necessary for them to choose between those goods and services they will either purchase or produce and those they will forgo. In analyzing how people make their choices, economists speak of trade-offs and opportunity costs.

Making Economic Choices

The many segments of society—individuals, businesses, government—make decisions about how to use available resources to produce the quantity and quality of goods and services that consumers desire. How well a society provides what consumers want reflects its economic efficiency—or inefficiency.

Trade-offs As you learned in Topic 1.1, economics is the study of scarcity and choice. Economic decisions (such as whether to buy, produce, or invest) involve trade-offs. A **trade-off** takes place when one thing is given up in order to obtain something else. The answer to each of the following questions involves a trade-off:

- Should a recent high school graduate go to college or enter the job market?
- Should a company automate its production facility or provide advanced training for its sales force?
- Should a city redevelop land reclaimed from the demolition of abandoned buildings or leave the land as green space?

Opportunity Costs The trade-off of the value of one good or service for the value of another is the **opportunity cost** of the choice. If a high school graduate opts to enter the job market rather than go to college, the opportunity cost could be lower lifetime earnings. If a business chooses to automate its production rather than further training its salespeople, the opportunity cost could be fewer sales in the short-term.

Source: Getty Images

What might be the possible opportunity cost if you choose to go to the skate park rather than study?

Some opportunity costs are not so clear. The opportunity cost of redeveloping cleared land in a city rather than leaving it as green space might be a lower quality of life. However, the opportunity cost of leaving it as green space rather than redeveloping it might be lower property tax revenues to help finance municipal services, including public schools. As this example shows, no matter which choice is made, the trade-off results in an opportunity cost.

The Production Possibilities Curve (PPC)

Scarcity forces individuals and societies to choose among the things they want. If they choose one combination of goods and services, they must give up another. To illustrate the concept of scarcity, economists use a simple model based on these assumptions:

- The society produces only two types of goods, and it is making use of all of its resources.

- The society is using all available resources efficiently. (In other words, it is using all available natural resources and capital, and the labor force is fully employed.)
- The society is using the best available technology and working as efficiently as possible.

Consider an imaginary country called Altruria that produces two types of goods: consumer goods and capital goods. Consumer goods are goods such as electronics, automobiles, household appliances, food, and clothing that people buy to satisfy their wants or needs. Capital goods are goods used to produce other goods or services, such as factories, machinery, equipment, and vehicles such as ships and delivery trucks.

Assuming that the labor force is fully employed, Altruria has a number of options available:

- If it produces nothing but consumer goods, Altruria produces 24 million units per year.
- If it produces nothing but capital goods, Altruria produces 15 million units per year.
- If it chooses to produce both consumer goods and capital goods, the country produces various combinations of each type of good.

The Production Possibilities Table (below) shows some of the combinations that Altruria can produce in a given year. Assume that Altruria normally produces 14 million units of consumer goods a year and 12 million units of capital goods. Suppose, however, that Altrurians want to increase the number of consumer goods available to 18 million units. Would it be possible for them to produce the additional 4 million units? Yes, but to do so, they would have to shift some of the resources that have been used in the production of capital goods to consumer goods. According to the table, producing 18 million units of consumer goods will result in a 25 percent reduction in the production of capital goods, from 12 million units to 9 million units. In economic terms, the opportunity cost of producing an additional 4 million units of consumer goods is 3 million units of capital goods.

By transferring the information in the table to a line graph and connecting the plotted points, we can create a production possibilities curve. The **production possibilities curve**, or **PPC**, illustrates the trade-offs and opportunity costs associated with the production of two goods or services. (The PPC is sometimes referred to as the *production possibilities frontier*, or *PPF*, which points to the fact that in some instances, the "curve" appearing in a graph may actually be a straight line.) Each point along a production possibilities curve shows the maximum combination of two products that can be produced when all resources (natural resources, labor, capital, and technology) are being utilized as efficiently as possible.

PRODUCTION POSSIBILITIES TABLE		
Consumer Goods (millions of units)	Capital Goods (millions of units)	PPC Points
0	15	A
8	14	B
14	12	C
18	9	D
22	5	E
24	0	F

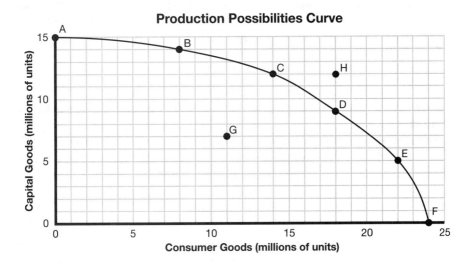

Production Possibilities Curve

Interpreting the PPC At point A, the society is using all of its resources to produce capital goods; at point F, all resources are being used as efficiently as possible to produce consumer goods. The other points along the curve represent the other combinations of capital goods and consumer goods from the Production Possibilities Table.

Suppose that Altruria's current production is at point G. The nation is producing 7 million units of capital goods and 11 million units of consumer goods. These amounts are well below capacity, which means that resources are being underutilized, or used inefficiently. As a result, Altrurians have fewer goods and services available to them than their economy is capable of producing.

Suppose, however, that Altruria wants to produce 12 million units of capital goods and 18 million units of consumer goods—point H on the graph. Is this possible? The graph shows that it is not possible under present conditions to expand production to point H. The PPC indicates a limit beyond which production cannot expand using current resources. Expanding the economy beyond the PPC would require additional resources or an expansion of trade.

Note that opportunity costs vary. To produce the first 8 million units of consumer goods (point B), Altruria's opportunity cost is 1 million units of capital goods. And between points B and C, the opportunity cost for producing 6 million more units of consumer goods is 2 million units of capital goods. This trend continues throughout the PPC, representing the idea of increasing opportunity cost. This increasing cost causes the possibilities curve to bend, rather than remaining constant and straight.

If a constant opportunity cost were in place between each point in the figure—2.5 million units of capital goods for every 4 units of consumer goods—the graph would be a straight line. While a constant opportunity cost has the advantage of simplicity, in most cases opportunity costs are increasing. For example, oil production initially came from sources that were simply stumbled upon. However, over time, producers had to actively search for additional sources of oil. This additional effort resulted in increasing opportunity cost.

Uses of the PPC

The production possibilities curve is very versatile in application. It can be used to determine possible outcomes of additional resources, such as the expansion of the labor force, better management techniques, or improved technology. Any or all of these resources could potentially allow workers to produce goods more efficiently. In other words, economic growth occurs through an increase in the quantity or quality of resources. In these cases, the resulting differences can be represented graphically.

The paired graphs "The Effects of Changes on the PPC" below show two types of shifts. In each graph, the original PPC is labeled *PPC1,* and the PPC that results from the shift is labeled *PPC2.* The first graph shows equal increases in production of both capital goods and consumer goods. The curve illustrates economic growth—an increase in the output of goods and services. (If the direction of the arrow was reversed and the labels were switched, the figure would illustrate economic contraction—a decline in output.) The second graph illustrates an increase in the production of consumer goods, but not capital goods.

The Effects of Changes on the PPC

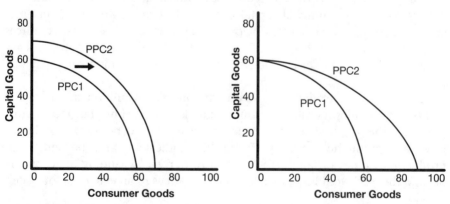

There are three main drivers of economic growth:

1. The introduction of new technology, such as assembly lines, robotics, and computers.

2. An increase in the labor force, such as a surge in immigration (like at the end of the 19th century) or a "baby boom" that enters the workforce

3. The discovery or exploitation of a new resource, such as the movement of industry from steam power to petroleum (oil and gas) or electricity

Limitations of the PPC Clearly, the PPC is a simplified version of reality. Only two commodities can be compared at a time, when in reality no society limits itself to the production of just two things. The PPC assumes that the natural resources, labor pool, and capital are constant and always available, when in fact they fluctuate. Managers can use a PPC to determine how much of one good they need to give up in order to increase production of another good, but it will not tell them how much of each good they *should* produce. But its inherent simplicity does not mean it is without value. Production possibilities curves are useful in providing rough estimates of what commodities are needed, how much should be produced, and what resources need to be adjusted.

ANSWER THE TOPIC ESSENTIAL QUESTION

1. Explain the purpose of a production possibilities curve and how economists use it.

KEY TERMS

trade-off	opportunity cost	production possibilities curve (PPC)

MULTIPLE-CHOICE QUESTIONS

Questions 1 to 3 refer to the graph below.

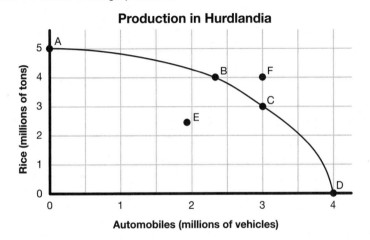

Production in Hurdlandia

1. Which of the following best explains this graph?
    (A) The graph provides a visual representation of how Hurdlandia shifted production from rice to automobiles over time.
    (B) The graph illustrates how agriculture and industry compete for resources in Hurdlandia.
    (C) The graph shows the growth of industry at the expense of agriculture in Hurdlandia.
    (D) The graph shows annual amounts of Hurdlandia's two major imports.
    (E) The graph shows the levels of production of Hurdlandia's two major exports.

2. What is the opportunity cost of raising automobile production from 3 million vehicles to 4 million vehicles?
    (A) 1 million vehicles
    (B) 2 million vehicles
    (C) 3 million tons of rice
    (D) 2 million tons of rice
    (E) It is impossible to determine the opportunity cost based on the information provided in the graph.

3. Production at point F on the graph might occur if
    (A) engineers improved the efficiency of auto production
    (B) manufacturers decreased production of autos
    (C) farmers in other countries increased rice production
    (D) people became willing to pay higher prices for autos
    (E) families in the country starting eating less rice and more wheat

1. A country produces both servers (capital goods) and smartphones (consumer goods). The PPC below shows how many of each can be produced per week in various combinations, ranging from all servers and no smartphones to no servers and all smartphones.

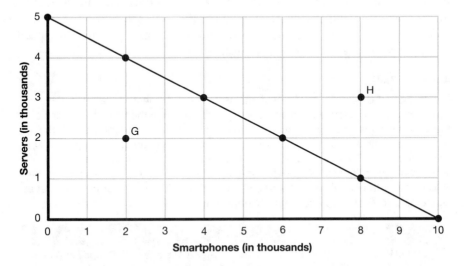

(a) What type of opportunity cost does this graph represent?

(b) How does this graph illustrate efficient production of the two products?

(c) Explain what is occurring in the economy at point G.

(d) Explain what is occurring in the economy at point H.

(e) Assume that the country increases production of smartphones from 4,000 per week to 6,000 per week. What is the opportunity cost of making this adjustment?

THINK AS AN ECONOMIST: *DRAW AN ACCURATELY LABELED GRAPH*

A production possibilities curve (PPC) plots the output of any two goods or services by a producer. It can be used to determine the optimal mix of goods or services to produce.

As you have seen, as long as a country or a producer has the same level of resources, the production possibilities curve remains the same. The frontier that marks maximum output cannot change. The PPC shifts if the level of resources increases, as the newly available resources allow increased production capacity. What happens when resources decrease?

Apply the Skill

The country of Concordia produces digital watches and wheat. Under normal conditions, it can produce the mix of these goods shown in the two left columns of the table. One year, though, Concordia is hit by a significant drought. The weather disaster has little impact on digital watch production. However, the drought hits wheat production hard. The new levels of output possible during the drought are shown in the two right columns. Use the data in the table to create one graph showing the PPC under both normal and drought conditions. Label the graph correctly so that an economist would understand what is being shown.

NORMAL CONDITIONS		DROUGHT CONDITIONS	
Digital Watches	Pounds of Wheat	Digital Watches	Pounds of Wheat
39,000	0	38,000	0
35,000	110,000	32,000	20,000
30,000	180,000	26,000	60,000
22,000	260,000	17,000	120,000
14,000	310,000	10,000	180,000
7,000	340,000	5,000	225,000
0	350,000	0	250,000

Topic 1.3

Comparative Advantage and Gains from Trade

"Under a system of perfectly free commerce, each country naturally devotes its capital and labor to such employments as are most beneficial to each."

David Ricardo, *On the Principles of Political Economy and Taxation* (1817)

Essential Question: How does engaging in trade increase overall production and consumption?

Two hundred years ago, the English economist David Ricardo suggested that, instead of trying to produce everything that its citizens needed and wanted, each country should specialize in those goods that it could produce more efficiently than other countries. Each country would then trade for other goods with the countries that specialized in producing them. England had become the world's leading producer of textiles as a result of the Industrial Revolution. But the English climate was not conducive to growing grapes on a large scale. Portugal, on the other hand, was a major grape-growing country, but its textile industry had not yet been mechanized. Thus, it made sense for England to manufacture textiles and not grow grapes and for Portugal to grow grapes rather than producing textiles. The two countries could then trade with one another to satisfy their wants.

Absolute Advantage and Comparative Advantage

A person, business, or country has an **absolute advantage** when it can produce more of a good or service than another producer that has the same quantity of resources. In the late 18th century, industrialization allowed England to produce textiles more cheaply than other European countries, giving it an absolute advantage over them. Today, the United States, with its skilled workforce, plentiful natural resources, and cutting-edge technology, has an absolute advantage over many countries in producing many goods and services, but not in all. Indonesia, because of its climate and the skills of its workforce, has an absolute advantage in the production of spices. Thus, the United States buys spices from Indonesia and sells Indonesia soybeans, a crop in which the United States has an absolute advantage. Australia has an absolute advantage in aluminum production, since it is the leading producer of bauxite, the main aluminum ore. The United States buys aluminum from Australia and sells Australia transportation equipment.

Comparative Advantage In some cases, however, it is advantageous for a country to import goods and services from another country even though they could be produced more cheaply at home. (To import goods is to purchase them from outside a country; to export goods is to sell them to another country.) The principle of comparative advantage helps explain why this is so. **Comparative advantage** is the ability to produce a good or service at a lower opportunity cost than another producer.

In addition to discussing absolute advantage in his 1817 book, Ricardo formulated the law of comparative advantage, which takes into account the opportunity cost of producing two goods or services. If two countries have different opportunity costs in the production of two goods or services, both countries would benefit from specializing in the goods it can produce in which its opportunity costs are lower—meaning they give up less to produce the good. The production of the other item would then be left to the other country. The two countries could then trade with each other.

A hypothetical case might use Ropistan and Wirania as the two countries and rope and wire as the two commodities. Ropistan might take 100 hours to produce a quantity of rope that could be produced in Wirania with 90 hours of labor. And for wire, Ropistan might take 120 hours to produce the same quantity as Wirania could produce with 80 hours of labor.

RICARDO'S COMPARATIVE ADVANTAGE		
Commodity	Hours of Work Needed to Produce 1 Unit	
	Ropistan	Wirania
Rope	100	90
Wire	120	80

In this scenario, Ropistan needs more labor to produce both goods. Thus, Wirania has an absolute advantage in production of both rope and wire. To determine which country has the comparative advantage, however, look at the opportunity costs. As you can see from the figures in the table above, it takes Ropistan about 10 percent more labor to produce the same amount of rope as Wirania, it takes 50 percent more labor for Ropistan to produce as much wire as Wirania. Ropistan is better off concentrating on the production of rope, since it requires 20 fewer hours of labor than wire production, and Wirania is better off concentrating on wire production, which requires 10 fewer hours of labor than producing rope would.

To determine the opportunity cost to each country of producing rope, divide the number of hours it takes to produce rope by the number of hours to produce wire:

Rope/Wire = Opportunity cost of rope

To determine the opportunity cost to each country of producing wire, divide the number of hours it takes to produce wire by the number of hours to produce rope:

Wire/Rope = Opportunity cost of wire

The table "Opportunity Costs" shows the opportunity costs of producing rope and wire for both Ropistan and Wirania.

OPPORTUNITY COSTS		
	Ropistan	**Wirania**
Opportunity cost to produce 1 unit of rope	100/120 = 0.833 units of wire	90/80 = 1.125 units of wire
Opportunity cost to produce 1 unit of wire	120/100 = 1.20 units of rope	80/90 = 0.89 units of rope

The country with the lower opportunity cost in producing a commodity has the comparative advantage. The opportunity cost of producing a unit of rope in Ropistan is 0.833 compared to 1.125 in Wirania, so Ropistan has the comparative advantage. The opportunity cost of producing a unit of wire in Ropistan is 1.20 compared to 0.89 in Wirania, so Wirania has the comparative advantage.

While it has the absolute advantage in production of both commodities, Wirania can exchange the wire for more rope than it could produce by diverting labor from wire production to the production of rope. Therefore, the opportunity cost of trading wire for rope is lower than the opportunity cost of producing the rope. Similarly, Ropistan has a comparative advantage in production of rope because the opportunity cost is lower than that of producing wire.

The example of Ropistan and Wirania is referred to as an input problem. This type of problem uses the amount of resources, usually hours of labor, that go into the production of a particular quantity of goods to assess comparative advantage. However, comparative advantage can also be assessed by comparing how much can be produced (output) when both countries employ an equal level of resources (input). This is known as an output problem.

Drawbacks The law of comparative advantage is a very simplistic two-good/two-country model. It makes many assumptions that, while being true, do not specifically reflect reality. The real world is much more complex, and most countries import and export a wide variety of goods and services. Also, comparative advantage does not take into account factors such as the value of one country's currency versus that of another (See Topic 6.2) and relative prices.

In addition, comparative advantage may change over time. The same factors that can result in changes in opportunity costs can also affect a country's comparative advantage. Such factors as improved technology or the depletion of nonrenewable resources have a positive or negative effect on opportunity costs, which in turn may change the comparative advantage one country has over another.

Specialization and Trade

In his book *The Wealth of Nations* (1776), British economist Adam Smith argued that **specialization** (focusing production on select goods to increase efficiency) and its accompanying **division of labor** (assigning different, specific tasks to workers) were the basis of economic progress. Smith believed that it made more sense for people to work at whatever they do most profitably and to use their earnings to buy the things they want. The same advice applies just as well to regions and countries, a fact that David Ricardo recognized in the passage that opens this topic.

One hundred years ago, there was a great deal of regional specialization in the United States. Cars made in Michigan were sold in Kansas, while baked

The Ten Leading U.S. Trading Partners, 2018
(figures in billions of dollars)

Canada
$298.7
$318.5

Japan
$75.0
$142.6

United Kingdom
$66.2
$60.8

South Korea
$74.3
$56.3

France
$36.3
$52.5

United States
Total Exports of Goods: $1,664.1
Total Imports of Goods: $2,542.8

China
$539.5
$120.3

Germany
$57.7
$125.9

India
$54.4
$33.1

Mexico
$346.5
$265

Italy
$54.7
$23.2

■ U.S. Exports   ■ U.S. Imports

Source: https://www.census.gov/foreign-trade/statistics/highlights/top/top1812yr.html

goods consumed in Michigan might have been made from Kansas wheat. Because of its location on the Great Lakes, availability of steel, capital, and growing workforce, Detroit became the center of the automobile industry. Kansas, on the other hand, had the right soil, climate, capital, and labor to produce wheat. For similar reasons, West Virginia became a major producer of coal, Florida of citrus fruits, and California of semiconductors. These days, however, production is much less regionalized. Automobiles, for example, are made in plants in many states.

As with states, countries tend to specialize in the production of certain goods and services. For example, Brazil is the world's largest producer of coffee beans, while Ecuador leads in the export of bananas. China is the leading exporter of electronics, while the United States produces much of the world's computer software. The United States is the world's largest exporter of services, including financial services, express delivery, energy services, information technology, and telecommunications. It is followed by the United Kingdom, which exports scientific and technical services, information and communication services, financial and insurance services, and travel and transport services.

Mutually Beneficial Trade Countries specialize in the production of certain goods and services for many reasons. These include availability of resources (including labor) in addition to absolute and comparative advantage. Specialization according to comparative advantage results in opportunities beyond those on the production possibilities curve (PPC). Trade between two countries allows for higher total output and consumption than would be possible domestically. **Gains from trade** result when two countries specialize in commodities in which they have a comparative advantage and exchange with one another, allowing each to benefit from increased consumption of goods they would not have without trade.

Returning to the examples of Ropistan and Wirania, if each country specializes in the commodity in which it has a comparative advantage and

Gains from Trade

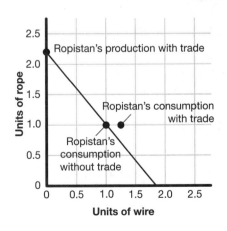 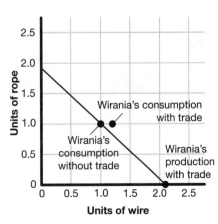

trades the surplus, both countries benefit. This is because the arrangement allows both countries to consume beyond their production possibilities. If Ropistan devotes 220 hours of labor to manufacturing rope, it can produce 2.2 units and trade the 1.2 surplus units for wire, and if Wirania devotes 170 hours to making wire, it can produce 2.125 units and trade the 1.25 surplus units for rope. Each country benefits by being able to consume more of the commodity that it imports from the other than it was able to before trade took place.

Keep in mind, though, that trade-offs occur as a result of this specialization. For example, workers in some industries lose their jobs when a country no longer specializes in a certain industry. Also, increases in manufacturing can have negative environmental effects.

While comparative advantage and opportunity costs play a part in determining the terms of trade, other factors also come into play. For example, the United States must be able to import manufactured goods from China at lower cost than those items can be produced domestically. The terms of trade are the ratio between the prices of a country's exports, or goods it sells abroad, and its imports, or goods it buys from other countries. The terms of trade are calculated using this formula:

Price of exports/Price of imports x 100 = Terms of trade

As you can see, if from one year to the next, the price of a country's exports goes up (or imports goes down), the country's terms of trade improve. In either situation, the country stands to improve its standard of living as a result.

When two countries such as the United States and China have a rate of exchange that is profitable for both, **mutually beneficial trade** can take place. As a result, both countries are able to enjoy gains from trade.

ANSWER THE TOPIC ESSENTIAL QUESTION

1. In one to three paragraphs, explain how engaging in trade increases production and consumption.

KEY TERMS

absolute advantage	division of labor
comparative advantage	mutually beneficial trade
specialization	gains from trade

1. In what term is the opportunity cost of a commodity expressed?

   (A) Resources

   (B) Hours of labor

   (C) Another commodity

   (D) Gains from trade

   (E) Money

2. If a country possesses a skilled workforce and cutting-edge technology, this means that it would

   (A) have an absolute advantage over many other countries in the production of a variety of goods

   (B) have a comparative advantage over many other countries in the production of a variety of goods

   (C) not be subject to the types of trade-offs that other countries must face when engaging in trade

   (D) be virtually guaranteed a trade surplus each year

   (E) have difficulty finding trading partners with whom it can engage in mutually beneficial trade

3. Which of the following is a basic economic concept that makes mutually beneficial trade possible?

   (A) Absolute advantage

   (B) Specialization

   (C) Trade-offs

   (D) Scarcity

   (E) Opportunity cost

FREE-RESPONSE QUESTIONS

1. Suppose that countries A and B produce only two goods: cheese and fish. The table below summarizes the average hourly worker productivity for each country and commodity.

NUMBER OF KILOGRAMS PRODUCED PER HOUR		
Country	Fish	Cheese
A	80	40
B	100	20

(a) Which country has an absolute advantage in the production of fish?

(b) Draw a production possibilities curve that includes both countries. Place *Fish* on the vertical axis and *Cheese* on the horizontal axis, and label each country on the graph.

(c) Calculate the opportunity cost of Country A to produce 1 unit (kilogram) of cheese.

(d) Calculate the opportunity cost of Country B to produce 1 unit (kilogram) of cheese.

(e) Which country has the comparative advantage in producing cheese? Explain.

THINK AS AN ECONOMIST: *IDENTIFY AN ECONOMIC CONCEPT USING CALCULATIONS*

Economists use calculations to explain and identify economic concepts. In this lesson, you learned how to determine the comparative advantage of two countries when considered as an input problem. In an input problem, the amount of inputs (labor, in the text example) varies but the output (the quantity produced) is fixed. Economists calculate the opportunity cost of inputs by dividing the labor required to produce one unit of a good by the labor needed to produce one unit of a second good. The country with a comparative advantage in producing a good is the one with the lowest opportunity cost. In the text example given in this topic, Ropistan had a comparative advantage in producing rope, and Wirania had a comparative advantage in producing wire.

Apply the Skill

Economists also consider the comparative advantage in terms of outputs--the quantity of two goods that can be produced with a fixed set of inputs. The calculation is similar. You compare the output of two goods in two countries based on a specific level of inputs. The country with the comparative advantage for producing a good has the lowest opportunity cost for making that good. Study the table, which shows the output of pounds of chocolate or individual step counters that two countries can produce with 10 units of labor. Calculate the comparative advantage of each country in terms of output. Which good should each country specialize in?

OUTPUT PER 10 UNITS OF LABOR		
	Sweetonia	Sweatistan
Chocolate (pounds)	45	20
Step counters (units)	15	4

Topic 1.4

Demand

"The market price of every particular commodity is regulated by the proportion between the quantity which is actually brought to market, and the demand of those who are willing to pay the natural price of the commodity.

Adam Smith, *An Inquiry into the Nature and Causes of the Wealth of Nations* (1776)

Essential Question: What effect does the price of a good or service have on consumer demand?

The price people pay for goods and services plays a crucial role in the choices they make as consumers, and hence in the economic system. If the price is too low, sellers will not sell. If it is too high, buyers will not buy. In general, buyers will purchase more of an item at a lower price and less at a higher price. But price is only one of several factors that affect demand and, therefore, the prices consumers pay. To understand how a nation's economy functions, it is necessary to have some understanding of that nation's price system. And to understand the price system, it is necessary to understand the law of demand.

The Law of Demand

In economics, **demand** refers to consumers' desire and ability to purchase goods and services. The **law of demand** describes the relationship between the quantity of goods and services that are demanded and the price. When all else is equal, there is an inverse relationship between price and quantity demanded. So, as prices increase, the quantity demanded decreases, and as prices decrease, the quantity demanded increases. Several factors explain these relationships. At a lower price, more people can afford to buy a product, and they often buy larger quantities of the product. At higher prices, fewer people can afford to buy the product, and those who do will purchase smaller quantities.

Determinants of Demand

When an individual consumer considers buying a ticket to a movie, more than just the specific price of that ticket affects the decision. For example, if a consumer is poor, the price might feel high. If a consumer is wealthy, the price might seem low. At the macro level, non-price factors also influence total demand for a good or service. These factors, called **determinants of demand** (or shifters of demand), affect how much consumer will purchase at every price. Five are particularly important.

Change in Disposable Income People make many of their purchasing decisions based on their incomes. A rise in income is usually accompanied by an increase in demand, while a fall in income is usually accompanied by a decline in demand. In some cases, though, the demand for a good or service may increase as income falls. For example, a decline in consumer income might cause people to shop more for second-hand clothing.

Change in Availability of Related Goods or Services Some goods are **substitutes**, ones that can be purchased in place of a certain good or service. Many consumers consider butter and margarine substitutes for each other. If the price of one rises significantly, they will buy less of it and more of the other.

Other good are **complementary**, meaning that they are purchased along with a particular good or service. Automobiles and gasoline are complementary goods. In the 1970s, several large oil-producing countries protested U.S. policies in the Middle East by ending the sale of oil to the United States. This led to a steep rise in the price of gasoline. In response, consumers purchased fewer large gas-guzzling cars and more small, fuel-efficient ones.

Source: Bob DuHamel

In the 1970s as the price of gas rose, demand for cars that used less gas rose as well.

Change in Tastes or Preferences Buyers often base their choices on their opinion of a particular product, which can be shaped by advertising. Advertising attempts to increase the desire for a particular good or service by appealing to a consumer's emotions or self-image. Consumer tech companies have waged an ongoing battle to position their smartphones, laptops, or tablets as *the* product for savvy users and trend-setters. At the same time, they have tried to position their competitors as sellers of yesterday's technology for those who are followers, not leaders.

Change in Expectations About the Future If people think that the price of an item is going to rise, they may decide to purchase it right away instead of waiting. In 2019, when President Donald Trump threatened to impose additional tariffs on imports from China, for example, many people made purchases before the anticipated price increases. On the other hand, if people expect prices to drop, they may delay purchases. Many people hold off purchasing expensive items such as large televisions in the expectation that retailers will offer deep discounts during holiday sales.

Change in Number of Buyers in the Market As more buyers enter the market, demand rises even if prices don't change. Conversely, as the number of potential buyers drops, so does demand.

Other Factors Influencing Demand Several other factors also shape demand, but most of these have only short-term effects. For example, the demand for some goods varies by season. There is a greater demand for fans and air conditioners in the summer and a greater demand for electric heaters in the winter. Health news can be very influential on demand for food. In 1959, just days before Thanksgiving, preliminary tests indicated that a batch of cranberries might include chemicals that caused cancer. Suddenly, no one was buying cranberries for their Thanksgiving dinner. Though later tests showed that the danger was very limited, the scare devastated the cranberry industry for that year.

Graphing Demand

The demand for a good or service can be shown in a chart of data or a line graph. Either provides a simple way to analyze how much people want to purchase at various prices.

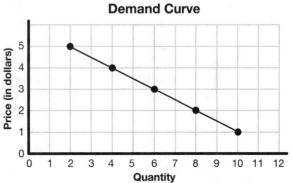

DEMAND SCHEDULE	
Price	Quantity Demanded
$5	2
$4	4
$3	6
$2	8
$1	10

Demand Schedule A demand schedule is a table showing the relationship between the price of a good or service and the quantity demanded when all other determinants are equal. It usually consists of two columns. The first column lists different price levels in either ascending or descending order, while the second column lists the quantity of the product that will be demanded at that price.

Demand Curve A graph of the demand table can be created by plotting the price on the vertical axis (often referred to as the y-axis) and the quantity demanded at that price on the horizontal axis (often referred to as the x-axis). By connecting the points, we have a downward-sloping line that relates the price and quantity demanded. This is called the **demand curve**. The table and graph below are a simple demand schedule and demand curve.

Any change in the determinants of demand can shift the demand curve to the right or to the left. When a change increases the quantity demanded at every price, the demand curve shifts to the right. This is referred to as an *increase in demand*. If, conversely, a change reduces demand at every price, the demand curve shifts to the left and is called a *decrease in demand*.

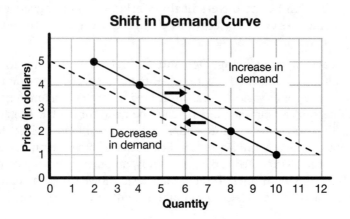

Shift in Demand Curve

Shifting the Demand Curve A demand curve shows how the quantity demanded of a good or service changes as its price changes. An increase or decrease in price does not shift the curve; it just moves to a new point along the existing curve. However, if one of the determinants of demand changes, it creates an entirely new curve. If a change in one of the determinants of demand causes overall demand to increase at every price, the curve shifts to the right. If the change causes demand to decrease at every price, the curve shifts to the left.

Slope of the Demand Curve The law of demand states that a change in the price of a good or service results in a corresponding but inverse change in the quantity that consumers will demand. It does not, however, predict how much the quantity demanded will increase or decrease with each change in price. The sensitivity of the quantity demanded to a change in price is called the price elasticity of demand.

- If people perceive a good as hard to replace and its price low, such as salt, a 10 percent increase in price might change the quantity demanded very little. Its price elasticity is low, so its curve will be more vertical.

- If people perceive a good as easy to replace and its price high, such as fresh halibut, a 10 percent increase in price might change quantity demanded significantly. Its price elasticity is high, so its curve will be more horizontal.

1. In one to three paragraphs, explain the effect the price of a good or service has on consumer demand

KEY TERMS	
demand	substitute
law of demand	complementary
determinants of demand	demand curve

MULTIPLE-CHOICE QUESTIONS

1. The law of demand states that the quantity of a good or service demanded varies
   (A) directly with its price
   (B) inversely with its price
   (C) in the same direction as total supply of the good
   (D) according to geography and season
   (E) based on tradition and government regulation

2. If consumers buy more of Good B when the price of Good A rises, what is the relationship between the two goods?
   (A) Good A is more of a luxury than Good B.
   (B) Good B is more expensive than Good A.
   (C) Both goods are necessities.
   (D) The goods are substitutes for each other.
   (E) The goods are complementary to each other.

3. Unlike a change in price, a change in a determinant of demand results in
   (A) a decrease in quantity demanded overall
   (B) an increase in prices overall
   (C) an increase in the price demand of elasticity
   (D) a new demand schedule but not a new demand curve
   (E) a new demand schedule and a new demand curve

1. With electric cars in mind, use the following mock headlines to determine whether demand increases, decreases, or remains the same and explain what prompted the change in demand (change in buyer's tastes, change in expectations, change in income, change in the price of related goods, or change in the number of buyers or size of the market).

   (a) Gasoline Prices Triple in the United States

   (b) Government Lowers Driving Age to 15

   (c) Personal and Public Electric Car Charging Stations to Become Less Expensive

   (d) Cybersecurity Experts Report Electric Cars Are Difficult to Steal

   (e) U.S. Recession Over; Unemployment Drops to 5.2 Percent

THINK AS AN ECONOMIST: *DRAW AN ACCURATELY LABELED GRAPH TO REPRESENT AN ECONOMIC MARKET*

Market demand is consumers' interest in and ability to purchase a good or service. It reflects the cumulative effect resulting from combining the demand of all individual consumers in the market. The desire to buy a product does not equal demand; consumers must also have the economic resources to make a purchase. Economists use demand curves to graph demand, which generally has a downward slope since demand decreases as price increases.

Apply the Skill

Here is the demand schedule for a type of entertainment: tickets to an NBA basketball game. Graph the demand curve and label it correctly.

DEMAND SCHEDULE	
Quantity demanded (in thousands)	Price
10	$110
20	$90
30	$75
40	$65
50	$50
60	$35
70	$20
80	$10

Topic 1.5

Supply

"A given change in price tends to have a larger effect on amount supplied as the time for suppliers to respond increases."

Paul Samuelson, *Economics: An Introductory Analysis* (2009)

Essential Question: What influences the supply of goods in a competitive market?

The previous topic demonstrated that the price of a product affects the number of units that people are willing and able to buy—in other words, the quantity demanded. Price also affects the quantity of an item that is supplied. The term **supply** refers to the amount of a good or service a producer is willing and able to sell at a given price. Producers in a free market compete with each other for profits, so businesses shift their resources from less-profitable goods or services to those that are more profitable. This causes the supply of more-profitable goods and services to increase while the supply of less-profitable ones decreases.

The Law of Supply

The **law of supply** states that, when all other factors are equal, there is a positive relationship between price and quantity supplied. In other words, the quantity of a good or service supplied varies directly with its price, so an increase in price usually leads to an increase in the quantity supplied. Not only will existing producers increase their output at the higher price but higher prices will cause new producers to enter the market. Conversely, a decrease in price usually decreases the quantity supplied.

Determinants of Supply

Price is not the only factor that affects supply, just as it is not the only factor that affects demand. Suppliers may shift production—and, therefore, supply—for a variety of reasons not directly related to price. Factors other than price that affect how much of a good producers are willing or able to supply are called **determinants of supply** (or shifters of supply). These affect supply at every price.

Change in Prices of Related Goods or Services Businesses that are able to produce related products may shift production to another product if they can make greater profits. For example, in the months leading up to summer, a manufacturer of refrigerators may switch to making air conditioners, causing production of refrigerators to drop. Or a farmer may switch from growing wheat to growing oats, resulting in a drop in total wheat production.

Change in Technology Technological advancements make it possible to produce goods and services more efficiently, often using fewer workers. The shift, over time, from production via individual artisans, to assembly lines, to modern facilities using automation and robotics illustrates this fact. Improvements in technology make it possible to cut production costs while increasing production and profits.

Source: Getty Images

The evolution of agricultural technology, from horse powered to petroleum powered, has had a massive effect on the world's supply of food.

Change in Price of Resources The cost of land, labor, energy, and raw materials directly affects production costs. Supply is inversely proportional to the cost of any of the resources needed to produce a product. As those costs rise, profits shrink, and the supply is reduced. The impact of each of these factors varies by the nature of the industry involved. For example, a rise in the cost of land has a big impact on the cost of producing more crops but a small to negligible impact on increasing production at a manufacturing facility.

Change in Number of Producers As the number of producers of a particular good or service increases or decreases, so, too, does the amount of goods or services available. For example, when a new mall opens, it might only have one store that sells shoes. Over time, more shoe stores arrive. And while this increase in the number of suppliers does change (increase) the quantity of shoes supplied, its does so at every price point.

Change in Expectations Producers' expectations about the future price of a good or service can directly affect the amount they supply. Manufacturers may increase production if they expect prices to rise. For example, if farmers expect the price of a commodity to increase in the future, they may be able to withhold all or part of their crops until they can benefit from the higher price, thus reducing the supply in the short run.

Change in Government Policies Government policies include environmental and health regulations, labor and minimum-wage laws, zoning, and land-use regulations. Most of these adversely affect the supply of a good or service because they add to the cost of production. Taxes and subsidies have a more direct effect on supply. Tax increases tend to reduce supply, while tax cuts increase it. Government subsidies reduce the cost of production and usually lead to an increase in supply.

Other Factors Many other factors can affect the supply of goods and services. For example, a change in the weather in one season can have short-term effects on supply.

Graphing Supply

The supply of a good or service can be shown in a chart of data or in a line graph. Either provides a simple way to analyze how much producers are willing to provide at various prices.

Supply Schedule A table showing the relationship between the price of a good or service and the quantity supplied when all other determinants are equal is called a **supply schedule**. It usually consists of two columns. The first column lists different price levels in either ascending or descending order, while the second column lists the quantity of the product that will be supplied at that price.

Supply Curve A supply schedule, like a demand schedule, can be plotted on a graph. Again, the price is plotted on the vertical axis and the quantity supplied at that price on the horizontal axis. By connecting the points, a line that slopes upward from the left to right emerges. This is called the **supply curve**. The following table and graph are a simple supply schedule and supply curve.

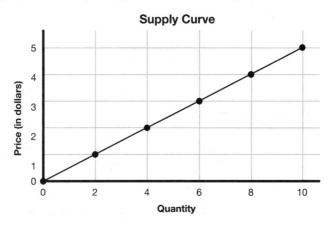

SUPPLY SCHEDULE	
Price	Quantity
$0	0
$1	2
$2	4
$3	5
$4	8
$5	10

As you can see in the Supply Curve above, the quantity supplied changes in direct proportion to the price.

Shifting the Supply Curve Changes in price causes movement along an existing supply curve. However, any change in the determinants of supply can shift the entire supply curve to the right or to the left. For example, if the cost of buying milk increases, makers of cheese will find making cheese more expensive. At any given price, they will produce less cheese. So, the supply curve shifts to the left. After World War II ended in 1945, the federal government provided large subsidies to encourage construction of homes. This caused the supply curve to shift to the right.

Slope of the Supply Curve Supply, like demand, varies in elasticity. The price elasticity of supply shows the extent to which the quantity supplied responds to changes in price. The supply of some commodities is more sensitive to price changes than the supply of others.

- Supply is elastic if a change in price leads to a substantial change in the quantity supplied. For example, the supply of oil is fairly elastic. Oil companies often operate oil wells at less than full capacity and own some wells that are not profitable at low prices. If the price of oil increases, oil companies can increase production at existing wells and activate additional wells.

- Supply is inelastic if a change in price only leads to a slight change in the quantity supplied. For example, the supply of many rare metals is fairly inelastic. Even a large increase in price does not increase the amount available to be mined.

ANSWER THE TOPIC ESSENTIAL QUESTION

1. In one to three paragraphs, explain what influences the supply of goods and services in a competitive market.

KEY TERMS

supply	determinants of supply	supply curve
law of supply	supply schedule	

MULTIPLE-CHOICE QUESTIONS

1. A decrease in the number of televisions produced in a country in response to a fall in price demonstrates
   (A) the law of supply
   (B) the difference between elasticity and inelasticity
   (C) the influence of supply determinants
   (D) a shift in the supply curve
   (E) a change in demand for televisions

2. Which of the following would most likely cause the supply curve to shift to the right in the supply of doctors in the United States who practice general medicine rather than a specialty?

(A) An increase in the salaries of doctors who specialize in a particular field

(B) An increase in the cost of attending medical school

(C) An increase in government subsidies to students who want to practice general medicine

(D) A decrease in the number of students admitted to medical school

(E) A decrease in the number of general-medicine doctors that hospitals plan to hire

3. Which best explains why supply curves slope upward?

(A) Supply and price have an inverse relationship.

(B) Prices have a positive relationship with supply.

(C) Elasticity of supply varies depending on the good or service.

(D) Determinants of supply vary depending on the good or service.

(E) Non-price factors determine the shape of a supply curve.

FREE-RESPONSE QUESTIONS

1. Many factors besides price can affect the supply of a product. Explain how each of the following situations would most likely affect the supply of a given product or service.

(a) Congress votes to provide a subsidy to encourage the construction of affordable housing.

(b) Oil-exporting countries cut off shipments of oil to the United States in retaliation for changes in U.S. foreign policy.

(c) Universities in South Korea begin to train lawyers with skills identical to those trained in U.S. law schools.

(d) Researchers at a state university develop new technology to make production of eyeglasses more efficient and less labor intensive.

(e) The price of corn rises significantly as a result of the construction of new plants that make ethanol, a type of fuel made from corn or other plants.

THINK AS AN ECONOMIST: *DRAW AN ACCURATELY LABELED GRAPH TO REPRESENT AN ECONOMIC MARKET*

As with demand, economists use a graph to display the supply of a good or service in a market. The demand curve slopes upward, indicating that quantity supplied increases as price increases. As with demand, certain factors function as determinants of supply. This reflects producers' response to economic incentives; the higher the price, the more money they make.

The determinants of supply can shift the supply curve either to the left or the right. Those that represent benefits to the producer move the curve to the right. Those that work against a producers' interests move it to the left.

Apply the Skill
The table shows the supply schedule for Acme Widgets, the finest widget maker in the country. The center and right columns show the quantity supplied under two scenarios. One indicates the original supply curve; the other represents the supply curve after Acme adopted a new cost-cutting production technology. Graph the two supply curves, correctly label them, and use an arrow to show the direction in which the supply curve moved.

QUANTITY SUPPLIED (IN THOUSANDS)		
Price (per unit)	Scenario 1	Scenario 2
$5	7	10
$10	11	14
$15	15	18
$20	18	23
$25	22	29
$30	26	34
$40	31	41
$45	34	45

When you decide to buy a new phone, hire a tutor, or purchase any other good or service, you probably expect that the benefits you receive will outweigh your costs. You are acting in your self-interest as you see it. However, economists disagree on whether such decisions are always as rational people think.

The Neoclassical Approach In the late 1800s, thinkers who are today referred to as neoclassical economists assumed that people always acted rationally. For example, a business would continue to increase production as long as doing so increased profits. Based on the belief that people made rational decisions, economists could develop clear models and mathematical equations that predicted how consumers and producers would behave. These neoclassical assumptions remain the basis of most economic analysis today.

The Keynesian Approach However, despite constant improvements in their models, economists found that individual behavior and markets could be very unpredictable. Rather than conclude that they simply needed better models, economists questioned the assumption of rationality. They recognized that people sometimes made decisions based on emotion rather than reason. For example, British economist John Maynard Keynes (1883–1946) observed that consumers and producers sometimes made decisions out of a "a spontaneous urge to action" that could be best explained by "animal spirits." If stock prices were going up, people might buy more stocks because they hoped the prices would continue to increase, even if past experience warned them that stock prices would decline.

The Behavioral Approach Building on the observations of Keynes and others, some economists in the late 20th century focused on how irrational decisions shaped economic choices. These individuals became known as behavioral economists. For example, two scholars with expertise in both psychology and economics, Daniel Kahneman and Amos Tversky, looked at how ideas of fairness, altruism, and overconfidence influenced how people made economic decisions.

A one-time colleague of Kahneman and Tversky, Richard Thaler, believed that people acted irrationally in ways so consistent that economists could accurately predict their behavior. In 2017, Thaler won the Nobel Prize in Economics. When asked what he would do with the $1.1 million cash award, he responded, "I will try to spend it as irrationally as possible."

Market Equilibrium, Disequilibrium, and Changes in Equilibrium

"The concept of equilibrium is very useful. It allows us to focus on the final outcome rather than the process that leads up to it. But the concept is also very deceptive. . . . Equilibrium itself has rarely been observed in real life—market prices have a notorious habit of fluctuating."

George Soros, *The Alchemy of Finance* (1987)

Essential Question: How do demand for and supply of a good or service determine the equilibrium price in a competitive market?

Up to now, the concepts of demand and supply have been investigated separately—the quantities that consumers and producers are willing to consider at different prices and how these quantities fluctuate in response to changes in price. But people are not always able to do what they are willing to do. Both consumers and producers are limited by what they can afford. This topic looks at how the prices of goods are set in the U.S. market system.

How Supply and Demand Determine Price

The law of supply says that as price increases, the quantity of goods or services offered for sale increases, while the law of demand says that as price increases, the quantity that consumers are willing and able to buy decreases. How can these two economic laws that seem to be diametrically opposed be reconciled?

Equilibrium and Market Price As it turns out, there is a price at which supply and demand are equal. On a graph, this price is the point at which the demand and supply curves intersect. This price is referred to as the **equilibrium price** because it is the price at which supply and demand are in balance, or equal. In other words, the price at which the quantity of goods or services demanded is equal to the quantity supplied is the price at which sales take place.

The graph "Supply/Demand Equilibrium" charts both the demand and supply curves for an item. Here the equilibrium price is $2.50. At that price, 5 units of the item are demanded, and 5 units are supplied. As long as demand and supply do not change, this is the only price at which all of the items can be sold. At the equilibrium or market price, the market is cleared—that is, all possible sales are made. The quantity demanded by consumers equals the quantity supplied by producers so that there is no leftover supply or demand.

Supply/Demand Equilibrium

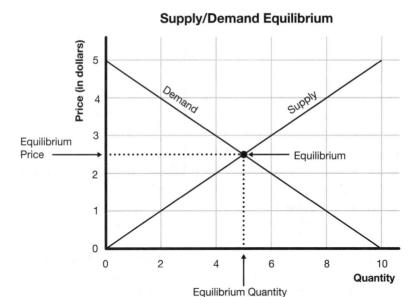

Market Imbalances Market pressures push prices toward equilibrium, but prices never quite reach it. Rather, they are at **disequilibrium prices**, ones that have some type of imbalance.

- At any price higher than the equilibrium price, producers will be left with **surplus** items, excess supply for that price. If producers want to sell all they have produced, they have to accept a lower price.

- At prices lower than the equilibrium price, consumers will find a **shortage** of items, a supply too small to fill demand at that price. If consumers want to buy the item, they have to be willing to pay a higher price.

Graphing Surpluses and Shortages The paired graphs "Markets Not in Equilibrium" shows how markets may be out of equilibrium. In the first graph, the price is $3, which is above the equilibrium price of $2.50. The quantity supplied at that price is 6 units, but the quantity demanded is 4 units, so there is a surplus of 2 units. Producers can try to increase sales by cutting prices, moving the price toward the equilibrium price so that they can get rid of their surplus.

In the second graph, the price is $2, which is below the equilibrium price of $2.50. The quantity supplied at that price is 4 units, but the quantity demanded is 6, so there is a **shortage** of 2 units due to excess demand. In other words, producers will run out of the item. Because demand exceeds supply, producers can raise the price without losing sales. In both cases, price adjustments move the market toward the equilibrium of supply and demand.

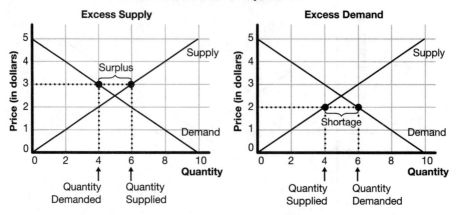

Markets Not in Equilibrium

Whether the price of a good or service starts out too high or too low, the activities of many consumers and producers push the market price toward the equilibrium price. Surpluses and shortages are usually temporary since prices generally move toward their equilibrium levels.

Changes in Equilibrium Price

The equilibrium price increases or decreases depending on the positions of the demand and supply curves. If one of the determinants of demand (see Topic 1.4) or determinants of supply (see Topic 1.5) change, the equilibrium price also changes. You can analyze how an event affects the equilibrium in three steps:

1. Determine whether the shift affects the demand curve, the supply curve, or both curves.

2. Determine whether the curve shifts to the left or to the right.

3. Use the supply-and-demand graph to compare the original equilibrium with the new one.

   Graphing Changes in Equilibrium Price The paired graphs "Changes in Demand and Supply" show how changes in demand and supply affect the equilibrium price. The first graph shows an increase in demand, and the second one shows a decrease in supply. To see how a decrease in demand would affect the equilibrium, draw a new demand curve to the left of and parallel to the original one. To see how an increase in supply would affect the equilibrium, draw a new supply curve to the right of and parallel to the original one.

These examples illustrate two principles:

- Price varies directly with changes in demand.
- Price varies inversely with changes in supply.

Since there can be changes in either demand or supply, it should come as no surprise that both may change. If both the demand and the supply shift, the

Changes in Demand and Supply

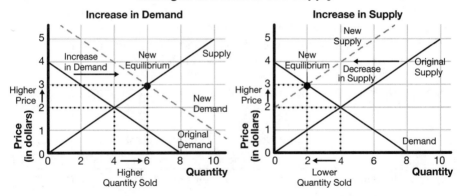

new equilibrium price and quantity cannot be predicted without knowing the amount and direction of each shift.

Competition and Prices in a Market Economy This analysis of market price has been based on a concept known as perfect competition, which holds that price is determined solely by supply and demand. Perfect competition assumes the existence of several conditions:

- There are many consumers and producers.
- Competing products are virtually identical.
- All consumers and producers have full knowledge of market conditions.
- Consumers are free to buy or not to buy and producers are free to sell or not to sell.

However, these conditions are rarely met in real life. One company may control the production of an item. Similar products usually are not identical. Consumer demand may be influenced by advertising or brand loyalty rather than the intrinsic value of an item. These are just some of the reasons that the laws of supply and demand do not operate in the real world as they do in the model. But in spite of its limitations, perfect competition highlights the forces that influence prices. And prices are what make the market system work. Prices play several roles in a market economy:

- **They act as signals to consumers and producers.** When prices are low enough, they send a signal to consumers to buy. When they are high enough, they send a signal to producers to sell.
- **They encourage efficient production.** Producers strive for efficient use of resources as a way of increasing their profits. In turn, consumers benefit because they are provided with the things they want at lower prices.
- **They determine who will receive goods and services.** Prices help determine who will be able to afford an economy's output of goods and services.

Prices make things happen. If consumers want something sufficiently enough and have enough money, they will pay more for it. If producers want to sell something sufficiently enough, they will lower its price. Prices react to demand and supply. The changes in demand and supply and their affect on the equilibrium price are summarized in the chart below.

EFFECT ON EQUILIBRIUM PRICE OF CHANGES IN SUPPLY AND DEMAND			
		Supply	
		Increases: *Curve shifts right*	**Stays Constant:** *Curve does not shift*	**Decreases:** *Curve shifts left*
Demand	**Increases:** *Curve shifts right*	Varies	Increases	Increases
	Stays Constant: *Curve does not shift*	Decreases	**Stays Constant**	Increases
	Decreases: *Curve shifts left*	Decreases	Decreases	Varies

ANSWER THE TOPIC ESSENTIAL QUESTION

1. In one to three paragraphs, explain how demand for and supply of a good or service determine the equilibrium price in a competitive market.

KEY TERMS

equilibrium price   surplus
disequilibrium price   shortage

MULTIPLE-CHOICE QUESTIONS

1. When the demand curve shifts left and the supply curve does not change, what happens to the equilibrium price?

   (A) It decreases.

   (B) It stays the same.

   (C) It shifts right.

   (D) It increases.

   (E) It is no longer on the supply curve.

2. Which of the following correctly describes how price adjustments eliminate a shortage?

(A) As the price rises, the quantity demanded increases while the quantity supplied decreases.

(B) As the price rises, the quantity demanded decreases while the quantity supplied increases.

(C) As the price rises, both the quantity demanded and the quantity supplied increase.

(D) As the price falls, the quantity demanded increases while the quantity supplied decreases.

(E) As the price falls, the quantity demanded decreases while the quantity supplied increases.

3. A surplus of goods in a market sends a signal to

(A) producers to increase supply of the good in order to increase their sales

(B) producers to raise prices to cover the expense of making goods that are unsold

(C) producers and consumers that the equilibrium price is too low

(D) consumers that the price for that good might decrease

(E) consumers that they should buy more of that good

FREE-RESPONSE QUESTIONS

1. Many factors can affect the equilibrium price and quantity of a product. Lightnings and Stealthys are two brands of running shoes, and each has a price of $80. How would the supply or demand and the price and quantity for Stealthys change given each scenario?

(a) The price of rubber used in the sole of the two running shoes increased.

(b) The federal government offers a subsidy for companies who make fitness equipment and clothing.

(c) An Italian company comes out with a running shoe that is superior to and less expensive than the current popular US running shoe.

(d) The price of Lightnings increases to $100.

(e) Researchers publish findings showing that running is good for your heart.

Economists can demonstrate the effects of a change by using accurately labeled visuals. For example, look back at Figure 3 in the topic text. The supply-demand curve on the left shows how an increase in demand pushes the demand curve to the right, resulting in a new higher equilibrium price and a higher quantity produced. The curve on the left shows the result of a decrease in supply. The supply curve shifts to the left, resulting in a higher price and reduced demand, which means that quantity goes down.

Apply the Skill

Consider this situation. Supply (S) and demand (D) for Boost Energy Bars were at a market equilibrium point (e) at quantity Q and price P. Then Boost was jolted when new ads came out in which a famous athlete proclaimed her increased stamina from eating a rival company's energy bars. Demand for Boost bars crashed, creating a new demand curve D1. Use this information to create a supply and demand curve showing the original supply, demand, price, quantity, and equilibrium and the resulting changes in price (P1), quantity (Q1), and equilibrium (e1). Include arrows showing the direction of change in demand, price, and quantity.

UNIT 1

Long Free-Response Question

1. The countries of Jamandy and Saramy make 2 products—phone chargers and sunglasses. Jamandy can make 300 phone chargers or 400 sunglasses while Saramy can make 400 phone chargers or 200 sunglasses given equal amounts of resources.

   (a) Draw one correctly labeled production possibilities curve for the country of Jamandy. Include phone chargers on the vertical axis and sunglasses on the horizontal axis.

   (b) On the graph in part (a), include the production possibilities curve for the country of Saramy.

   (c) Which country has the absolute advantage in producing phone chargers?

   (d) Calculate the opportunity cost of a phone charger in Saramy.

   (e) Which country has the comparative advantage in producing phone chargers?

   (f) Which country should export sunglasses?

   (g) Explain why the country you identified in item (f) should export sunglasses.

   (h) If production triples in Saramy, which country would have the comparative advantage in the production of sunglasses?

   (i) Assume Jamandy discovers a new, less expensive resource which will assist in increasing production of phone chargers to 500. Draw a new production possibilities curve for Jamandy which includes the old PPC and the increase in production due to the new resource.

   (j) Draw a correctly labeled demand and supply curve for Jamandy's phone chargers and illustrate on that graph what would happen to equilibrium price and quantity with the discovery of the new resource.

UNIT 2

Economic Indicators and the Business Cycle

There are many different ways of measuring the health of an economy. These economic indicators include the gross domestic product (GDP), the unemployment rate, and the rate of inflation. A rising GDP is generally a sign of a healthy economy, as are low rates of unemployment and inflation.

At the end of January 2020, a National Association for Business Economics survey reported that two-thirds of its respondents expected the GDP to grow by 1.1–2 percent, while another 30 percent expected it to grow by as much as 3 percent. Unemployment was at a record low, and consumer confidence was high as wages and salaries were growing. The economy had recovered from the Great Recession of 2007–2009, and seemed poised to keep growing.

Four months later, a very different story emerged. The onset of the COVID-19 pandemic forced states to shut down large parts of their economies. Revised projections pointed to a 6.5 percent contraction in GDP for the year. With 40 million people out of work, unemployment hovered around 20 percent. In a matter of months, the U.S. economy went from very healthy to the sort of crisis not seen since the Great Depression of the late 1920s and 1930s.

Boom and bust: that's what business cycles are all about. But most of them are not this dramatic. There were 33 business cycles between 1854 and 2009, averaging 56 months in length. The latest one lasted for 10 years, from 2010 to 2020. In this unit, you will learn more about economic indicators and the business cycle.

"Do you promise to love, honor, and to contribute to the Gross National Product?"

CartoonStock.com

Topic Titles and Essential Knowledge

Topic 2.1 The Circular Flow and GDP

- GDP is a measure of final output of the economy.
- GDP as a total flow of income and expenditure can be represented by the circular flow diagram.
- There are three ways of measuring GDP: the expenditures approach, the income approach, and the value-added approach.

Topic 2.2 Limitations of GDP

- GDP is a useful indicator of a nation's economic performance, but it has some limitations, such as failing to account for nonmarket transactions.

Topic 2.3 Unemployment

- The unemployment rate is the percentage of the labor force that is out of work.
- The labor force participation rate is another measure of the labor market activity in an economy. The labor force participation rate is the percentage of the adult population that is in the labor force.
- The measured unemployment rate is often criticized for understating the level of joblessness because it excludes groups such as discouraged workers and part-time workers.
- Economists primarily focus on three types of unemployment: cyclical, frictional, and structural.
- The natural rate of unemployment is the unemployment rate that would exist when the economy produces full-employment real output. It is equal to the sum of frictional and structural unemployment.
- The deviation of the actual unemployment rate from the natural rate is cyclical unemployment.
- The natural rate of unemployment can gradually change over time because of such things as changes in labor force characteristics.

Topic 2.4 Price Indices and Inflation

- The consumer price index (CPI) measures the change in income a consumer would need in order to maintain the same standard of living over time under a new set of prices as under the original set of prices.
- The CPI measures the cost of a fixed basket of goods and services in a given year relative to the base year.
- The inflation rate is determined by calculating the percentage change in a price index, such as CPI or the GDP deflator.
- Real variables, such as real wages, are the nominal variables deflated by the price level.
- The CPI as a measure of inflation has some shortcomings, such as substitution bias, causing it to overstate the true inflation rate.

Topic 2.5 Costs of Inflation

- Unexpected inflation arbitrarily redistributes wealth from one group of individuals to another group, such as lenders to borrowers.

Topic 2.6 Real v. Nominal GDP

- Nominal GDP is a measure of how much is spent on output. Real GDP is a measure of how much is produced.
- Nominal GDP measures aggregate output using current prices. Real GDP measures aggregate output using constant prices, thus removing the effect of changes in the overall price level.
- One way of measuring real GDP is to weigh final goods and services by their prices in a base year. Because this can lead to overstatement of real GDP growth, statistical agencies actually use different methods.
- Nominal GDP can be converted to real GDP by using the GDP deflator.

Topic 2.7 Business Cycles

- Business cycles are fluctuations in aggregate output and employment because of changes in aggregate supply and/or aggregate demand.
- The phases of a business cycle are recession and expansion.
- The turning points of a business cycle are peak and trough.
- The difference between actual output and potential output is the output gap.
- Potential output is also called full-employment output. It is the level of GDP where unemployment is equal to the natural rate of unemployment.

Source: *AP® Macroeconomics Course and Exam Description.* Effective Fall 2019 (College Board).

The Circular Flow and GDP

*When you can measure what you are speaking about,
and express it in numbers, you know something about it.*

Lord Kelvin, *Popular Lectures and Addresses* (1889)

Essential Question: How is GDP (as represented by the circular flow model) measured, and what are its components?

Macroeconomic measurement—the tracking and analysis of the flow of money, goods, and services throughout the economy—is an important tool for entities and individuals in all sectors of an economy. Measuring and drawing conclusions from economic data helps in several ways:

- It allows for comparison over time, helping in the identification of short- and long-term economic trends.
- It helps policy makers respond to short-term shocks (such as recessions or environmental disasters) and lay the groundwork for long-term growth.
- It helps decision-makers in business and government evaluate whether or not their policies are having the desired effects.

One of the most important tools of macroeconomic measurement is the **gross domestic product (GDP),** which is the total value of all final goods and services produced within a country in a specific time period. One way to measure it is by adding together all the money spent by consumers, saved in investments, and paid in taxes, with adjustments for imports and exports. (It will be defined more precisely later in the topic.)

GDP and changes in GDP are commonly used to evaluate a country's economic strength. An increase in GDP can indicate that the economy is doing well. A significant decrease can signal a recession or economic decline. It is often represented within a **circular flow model,** a graphic representation of how different units of the economy interact. GDP, as represented by the circular flow, is a basic and essential tool of economic analysis.

History of the Gross Domestic Product

In the 19th and early 20th centuries, policy makers had very incomplete, limited, and fragmentary economic data (the raw factual information that is collected and used for analysis). As a result, they had no standardized way to evaluate the economy. Economists tried to use a patchwork of information, such as banking and financial statistics, industrial production, and retail sales. These, however, provided only a narrow indication of the overall health of the economy. The limitations were clear when the National Bureau of Economic Research (NBER) touted a steady two-decade increase in the national income just two months after the 1929 stock market crash ushered in the Great Depression, the worst economic downturn in the history of the moderrn industrial world.

The desire for more accurate economic tools, prompted by the hardships of the Great Depression, led economists to develop more refined statistics, including a more precise measure of national income. During World War II, the **gross national product (GNP)**, an estimate of total value of goods and services produced by the country's residents both at home and abroad, became the most significant statistic determined by the Bureau of Economic Analysis (BEA). Then, in 1991, the BEA began featuring the GDP rather than the GNP. The key difference is that the GNP includes income produced abroad, but the GDP does not. This made U.S. data align better with international standards and allowed the United States to compare its economy with that of other countries. The BEA continues to produce both statistics.

The Circular Flow

Money is always on the move in a free market. Yet cash doesn't flow through society in a straight line like a river. Instead, money flows in an endless cycle, which economists call the "circular flow model."

The circular flow economic model illustrates how people, businesses, governments, and financial markets exchange money, goods, and services included in the GDP. As you know, a market economy is an economic system in which buyers and sellers easily exchange goods and services for a price. Goods and services flow in one direction and money in the other.

Money flows as wages from producers to workers. In turn, money in the form of payments flows back to the producers. That's the basic explanation, yet circular flow comes in several different forms. Their complexity varies depending on how many elements are included. Each model describes activity in a market economy. The models generally assume an equilibrium in which the amount of money spent equals the value of the goods and services purchased.

Two-Sector Model The two-sector model is the least complicated. In it, there are only two segments in this model: businesses, or firms, that produce goods and services, and households that consume those goods and services. Households may be a single individual or group of consumers, such as a family, that makes decisions about satisfying their wants. They also own the **factors of production** (labor, land, capital, and entrepreneurship) and sell them in exchange for the income that they later use to buy goods and services.

Firms, on the other hand, are organizations that produce and sell goods and services to make a profit. Firms employ household members and pay them wages, interest, and profits. In the two-sector model, the government isn't involved in economic decisions, and businesses do not import or export goods or services. Nor are the financial markets involved. As you can see from the diagram below, the two-sector model is closed.

Circular Flow Two-Sector Model

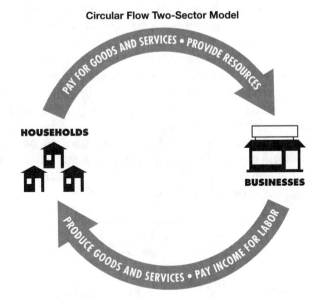

Here's how this model works: In each household are people who consume goods and services to satisfy their wants. Directly across from the household sector are businesses. These are the producers that satisfy the wants of those consumers. At the top of the circle are the **product markets** where consumers exchange goods and services with producers. In other words, the market is the place where people purchase what they want. At the bottom of the circle is the **resource market**. This is where businesses purchase the resources they desire to produce the goods consumers demand.

Money flows out of the household and moves clockwise. For example, as happens every year during the holiday season, one toy becomes the "must-have" item for kids. Parents across the country buy every available one. This year it's the "Freddy Bear," an adorable update of a classic. The money people pay for the stuffed animal flows between the household and the product market—the place where the Freddy Bear is sold. Economists call this **consumption**.

Once people purchase the bear, their money flows from the product market to the manufacturer—in this case, the maker of the toy. However, the company has a lot of payments to make to the resource market such as paying workers, renting a factory, and purchasing raw materials. The income earned by the factors of production then flows to the household. The cycle repeats itself as people use that income to consume more products.

Three-Sector Model As you might have noticed, the two-sector model does not include an essential economic agent—the government. Yet governments, whether local, state, or federal, affect the economy in multiple ways, primarily through taxing both consumers and businesses and spending the money on such benefits as education, public health, and infrastructure, among others. The three-sector model includes actions by the government but does not include those taken by the financial and foreign sectors.

Going back to the Freddy Bear example, each purchase nationwide includes the addition of some level of government taxation in addition to the purchase price. The three-sector model takes this into account. Taxes are the lifeblood of local, state, and federal governments. As you can see from this diagram, taxes flow from the household and business sectors to the government. Taxes come in many forms. Some are direct taxes like income taxes and corporate taxes, while others are indirect, including sales taxes. The price of the Freddy Bear might include a local or state sales tax.

The revenue generated by these taxes flows back to households and businesses in the form of subsidies, payment transfers, and payments for goods and services, among other things. Governments also hire and pay individuals for their work—another flow of money in this model.

Circular Flow Three-Sector Model

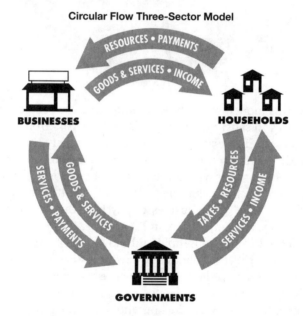

Four- and Five-Sector Models Even adding the government to the circular flow model does not, however, account for other elements essential to understanding a nation's economy and its place in the world. Among these are financial institutions, such as banks, credit unions, and investment companies, and the foreign sector. Adding one of these elements results in a four-sector model, and adding both creates the five-sector model. These complex models more closely match the real world, where global trade plays an important role, and financial institutions account for savings and investments.

The four-sector model includes all governments, businesses, and households in foreign countries. Not only do these countries import goods and services from other nations, but they are also exporters.

What does that mean? If a country exports more than it imports, then the factor payments to the domestic economy as well as the value of goods and services produced by a country are large. This means there is more income for households, businesses, and governments. If a country imports more than it exports, the opposite happens as the total flow is smaller, which means there is less income available for each sector. The impact of trade on a country's prosperity is varied, helping some people more than others. While having more exports than imports increases the money for each sector, countries are often better off overall purchasing better or lower-cost goods from abroad than trying to produce them domestically. (See Unit 6.)

The last circular model, the five-sector model, includes all those sectors in addition to the financial markets. Financial markets are an umbrella term that describes where stocks, bonds, and other securities are traded. Investors make these funds available to borrowers, which injects money into the economy.

The financial markets give individuals the opportunity to borrow money for, say, a new home or car. It also provides businesses with cash to expand production, purchase equipment, or help meet payroll. Companies can also generate new capital by issuing stocks and bonds and by borrowing money from banks.

Measuring the GDP

Although the GDP is always a measure of the final purchases by households, businesses, and governments in a particular period, three distinct approaches can be taken to calculate it:

- The expenditures approach
- The income approach
- The value-added approach

Even though the method of calculating the GDP may be different, the results of each are theoretically the same.

Expenditures Approach The **expenditures approach** is also called the demand approach since it focuses on the demand for goods and services. Economists calculate the GDP as the sum of four types of spending within an economy. They are:

- Consumption (C) includes any money a household spends on goods or services. Examples include buying food, paying a doctor, or purchasing a new car.

- Investment (I) includes money businesses pay for equipment and supplies to operate their businesses. Examples include vehicles for transport and new computers and software.

- Government spending (G) includes government spending on public goods and services. Examples are defense spending and road construction.

- Net exports (Xn) are the value of a nation's total export goods and services minus the value of its total imported goods and services. (This is also commonly expressed as X–M, or "Exports minus Imports.")

An export example is a car manufactured in the United States that is purchased by a business in Buenos Aires and whose value would be added to the net exports. An import example might be a computer manufactured in China and purchased for a household in the United States whose value would be subtracted from the net exports.

The formula for calculating the GDP in this approach is as follows:

$$C + I + G + Xn = GDP$$

While this formula may seem simple, you have to look a bit deeper to totally understand it. For example, a firm's inventory is baked into the investment component. When a producer manufactures a product, it can either sell it or stockpile it in its inventory. Inventories increase when companies produce more than they sell and decrease when companies sell more than they produce.

Regardless, accountants and economists count inventories as part of a company's capital stock—the equipment, plant, and other assets used in production. As a result, any change in inventory is considered a part of investment.

Investment also includes the building of machines, houses, factories, and offices. Construction investment comes in two forms: residential and public. Residential construction is the amount spent on the building of homes and apartment buildings by private firms. Public construction is undertaken by governments that provide capital to build schools, hospitals, roads, canals, bridges, and many other types of public work projects.

The Income Approach The **income approach** measures the total income earned through the factors of production—labor, land, capital, and entrepreneurship. The income from these factors are represented by the following formula:

$$GDP = W + R + I + PR$$

Here, wages for labor are W, rent for land is R, interest on capital is I, and profits from entrepreneurship are PR. The final GDP also includes some adjustments for taxes and subsidies.

The Value-Added Approach The **value-added approach**, also called the production approach, involves determining the value of goods and services (the output of the production process) and subtracting the goods and services that were used in generating that output (referred to as intermediate consumption). Therefore:

$$GDP = Value\ of\ production - Value\ of\ intermediate\ goods$$

Trade and GDP Since GDP attempts to measure the value of goods and services produced in a single country, the data is adjusted to account for trade. Goods and services are part of the GDP of the country where they are made, regardless of where the company is headquartered:

- When a U.S.-based automobile manufacturer produces cars in China, those sales are not counted as part of the U.S. GDP.

- When a Japanese-based automaker produces cars in the United States, that production is included in the U.S. GDP.

What GDP Leaves Out Although the GDP attempts to measure a country's economic health, it does not count many types of transactions. These exclusions and others are explained in the next topic.

ANSWER THE TOPIC ESSENTIAL QUESTION

1. In one to three paragraphs, explain the circular flow model and how GDP is measured.

KEY TERMS

gross domestic product (GDP)	resource market
circular flow model	consumption
gross national product (GNP)	expenditures approach
factors of production	income approach
product market	value-added approach

MULTIPLE-CHOICE QUESTIONS

1. Why is the GDP considered to be an essential economic measurement?
   (A) It is the sum of final goods and services the economy produces in a given time period.
   (B) It identifies the different factors of production.
   (C) It is the result of adding the value of goods produced minus the value of exports.
   (D) It is useful to the president, Congress and the Federal Reserve.
   (E) It focuses on household income.

2. The circular flow of economic activity between consumers and producers includes which of the following?
   (A) Households buy factors of production from firms and firms sell factors of production to households.
   (B) Households buy goods and services from firms and sell factors of production to businesses.
   (C) Firms sell factors of production to households and buy factors of production from the government.
   (D) The government buys factors of production from firms and firms pay taxes to households.
   (E) Firms buy factors of production from both households and the government.

3. Which of the following is NOT included in the income approach to calculating GDP?

(A) Money earned by a boat dealer

(B) Money the government spends on military equipment

(C) Money received by a landlord

(D) Income of a farmer

(E) Money received from a barber for cutting a client's hair

FREE-RESPONSE QUESTIONS

1. Use the passage below to answer all parts of the questions that follow.

Economics is a science of thinking in terms of models joined to the art of choosing models which are relevant to the contemporary world. It is compelled to be this, because, unlike the typical natural science, the material to which it is applied is, in too many respects, not homogeneous through time. The object of a model is to segregate the semi-permanent or relatively constant factors from those which are transitory or fluctuating so as to develop a logical way of thinking about the latter, and of understanding the time sequences to which they give rise in particular cases.

Good economists are scarce because the gift for using "vigilant observation" to choose good models, although it does not require a highly specialized intellectual technique, appears to be a very rare one.

John Maynard Keynes, letter to Roy Harrod, July 4, 1938

(a) Why does economics require models?

(b) According to Keynes, why is it difficult for economists to choose good models?

(c) What is the important object of creating models?

(d) Does the circular flow model meet Keynes' criteria of including both constancy and change?

(e) Does the circular flow model stand up to the "vigilant observation" of the real world?

THINK AS AN ECONOMIST: *DESCRIBE ECONOMIC MODELS*

Economists use economic models to analyze situations and explain how economic outcomes occur. To do so, they take these steps:

- Identify the economic actors involved in a situation.
- Describe how those economic actors interact with one another and what forces drive or shape those interactions.

For example, economists explain that consumers and producers are the relevant economic actors. They interact through the dynamic of demand and supply, driven by the law of demand and the law of supply. According to these laws, quantity demanded diminishes as price increases, and quantity supplied diminishes as price decreases. The two forces of demand and supply meet at a point called the equilibrium price, which sets the price for the market for a particular good or service.

Apply the Skill

Economists use the circular flow to model the interaction of economic actors in a national economy. Study the model of the circular flow with three economic sectors in the topic text. In a paragraph, explain what economic actors are involved in this model, how they interact, and what forces shape their economic activity.

The Limitations of GDP

GDP is a poor way of assessing the health of our economies, and we urgently need to find a new measure.

Erik Brynjolfsson, at the World Economic Forum in Davos, 2016

Essential Question: What are some limits of GDP as a measure of economic performance?

Since World War II, gross domestic product (GDP) has been viewed as a metric for evaluating a country's **economic well-being,** which consists of the material living conditions that people experience and their access to goods and resources. However, GDP does not include every transaction. Some it leaves out because they are considered intermediate transactions that don't represent actual production. Some it leaves out because they are hard to measure. Further, critics point out that GDP focuses on the quantity of production without regard to the effect on the quality of people's lives.

Exclusion of Intermediate Transactions

Since GDP attempts to measure final production, it does not include **intermediate goods,** ones used to produce final goods. A **final good** is one sold to the consumer who will actually use it. For example, when a glass company sells glass to a company that makes solar panels, the glass is an intermediate good, and the solar panel is a final good. Other intermediate transactions that GDP does not include are payment transfers such as a tax refund to a taxpayer and many financial trades, such as buying stock.

Exclusion of Non-Recorded Transactions

Many of the essential economic activities that are not included in GDP calculations contribute in important ways to the country's economy. But since the transactions do not go through the traditional markets, and it is difficult to place a monetary value on them, they have been excluded from GDP. The activities generating these transactions are sometimes called the **underground economy**.

   Nonmarket Transactions Domestic activities, such as cooking, cleaning, and childcare make up a large share of economic activities known as **nonmarket transactions**. If there is no specific money value associated with them, despite their clear economic value, they are not included in the GDP. However, if the same tasks are done for pay, they become part of GDP's economic measurement. For example, if you fix your own car, GDP is not affected. But if you pay a mechanic to fix your car, the exchange increases GDP. So the GDP is not measuring the actual worth of activities but only the exchange in money.

A nurse's work helping an elderly patient is part of GDP, but a family member providing similar assistance to a parent is not counted in GDP.
Source: Getty Images

Unreported Activities Some activities are legal activities that should be included in GDP but are not. For example, tips to restaurant workers are legal, and if they are reported to the government, they are included in GDP. However, if people try to avoid paying taxes on this income by failing to report it, they are breaking the tax laws.

Illegal Activities Since activities such as drug dealing and identity theft are illegal, people committing them try to avoid detection by the government. These transactions are not accounted for in GDP.

GDP as a Measure of Economic Well-Being

The GDP was originally intended to allow the government to measure country's production output. Yet shortly after the government began calculating it, people began to associate it with how well the country's individuals were doing. People interpreted an increasing GDP as a sign of increasing prosperity and economic progress.

But economists have challenged relying on the GDP as a measure of a country's economic health or as a guide for formulating economic policies. In order to fill this gap, they have developed alternatives and complements to GDP. One example, adopted by several states and increasingly used internationally, is the Genuine Progress Indicator (GPI), which assigns values to the indispensable functions of households, communities, and the natural environment, and it accounts for the negative consequences of economic growth. The GPI, for instance, includes unpaid domestic work when calculating production values and subtracts the destructive effects of consumer consumption, such as pollution and the depletion of natural resources.

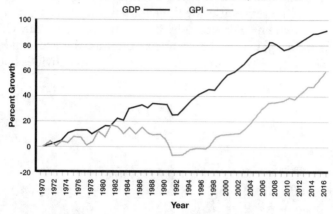

Growth in GDP vs. GPI for New Zealand, 1970-2016

GDP ——— GPI ———

Percent Growth (y-axis)

Year (x-axis)

Even for a country such as New Zealand, which perennially outperforms the vast majority of the world's countries in every major index of progress and development, year-by-year growth of GPI lags well behind that of GDP.

Another measure, the Human Development Index (HDI), was devised in 1990 by economists involved in work with developing nations. The underlying premise of the HDI is that measures such as GDP do not adequately measure the extent to which people's lives are improving. Like the GPI, the HDI takes into account more than just production and wealth. It is based on three dimensions:

1. A long and healthy life, as measured by the life expectancy each country's citizens at birth

2. Knowledge, as measured by expected years of schooling for children just entering school and the average years of schooling attained by adults over 25

3. A decent standard of living, as measured by the Gross National Income (GNI) per capita. GNI differs from GDP in that it measures income rather than production. It takes into account all of the income of all of a country's businesses and residents, including money earned abroad as well as foreign investment and aid. These differences are important when measuring the financial well-being of developing nations.

The creators of the HDI felt that when a person can live a healthy life, obtain knowledge, and have a decent standard of living, he or she will have greater opportunities. These are opportunities that people in developed countries take for granted: to decide about one's future, to control one's surroundings, to be free from violence, and to enjoy leisure time.

Income Inequality When income is distributed unevenly, even if GDP is growing, many people do not benefit from increasing economic output because they still cannot buy most of the goods and services produced. According to the Congressional Budget Office, while average income increased by 60 percent between 1979 and 2016, the lowest-income groups increased only by 33 percent, while the highest groups increased by 99 percent. For the top 1 percent, the income increase was 218 percent. While the GDP grew, so did income inequality. GDP looks at the overall economy. It does not account for variations in changes among groups within the population.

Negative Outputs The GDP also ignores the cost of economic activity that is damaging and unsustainable, such as pollution and resource depletion. A surge in lithium mining in Chile's Atacama Desert feeds the growing desire in developed countries for lithium batteries for electric cars. But the mining removes large quantities of water and pollutes the remaining supply, putting a severe strain on local farmers. So any calculation of the impact of mining on the economy should include the environmental impact as well as the economic significance.

Quality of Life Many factors that contribute to the quality of life are subject to measurement, such as housing, education, life expectancy, and clean air and water. Yet even though they can be measured, they are not included in the most pervasive measure of the economy—GDP. And other factors that contribute to the quality of life are even more elusive. Senator Robert F. Kennedy, in a 1968 speech at the University of Kansas, famously spoke of the limitations of using the GDP as a measure of quality of life:

Too much and for too long, we seemed to have surrendered personal excellence and community values in the mere accumulation of material things. Our Gross National Product counts . . . ambulances to clear our highways of carnage. It counts special locks for our doors and the jails for the people who break them. It counts the destruction of the redwood and the loss of our natural wonder in chaotic sprawl. It counts . . . the television programs which glorify violence in order to sell toys to our children. Yet the gross national product does not allow for the health of our children, the quality of their education, or the joy of their play. It does not include the beauty of our poetry or the strength of our marriages. . . neither our compassion nor our devotion to our country; it measures everything in short, except that which makes life worthwhile.

1. In one to three paragraphs, explain the limitations of GDP.

KEY TERMS

economic well-being   nonmarket transactions
intermediate goods   underground economy
final good

MULTIPLE-CHOICE QUESTIONS

---

1. Which of the following items are used to calculate GDP?
   (A) The purchase of glass by a car manufacturer to make cars
   (B) The purchase of paint by a house painter.
   (C) The purchase of sweet corn by a consumer.
   (D) The payment for babysitting services done by a teen on a Friday evening
   (E) The graduation gift received by a student from his or her family member

2. Identify which transaction is included in the expenditures approach to GDP.
   (A) the purchase of a new car
   (B) the services of a barber cutting his child's hair
   (C) mowing your neighbor's lawn
   (D) income received from selling shares of purchased stock
   (E) glass purchased by a car manufacturer

3. Genuine Progress Indicator (GPI) and Human Development Index (HDI) are considered measurements that
   (A) track income inequality
   (B) fill in gaps in GDP
   (C) reveal gaps in government spending
   (D) track non-market transactions
   (E) work best for less-developed countries

1. (a) Explain the difference between an intermediate good and final good.

   (b) Provide an example of an intermediate good.

   (c) Provide an example of a non-market transaction.

   (d) In your own words, explain why the underground economy is not counted as part of a country's gross domestic product.

   (e) In your own words, why is GDP not the most accurate measurement of the economic well-being of a country?

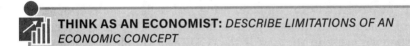

THINK AS AN ECONOMIST: *DESCRIBE LIMITATIONS OF AN ECONOMIC CONCEPT*

Gross domestic product (GDP) is an economic concept—an attempt to explain and quantify economic activity. Because of the complexity of economic behavior, no concept can perfectly explain what is taking place in an economy.

To describe the limitations of an economic concept, economists consider these factors:

- What activities does the concept not include?
- What economic value do those activities have?
- How can the concept be refined to include those activities?

Consider the concept of the law of demand. According to this law, the quantity demanded for a good or service decreases as price increases. However, economists recognize that demand for a given good or service can be affected by demand for other goods and services. The availability of substitute goods, for instance, can affect the demand for a good. In light of that, economists modify the concept of the law of demand to reflect that fact.

Apply the Skill

Economists recognize that the concept of the GDP does not perfectly represent the economic activity in a country. Identify and analyze one limitation in GDP and explain how the concept might be refined to include that activity.

It is with great fanfare that the media reports on the latest Gross Domestic Product (GDP) figures each quarter. Positive growth of GDP is an indicator of a growing economy. Negative growth is evidence of a looming or current recession of the economy. Many politicians will point to these GDP assessments as evidence that the fiscal policies of the government are working or falling short of expectations. Leaders of countries will point to their GDP, in comparison to those of other countries, to show how competitive, innovative, or vibrant their economy is in comparison. In short, the GDP number is king among measures of economic growth.

But should it be our main measurement of an economy?

Arguments for GDP as the Main Measure of the Economy Much of the support for GDP as a measure of the economy is that it has been used so long, that it is the easiest tool to compare, using real dollars, the economic performance of a country from one year to another. The other argument that economists have made in the past is that GDP is a simple equation to understand and use to explain economic growth or recession. Lastly, GDP is often used to measure a population's standard of living.

Arguments for Alternative Measures of the Economy Perhaps the best reason for using other measures of economic well-being is that GDP can rise due to production or consumption of products or services that might be viewed as negative to people's well-being. For instance, GDP growth might be attributed to rising costs of health care or in times of war or costs associated with higher crime rates. GDP also neglects, in measuring the well-being of a nation, other indicators of its standard of living.

Economists point out that GDP has other limitations. For instance, GDP is geared more to the manufacturing economies of the past, not the information technology, or "gig," economy of the modern era. Measuring an economy that is, more and more, experience- and idea-oriented, rather than object- or product-oriented, is more difficult than what is possible through the simple equation of GDP. This is because much of the activity of the modern economy is difficult, if not impossible, to measure. Think about all the hours of entertainment provided by social media for which consumers don't pay.

Alternatives to GDP In 1972, the Kingdom of Bhutan, a small nation that borders India, declared that it would no longer measure its economy in terms of GDP but rather on Gross National Happiness. Bhutan would now consider the country's living standards, health, good governance, ecological diversity, resilience, leisure vs. work time, psychological well-being, cultural diversity and well-being, and community vitality. In 2015, Bhutan's GDP was among the lower third in the world; however, 43 percent of people in Bhutan claimed to be deeply or extensively happy.

Over time, other measures of a country's economic well-being were developed, including the Measure of Economic Welfare, Net National Welfare, the Index of Leading Cultural Indicators, the Thriving Places Index, and the Human Development Index. All of these alternatives place the emphasis on those activities that provide positive effects on society and eliminate those that produce negative effects.

Topic 2.3

Unemployment

We believe that if men have the talent to invent new machines that put men out of work, they have the talent to put those men back to work.

John F. Kennedy's speech in Wheeling, West Virginia,
September 27, 1962

Essential Question: What are the different types of unemployment, and why is the rate of unemployment difficult to assess?

The **unemployment rate** is the percentage of the **labor force** (people who are able and willing to work) who are not working. It is one of the most critical measures of a country's economic performance. Here is the formula to calculate the unemployment rate:

Unemployment rate = Unemployed/Civilian labor force

It is the driving force behind many national economic policy decisions that attempt to get the unemployed back to work. Several types of unemployment exist, and economists disagree on the best ways to measure them.

Types of Unemployment

Unemployment varies by cause and duration. As a result, economists have identified various types of unemployment.

Frictional Unemployment This temporary status results from a transition, such as a move from school to work. It occurs when workers are searching for jobs, perhaps because they are changing occupations, moving to a new city, or just looking for more satisfying employment. It is an expected part of economic activity and not a focus of policy concerns.

Structural Unemployment This results from shifts in the economy, such as the decline of a particular industry. Technological changes, for example the use of robots in factories, often result in structural unemployment. It could also be a result of other of changes, such as trade agreements that encourage the relocation of factories, displacing workers. It is often characterized by a mismatch between an employee's skills and an employer's needs. It is more difficult to address than other types of unemployment.

Cyclical Unemployment This occurs as a consequence of a downturn in the overall economy, such as an economic slowdown that leads to job losses. It is connected to an oversupply of goods or services or a decline in the demand that results in employee layoffs. During a downturn, unemployment often goes up to 7 or 8 percent. However, during the Great Depression, cyclical unemployment combined with a financial crisis to produce an unemployment rate of 24.9 percent in 1933. More recently, the business cycle combined with problems in the financial sector to produce the Great Recession. Overall unemployment rate reached 10 percent in October 2009.

Seasonal Unemployment An additional type of unemployment is seasonal unemployment. This is unemployment that occurs during times of the year when the demand for certain types of labor is low. Examples include agricultural work, which may require workers only during the harvest season, or some retail work, such as sales during the Christmas season.

Labor Force

The labor force, a basic employment concept, is the target of many policies that address unemployment. It consists of anyone age 16 or older who is employed, self-employed, serving in the military, or unemployed but looking for work. It does not include anyone who is not working but is not actively seeking employment, nor does it include students, retirees, or some persons with disabilities.

Labor Force Participation Rate The **labor force participation rate**, which is considered an indication of economic activity, compares the size of the labor force with the number of people who could potentially be part of the labor force—that is, anyone over the age of 16. Here is the formula to calculate the labor force participation rate:

Labor force participation rate = Labor force/Total population over age 16

So, for example, parents who are not working outside the home but are taking care of their children at home, are not considered part of the labor force, and their numbers reduce the labor force participation rate.

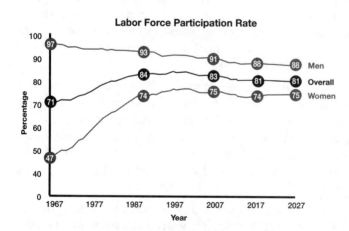

In the last half of the 20th century, the U.S. labor force participation rate increased significantly. The big jump came between 1967 and 1987, when the percentage of women in the job market increased from 47 percent to 74 percent.

Full Employment

The ideal employment rate within an economy is the **full employment rate,** a condition when anyone who wants to work can get work. This is not, however, equivalent to a zero-unemployment rate. The closest the United States has come to a zero-unemployment rate was during World War II when millions of men served as soldiers and millions of women filled the jobs the men had left. In 1944, the unemployment rate was 1.2 percent.

Economists define full employment differently based on their theories of how an ideal economy should function. Many think it means an unemployment rate somewhere between 3.5 and 4.5 percent. Some think reaching the full employment rate is not even desirable because it would cause a destabilizing increase in prices. A full employment economy is often defined as one in which frictional and voluntary unemployment are as expected, but structural and cyclical unemployment are not high enough to be problems.

Natural Rate of Unemployment The expected and acceptable unemployment rate has also been called the **natural rate of unemployment,** a concept formulated by economists Milton Friedman and Edmund Phelps to describe the proportion of the labor force that remains unemployed during a period of full employment. The natural rate of unemployment is a combination of frictional unemployment (FU) and structural unemployment (SU) divided by the labor force (LF) that remains when the economy is stable.

Natural rate of unemployment = (FU + SU)/LF

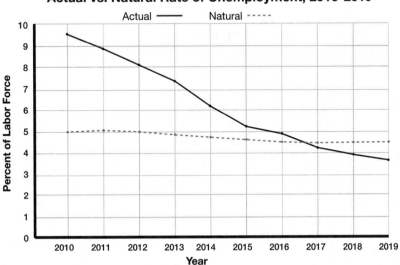

Actual vs. Natural Rate of Unemployment, 2010-2019

The difference between the actual unemployment rate and the natural unemployment rate is much greater during a time of economic difficulty (2010–2014). This difference represents the unemployment rate typical of cyclical unemployment.

The natural rate of unemployment accounts for workers being unemployed even when the economy is growing, because it incorporates the natural flow of workers from one job to another. The difference between the actual rate of unemployment and the natural rate of unemployment is considered the cyclical unemployment rate.

Cyclical unemployment rate =
Actual unemployment rate – Natural unemployment rate

Limitations of the Unemployment Rate

The current methods of measuring unemployment have some noteworthy limitations because they do not account for all the unemployed:

- Discouraged workers: These workers want a job but are not actively looking for one because they have given up trying to get work. An example might be an auto worker whose factory has moved overseas.

- Underemployed workers: These workers are mismatched with their current job, either by skills or wages. An example is a person with a nursing degree who is unable to find a job as a nurse, and so takes a lower-paying job as a medical technician.

- Part-time workers: Those workers who want full-time work but are able to find only part-time jobs are not considered in unemployment statistics.

- Chronically unemployed workers: These workers have been removed from the unemployment rate calculations after 27 weeks without work.

Because the commonly used unemployment rate does not include these categories of people, it underreports the number of potential workers who are actually without work. It makes the unemployment appear to be much lower than it really is.

ANSWER THE TOPIC ESSENTIAL QUESTION

1. In one to three paragraphs, describe the different types of unemployment and why the rate of unemployment is difficult to assess.

KEY TERMS

unemployment rate	seasonal unemployment
labor force	labor force participation rate
frictional unemployment	full employment rate
structural unemployment	natural rate of unemployment
cyclical unemployment	

Questions 1 and 2 refer to the following table.

Employment Data for a Medium-Sized City	
Total Population over 16	200,000
Employed	187,000
Unemployed	12,000
Discouraged/Chronically Unemployed/ Underemployed/Part-time Workers	1,000

1. Calculate the unemployment rate.
   (A) 4.2 percent
   (B) 6.03 percent
   (C) 6.4 percent
   (D) 12.01 percent
   (E) 24 percent

2. Calculate the labor force participation rate.
   (A) 10 percent
   (B) 20 percent
   (C) 60 percent
   (D) 93.5 percent
   (E) 99.5 percent

3. Which of the following are included in the labor force?
   (A) students
   (B) part-timers
   (C) retirees
   (D) volunteers
   (E) stay-at-home parents

1. Between 2000 and 2007, the U.S. unemployment rate varied from approximately 4 percent (2000) to 6 percent (2003) to 4.5 percent (2007), while the unemployment rate in the Eurozone varied from approximately 9 percent to 8.5 percent to 7.5 percent for the same time periods.

   (a) What do these figures tell us about labor force participation?

   (b) If this was a period of economic growth in both regions, what do these figures suggest about the natural rate of unemployment in the United States compared to the Eurozone?

   (c) What is the likely range for the natural rate of unemployment in the United States during this time period?

   (d) Assume that when its economy is stable, the Eurozone experiences 3 percent frictional unemployment and 2 percent structural unemployment. Given this data, what is their natural rate of unemployment?

   (e) Given your answer to (d), what type of unemployment was the Eurozone experiencing when it varied from 9 percent to 7.5 percent and what was the percentage of this type of unemployment?

THINK AS AN ECONOMIST: *ILLUSTRATE AN ECONOMIC CONCEPT BY AN EXAMPLE*

Economists use examples to clarify economic concepts. Being able to identify a specific example helps economists communicate effectively by making the abstract idea more concrete.

For example, in discussing service-sector industries, economists give examples ranging from bank employees meeting customers' banking needs to hair stylists working in hair salons.

Apply the Skill

Economists identify four groups of workers that unemployment statistics do not include. Name each type and give an example not in the text of a person in that situation.

Topic 2.4

Price Indices and Inflation

By a continuing process of inflation, government can confiscate, secretly and unobserved, an important part of the wealth of their citizens.

John Maynard Keynes. *The Economic Consequences of the Peace*

Essential Question: How is the consumer price index (CPI) related to inflation, deflation, disinflation, and real variables?

Inflation is an overall rise in the price of goods and services. For example, if you spent $1,000 one year for a mixture of clothes, food, and entertainment, and that exact same mixture cost $1,100 the following year, that would indicate inflation. Another way to think of inflation is a decline in the value of money. That is, $1 spent today buys less than it did in the past.

Inflation has many consequences, among them a decrease in the value of savings, an increase in the interest rates on loans, and a decrease in exports. A steady increase in prices is usually difficult for consumers. However, it benefits those who have borrowed money, because they are repaying loans with dollars that are worth less than the dollars they borrowed. Inflation also benefits the government. Since sales taxes are usually a percentage of the sales price, as prices increase so do government revenues. If incomes increase with inflation, government revenue can also go with added income tax receipts.

Consumer Price Index (CPI)

The government attempts to evaluate inflationary trends and establish policies to help deal with the effects of inflation. The most widely used inflation assessment tool is the **consumer price index (CPI)**, a measure that tracks the change in the average price of a group of consumer goods and services. The U.S. Bureau of Labor Statistics calculates the CPI using what it calls a "market basket"—a collection of over 200 categories of items that consumers purchase that includes, among other items, food, transportation, and medical services. Over time, the price changes are tracked for those basket items, providing a measure of the inflation that consumers experience in their daily lives.

What's In the CPI Market Basket?

FOOD AND BEVERAGES	HOUSING	CLOTHING	TRANSPORTATION
• Meat, Cereal, Restaurant Meals • Coffee, Milk, Juice	• Rent, Mortgage • Energy • Furniture	• Dresses, Pants, Coats • Jewelery	• Cars, Gas, Insurance • Airfare
MEDICAL CARE	**RECREATION**	**EDUCATION AND COMMUNICATION**	**OTHER GOODS AND SERVICES**
• Hospitalization, Medicine • Eyeglasses	• Movies, TV • Sports Equipment • Pet Supplies	• Tuition, School Supplies • Telephone, Internet	• Personal Grooming • Funerals

The government, businesses, and individuals use the CPI to make financial decisions. The CPI is also used to adjust income payments for over 80 million people so that the payments reflect price levels. These income recipients include the following:

- Social Security beneficiaries
- Military and federal civil service retirees
- SNAP recipients (a food assistance program)
- Some workers with collective bargaining agreements

Calculating the CPI The CPI for a given year is calculated by dividing the price of the market basket of goods and services in that year by the price of the same basket in the base year. (The current base year used by the government is 1982–1983, and the CPI in the base year always equals 100.) This ratio of the two baskets is then multiplied by 100. The formula is:

CPI = Cost of market basket in year a/Cost of market basket in base year × 100

Calculating the Inflation Rate During World War I, the **inflation rate**, the measure of the change in purchasing power, fluctuated wildly, ranging from below zero to almost 21 percent. The resulting concern led to instituting the CPI in order to have a more reliable gauge to help guide monetary policy.

The inflation rate can be calculated using the CPI in the following formula.

$$Inflation\ Rate = \frac{CPI_2 - CPI_1}{CPI_1} \times 100$$

(CPI_2 is the CPI in the second period; CPI_1 is the CPI in the previous period.)

The following table shows an example of using index values to calculate inflation percent changes.

	Item X	Item Y
Year I	112.5	225.0
Year II	121.5	243.0
Change in Index Points	9.0	18.0

Percent change   9.0/112.500 × 100 = 8.0
18.0/225.000 × 100 = 8.0

Real and Nominal Variables The difference between **real variables**, variables whose value is adjusted for and determined by their value in terms of goods and services, and nominal variables (discussed more in Topic 2.6) is inflation. The nominal variable is measured in money and does not include inflation. The CPI can be used to calculate the difference between real and nominal variables, for example, wages. For this calculation, use the following formula:

Real wage = Nominal wage/CPI × 100

Deflation and Disinflation The opposite of inflation is an overall drop in the price of goods and services. This is referred to as **deflation**. Far less common than inflation, it usually reflects severe economic problems. For example, the United States in the late 1800s experienced a general decline in prices accompanied by frequent financial panics and bursts of high unemployment. One cause of these problems was the normal interaction of supply and demand. Industrialization and improvements in farming techniques increased the supply of goods. However, low wages restrained the growth of demand. As a result, people were creating more goods than they could afford to consume. The combination of increasing supply and stagnant demand pushed prices down.

A second cause of deflation in the late 1800s was a shortage of money in circulation. Since money was in short supply, it became more valuable. That is, a dollar could purchase more goods than previously, another way of saying that prices were lower. The importance of the supply of money will be covered in Unit 4.

In contrast to deflation, **disinflation** is a marginal reduction in the inflation rate over a short period. While it often reflects a slowdown in economic growth, it is usually not a sign of economic trouble.

Inflation—Causes and Management

The most common cause of inflation is called **demand-pull inflation**. When consumers increase their demand, producers try to increase the supply. But when additional supply is unavailable, producers increase the price. For example, after the 2008 financial crisis, investors wanted gold as a protection against uncertainty surrounding the value of the Euro and the dollar. With a limited supply, gold prices went up to a record level, despite the general economic financial decline.

The government can combat high inflation in multiple ways, most of which reduce overall demand for goods and services. These efforts are explained in more detail in later topics on fiscal policy (3.8), monetary policy (4.6), and both types of policies (5.1):

- higher income tax rates that could reduce the amount of money consumers have available to spend

- higher interest rates that discourage borrowing and spending

- lower government spending so that the public sector is purchasing less

- changes in banking regulations that reduce the money available for making loans

Similarly, the government can combat deflation with efforts to increase overall demand.

CPI Limitations

Although it is a basic and essential economic indicator, the CPI is flawed. It has a number of important weaknesses, among them:

- **Inadequate representation of novelty** The actual cost of living may be temporarily skewed when a new product is introduced to the market and before the government adds it to the "market basket." When smartphones were introduced in the early 2000s, their price was not immediately reflected in the CPI.

- **No acknowledgment of changes in product quality** A consumer may derive significantly more benefit from a product whose quality has improved, even while its price has risen.

- **Substitution bias** For some products, a price rise can result in consumers purchasing less expensive alternatives, replacing, for example, steak with hamburger.

- **Lack of inclusion of buyer habits** Consumers whose preferences differ from the goods and services in the "market basket" may be underrepresented in inflation calculations. This may be a result of the consumers' location or, more likely, age, with younger consumers' buying habits underrepresented.

ANSWER THE TOPIC ESSENTIAL QUESTION

1. In one to three paragraphs, explain what the CPI is and how it helps to calculate inflation, deflation, disinflation, and real variables, such as wages.

KEY TERMS

inflation	deflation
consumer price index (CPI)	disinflation
inflation rate	demand-pull inflation
real variables	

MULTIPLE-CHOICE QUESTIONS

1. The Consumer Price Index (CPI) is used to measure
   - (A) changes in the prices of all goods and services in an economy over time
   - (B) change in the price of a select group of consumer goods and services over time
   - (C) changes in wages over a period of time
   - (D) the improved quality of a select group of goods and services
   - (E) the changes in spending habits of all consumers

2. In the country of Bornesia, CPI for 2008 was 100 and in 2009 the CPI was 120. Calculate Bornesia's inflation rate for 2009.
   - (A) 5 percent
   - (B) 10 percent
   - (C) 15 percent
   - (D) 20 percent
   - (E) 25 percent

3. Why is the CPI not an accurate measure of the economy?
   - (A) It does not include the value of improved quality.
   - (B) It is based only on goods from 1982 to 1983.
   - (C) It overestimates real wages.
   - (D) It has too many goods in its "market basket."
   - (E) It doesn't incorporate imported goods.

1. Country X has a CPI of 195 in year 1; 209 in year 2; 211 in year 3; 203 in year 4; 201 in year 5; and 208 in year 6.

   (a) Calculate the inflation rate for Country X between year 1 and year 2.

   (b) Calculate the inflation rate between year 3 and year 4.

   (c) What do the different rates tell you about the economy of Country X between year 1 and year 4?

   (d) What are some actions the government of Country X might decide to take in years 4 and 5?

   (e) What does the CPI tell us about real wages during that time period?

 THINK AS AN ECONOMIST: *INTERPRET AN ECONOMIC OUTCOME USING CALCULATIONS*

Government policy makers carefully monitor economic data, keeping watch on such factors as the GDP growth rate, the unemployment rate, and the inflation rate. They use this data to determine how the economy is performing and to predict the possible impact of policy decisions. One of the key indicators that policy makers watch is the consumer price index (CPI), the measure of prices of a standard market basket of more than 200 categories of goods and services. By comparing the CPI for one quarter to the CPI for the previous quarter, economists can determine if inflation is taking place. The formula for calculating the inflation rate is:

$$\textit{Inflation rate} = \frac{CPI_2 - CPI_1}{CPI_1} *100$$

(CPI_2 is the CPI in the second period; CPI_1 is the CPI in the previous period.)

Apply the Skill

Government statistics provide the CPIs for the first three quarters of the current year: Q1—252.8; Q2—253.9; Q3—255.1; Q4—257.7. The index for the fourth quarter of the previous year was 250.2. Use the data to determine the inflation rate for each quarter and the overall inflation rate for the year.

Cost of Inflation

*The central focus of what we are doing at the Fed is to keep
inflation from accelerating—and preferably decelerating.*

Alan Greenspan, Federal Reserve chair, 1987–2006

Essential Question: What are the costs to individuals, businesses, and
the economy of unexpected inflation?

Individuals cannot control the overall level of inflation in an economy, but they
can respond to its impact on their lives. Many economists view low inflation
as a sign of a healthy economy, and people plan for it. Over the past century,
inflation has averaged about 3 percent per year. However, unexpectedly high
inflation can cause significant economic problems. It can make planning for
the future difficult, discourage saving and investing money, and reduce the
standard of living for anyone whose income does not increase as prices go up.

Understanding Inflation

The basic working of supply and demand can cause the overall level of prices in
an economy to increase. **Aggregate demand** is the total demand for all finished
goods and services that consumers want at current prices. **Aggregate supply** is
the total amount of goods and services suppliers want to supply at those prices.
If these change at different rates, the difference can result in inflation:

- **Demand-pull inflation** occurs when aggregate demand increases faster
  than aggregate supply. For example, if consumers begin to save less and
  spend more, the increase in consumption can cause prices to increase.

- **Cost-push inflation** occurs when aggregate supply decreases. Any
  thing that increases the cost of production qualifies as cost-push
  inflation, from a trade conflict that reduces supply to a simple increase
  in the cost of raw materials for production.

In both types of inflation, the changing balance between aggregate demand
and aggregate supply results in a higher equilibrium price. (For more on
aggregate demand, aggregate supply, and inflation, see Unit 3.)

Effects of Inflation

Inflation is typical in the U. S. economy. Because it is common, people plan
for it in their economic decisions. The most obvious effect of inflation is

simply another way of describing it: as the cost of goods and services rises, the purchasing power of money decreases.

In general, any inflation benefits people who borrow money at the expense of people who loan money. This is because borrowers pay back their debt with money that is worth less than money was worth when they incurred the debt. Since both borrowers and lenders plan for inflation, they take some inflation into account when they agree to a loan. However, if inflation is higher or lower than expected, it will benefit one group far more than the other.

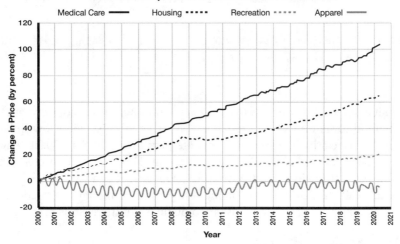

The prices for different goods and services vary at different rates, with some, such as medical costs, rising steeply and other, such as apparel, remaining stable.

Impact on Loans When a bank makes a loan, it figures into the cost of the loan how inflation will make the money it receives worth a little less each month. If inflation is higher than expected, the bank makes less profit, or possibly even loses money, on the loan. If inflation is lower than expected, the bank will make more.

For borrowers, higher than expected inflation means that the money they are using to repay the loan is worth even less than they expected. In general, this helps them. But the reality is more complex. If prices increase and wages do as well, then repaying the loan will be easier. However, if prices increase but wages do not, repaying the loan could be harder. As the cost of everything else goes up, repaying the loan might become more of a burden.

Devaluation of Savings When a person saves money in an account with a fixed interest rate, inflation reduces the value of the return on his or her savings. For example, if a saver puts $1,000 in an account with a 4 percent interest rate, he or she will have $1,040 at the end of the year. However, if the year's inflation rate was 8 percent, the purchasing power of that $1,040 would be only be about $960.

Fear of inflation is a serious problem in countries that have experienced multiple significant inflationary periods over the years. People are reluctant to save money because they know from experience that it could be worth much less in a few years.

Inflation can be particularly hard on savings for retirement because this money is often held for many years before it is used. In the 1970s, inflation was high, averaging over 7 percent per year. If a person in 1970 hid $100,000 under a mattress for retirement, by 1980, he or she would still have $100,000. But that money would purchase only what $50,000 would have purchased in 1970. In effect, the person would have lost half of the savings without spending a penny. If that person had invested the $100,000 in stocks, real estate, or other forms of investments, its value by 1980 would have depended on the return received. It might have kept pace with inflation, or it might have been worth far more than the equivalent of $100,000 or far less than $50,000.

In general, when prices increase and income does not, wage-earners and people living on a fixed income are among the groups that suffer from declining purchasing power. Their incomes often do not adjust rapidly with inflation.

Reallocation of Resources With inflation, the prices for different goods and services do not always rise at the same rate, and the inflationary effect is different for different groups. For example, a steep rise in medical costs has a greater impact on the elderly and people with diabilities than it does on most people between 18 and 30 years old. This can affect how resources are allocated. Seniors on fixed incomes may have to buy less expensive (and possibly less healthy) food in order to pay for their medical expenses. Similarly, a steep rise in the cost of post-high school education would affect people in their teens and twenties more than it would elderly people.

Imposition of Menu Costs When prices increase, businesses want to change their prices to meet the inflationary trend. This shift imposes certain expenses called menu costs: printing new menus with new prices is a straightforward example. But a wide range of wholesale and retail businesses incur costs associated with reprinting (catalogs and circulars), reprogramming (Web sites), remarking (price tags), and relabeling (signs). Most businesses wait until prices rise sufficiently to justify the expense of making physical and virtual price changes.

Responses to Inflation

One danger of inflation is that it can lead to more inflation, a situation known as an **inflationary spiral**. For example, if prices increase, workers might negotiate for higher wages, which then causes prices to increase even more.

If a country enters an inflationary spiral, or if inflation gets high enough to be a problem for any other reason, governments can respond through various policies. For example, a government can reduce aggregate demand by cutting government expenditures or raising taxes on consumers to reduce the amount of money they have to spend. It can also decrease the amount of money in circulation in the economy. The effect of this is to push interest rates on loans higher, which makes borrowing money more expensive. As consumers and businesses borrow less, aggregate demand decreases. (Responses to inflation are explained in more detail in Topics 3.8 and 4.6.)

ANSWER THE TOPIC ESSENTIAL QUESTION

1. In one to three paragraphs, explain the cost of inflation to individuals, businesses, and the economy.

KEY TERMS

aggregate demand	cost-push inflation
aggregate supply	inflationary spiral

MULTIPLE-CHOICE QUESTIONS

1. If Harry borrows $10,000 at a rate of 4 percent for a period of five years and inflation occurs at a rate of 6 percent during that time, who benefits from the high rate of inflation?

(A) The bank benefits.

(B) Harry benefits.

(C) Neither benefits, unless Harry pays the loan off early.

(D) Both benefit.

(E) Harry benefits, if he pays the loan off early.

2. Other things remaining constant, if a drought occurs or the price of oil increases, these events could cause

(A) An inflationary spiral

(B) An increase in real wages

(C) Demand-pull inflation

(D) Cost-push inflation

(E) Banks to make a higher profit.

3. The Federal Reserve Bank increases interest rates in order to

(A) keep the rate of inflation below 2 percent

(B) increase wages

(C) increase the amount of money in circulation

(D) counteract an inflationary trend

(E) implement wealth redistribution

1. The chart below compares inflation (left axis) and the price of crude oil (right axis) between the years 1969 and 1988. The shaded areas indicate a U.S. recession. Use the chart to answer the following questions.

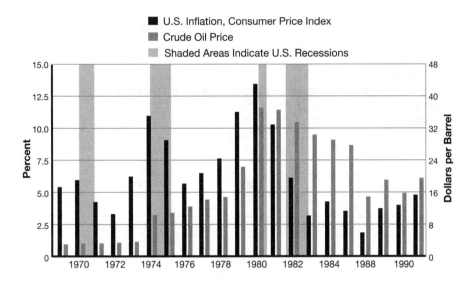

(a) Identify one trend based on the data in this chart and draw a conclusion based on that trend.

(b) In which year was the rate of inflation greatest?

(c) Roughly, how much did the inflation rate dip between 1982 and 1983?

(d) During which recession was the rate of inflation the lowest?

(e) What similarities existed between the recession of 1974–1975 and the recession of 1981–1982? Based on your reading, what type of inflation was at work during those periods? Explain your answers.

Economists use quantitative data and calculations to determine the outcome of a situation. A calculation they frequently make involves change over time, which is determined using this formula:

$$\frac{Period\ 2 - Period\ 1}{Period\ 1} \times 100 = Percentage\ change$$

Apply the Skill

Since 1975, Social Security benefits paid to retirees have increased each year based on cost of living allowances (COLAs). These are automatic increases that all recipients receive based on the inflation rate from the third quarter of the previous year to the third quarter of the current year. The increases go into effect in December of the current year.

	COLAs	CPI-W*
2015	0.0%	231.810
2016	0.3%	234.076
2017	2.0%	239.051
2018	2.8%	245.146
2019	1.6%	249.222

*CPI-W is the Consumer Price Index for Urban Wage Earners and Clerical Workers, the specific CPI on which COLAs are based.

Source: Social Security Administration

Consider a retiree who received a monthly Social Security benefit of $2,275 in 2015 before that year's COLA. What would that retiree's monthly benefit be in 2019? What was the overall percentage increase in that benefit from 2015 to 2019? How does that percentage compare to the overall percentage increase in the CPI-W for that period? What does that tell you about COLA increases?

Real vs. Nominal GDP

Just as a temperature gauge doesn't say much about how hot it will feel when you go outside because it doesn't measure humidity, statistics don't always capture economic reality for ordinary Americans.

Alister Bull, Federal Reserve correspondent,
Thomson Reuters news service, 2008

Essential Question: What is the difference between the real and nominal GDP, and how is it calculated using the GDP deflator?

The difference between nominal and real GDP is much like the difference between the actual experience of heat and the temperature reading on a thermometer. In the same way that the thermometer gauges only temperature but not humidity, wind speed, or other important aspects of the weather, the nominal GDP gauges only a specific aspect of the economy—the number of dollars paid for products and services in today's marketplace. However, the real GDP more closely portrays the actual experience of the country's economic condition by tracking a country's production output.

Nominal GDP

The **nominal GDP**, also called the unadjusted GDP, quantifies the total value in money, rather than units of production, of all the goods produced in a year. Because of this, it is said to quantify how much is spent on output, rather than how much is produced. To do this, nominal GDP uses the current price of goods. If the average person spent $200 on shoes in 2015 and $400 on shoes in 2020, it may mean that they bought four pairs of shoes for $50 each in 2015 and eight pairs of shoes for $50 each in 2020. It may, on the other hand, mean that they still bought four pairs of shoes in 2020, but each pair cost $100. So, if the nominal GDP increases, it may mean that prices, rather than production, increased.

The formula used to calculate the nominal GDP is:

$$GDP = C + I + G + (X - M)$$

In this equation, C is consumer consumption, I is gross private domestic investment, G is government spending, X is exports, and M is imports. Therefore, in a given year, if consumer spending was $10 trillion dollars, reported investments were $6 trillion, government spending was $7 trillion, exports totaled $1 trillion, and imports were $2 trillion, the nominal GDP for that year would be $22 trillion dollars.

$22 trillion = $10 trillion + $6 trillion + $7 trillion + ($1 trillion – $2 trillion)

Real GDP

Real GDP is nominal GDP adjusted for inflation and deflation. Since it is adjusted for changes in price, it better reflects the country's actual changes in the quantity of production. Both real and nominal GDP are reported by the U.S. Bureau of Economic Analysis. It changes a price-based measure—nominal GDP—into an index based on the economic output.

Box office receipts illustrate the difference between economic activity measured in current dollars (nominal) and activity adjusted for inflation. As of 2020, *Star Wars: Episode VII—The Force Awakens*, released in 2015, held the position of the top box office grossing film of all time with $936,662,225 in gross receipts. Yet if the box office receipts are adjusted for inflation, *Gone with the Wind*, released in 1939, has an adjusted gross that was 80 percent higher than *Star Wars: Episode VII*. The success of *Gone with the Wind* appears even more impressive when population is considered. The population of the United States was 200 million fewer than in 1939 than in 2020, and the global market for movies was far smaller when *Gone with the Wind* appeared.

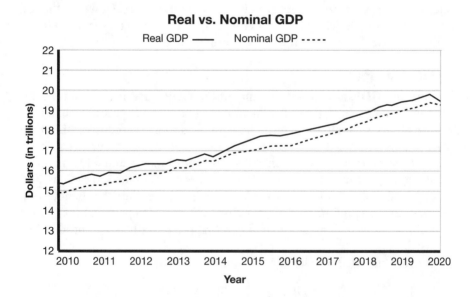

Calculating Real GDP Real GDP can be calculated by determining how much GDP has been affected by inflation since the base year established for the purpose of the calculation. The base year is the first in a series of years used as an economic index to determine economic growth.

Computing real GDP can be accomplished by taking the quantities of all goods and services in the year being measured and multiplying them by their prices in the base year. It can also be achieved by using the **GDP deflator,** a measurement used to determine price inflation or deflation in relation to a specific year.

The formula for finding real GDP divides the nominal GDP by the GDP deflator which, for the base year, is typically set at 100. Inflation will make the deflator rise in subsequent years, and deflation will cause the deflator to decrease. For example, if inflation rose by 1 percent the year following the base year, the GDP deflator for that year is 1.01. If the nominal GDP is $1,000,000,000,000, in order to determine the real GDP, that 1 trillion dollars is divided by 1.01. The resulting real GDP equals $990,099,009,900.9901.

Real GDP = Nominal GDP/Deflator (in hundredths)

If the GDP deflator has increased from the base year and the real GDP is lower than the nominal GDP, there is inflation; if the nominal GDP is lower, there is deflation.

GDP Per Capita

There are some measures that use real GDP that reveal more about a country's economic status. **GDP per capita,** calculated by dividing a country's GDP by its population, is a measure of a country's output per person. (Real GDP per capita is calculated in the same way, except that it uses real GDP as a starting point.) Because its elements (real GDP and population) are tracked worldwide and can be easily compared, real GDP per capita can function as a universal measure of prosperity, or standard of living.

Even when a nation has consistent economic growth, if its population is growing at a faster rate than the GDP, the change in its per capita GDP will be negative. For countries with a stable population, per capita GDP will grow as productivity grows, often as a result of technological developments that encourage greater output.

A Cambodian farmer tends her crops. Cambodia had a GDP per capita growth of 5.9 percent in 2018, one of the ten fastest growing in the world. However, poverty is still a serious problem in rural areas, where education and basic infrastructure are lacking.

Per capita GDP is, however, a very rough estimate of standard of living. It does not take into account quality of life. Are there quality schools? Are the streets safe? Is the environment livable? Is there any social safety net? None of these questions can be answered simply by a per capita GDP figure. Also, the question of income inequality remains unanswered by this measure. While GDP per capita divides figures evenly among the population, money within an actual society is not so equitably split.

ANSWER THE TOPIC ESSENTIAL QUESTION

1. In one to three paragraphs, explain the difference between real and nominal GDP and demonstrate how real GDP is calculated using the GDP deflator.

KEY TERMS

nominal GDP
real GDP
GDP deflator
real GDP per capita

MULTIPLE-CHOICE QUESTIONS

1. Calculate the nominal GDP for Country X given the data in the table below (in billions of dollars).

Consumption	850
Gross Private Domestic Investment	684
Government Spending	572
Depreciation	254
Exports	156
Imports	70

(A) $2,192 billion

(B) $2,446 billion

(C) $2,332 billion

(D) $2,586 billion

(E) $2,516 billion

2. Which statement best describes per capita GDP?
   (A) It is always higher in countries with large populations.
   (B) Its increase indicates a stable population.
   (C) It is considered a universally accepted measure of prosperity.
   (D) It grows when productivity slows.
   (E) It is difficult to compare globally.

3. A base year is
   (A) determined by the Federal Reserve Board
   (B) calculated by subtracting real GDP from nominal GDP
   (C) used for comparing changes in economic activity
   (D) always five years before the current year
   (E) given a value of 1,000

FREE-RESPONSE QUESTIONS

1. Country Z has the following output and prices for 2018 and 2019.

Goods	2018 Quantity	2018 Price	2019 Quantity	2019 Price
Hats	5,000	$8	5,000	$10
Scarves	2,000	$4	2,000	$5
Gloves	2,000	$4	3,000	$6

   (a) Calculate Country Z's nominal GDP in 2018, based only on consumer spending.
   (b) Calculate Country Z's nominal GDP in 2019, based only on consumer spending,
   (c) Calculate Country Z's real GDP in 2019 using 2018 as base year and its prices as constant prices, based only on consumer spending.
   (d) Why might an increase in nominal GDP be unrelated to increased economic growth?
   (e) What is the nominal GDP per capita for 2018 if the population of Country Z is 35 people?

Economists use quantitative data to explain and identify economic concepts. In doing so, they present the data, discuss it, and explain how it demonstrates the concept.

For example, to determine whether inflation is taking place, economists want to compare the prices of the same goods and services over time. They constructed the consumer price index as a tool that enables them to calculate the inflation rate from one period to another. The CPI provides quantitative data on the cost of this market basket of goods and services. It is useful for comparisons over a long period of time as well. Because the CPI uses the same market basket of categories of goods and services each year, economists can compare changes in the index over several years to track trends in inflation.

Apply the Skill

Gross domestic product (GDP) is a measure of a country's overall economic output. But using GDP alone to make comparisons from one country to another provides an incomplete picture of the productivity of a country's economy. A country with a vast population is sure to vastly outperform a smaller country. To compare national economies, economists look at GDP per capita.

Look at the data in the table. Use it to explain the value of using an index like per capita GDP to compare economic variables.

Country	GDP (in billions of dollars)	GDP rank	Population (in millions)	Population rank	GDP per capita
China	25,260	1	1,390	1	$18,200
United States	14,390	2	1,320	3	$59,800
India	9,470	3	333	2	$7,200
Bangladesh	690	33	163	8	$4,200
Singapore	528	38	6	110	$94,100
New Zealand	189	68	5	125	$39,000
Latvia	54	108	2	153	$27,700

Source: CIA World Factbook

Business Cycles

The whole reason that our capitalist system works the way it does is because there are cycles, and the cycles self-correct.

Seth Klarman (b. 1957), American billionaire

Essential Question: What is the business cycle, and what are its phases?

The economy is characterized by fluctuating periods of growth and decline in economic activity, known as the business cycle. Although each period may have a different length and intensity, the long-term trend is upward.

The Business Cycle

The business cycle is a mix of periods of economic expansion when production output and purchases increase, economic contraction when production and output and purchases decrease, and the transitions in between. These business cycles occur when there are changes in aggregate output and employment in response to changes in aggregate supply or demand. They do not occur at set intervals. An expansion could last for five years or even ten. Periods of contraction, generally known as **recession**, can last a few months to several years.

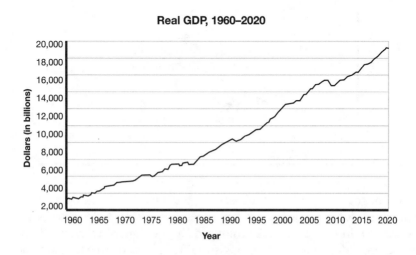

Real GDP, 1960–2020

This graph clearly shows the irregular intervals and lengths of economic recessions over the past 60 years.

The National Bureau of Economic Research, an independent non-profit organization, maintains a Business Cycle Dating Committee that provides a chronology of the business cycle, specifying dates for economic expansion and contraction. The committee uses various measures to determine its assessment of economic activity including:

- real GDP, measured on the product and income sides
- economy-wide employment
- real income

The NBER also occasionally uses indicators such as real estate sales data and the Federal Reserve's index of industrial production to help it pinpoint more exactly when recessions begin and end.

Business Cycle Phases

The business cycle consists of four phases:

- **Expansion** (or boom): This is a phase of increasing employment, economic growth, and pressure for price increases.
- **Peak**: This is the maximum growth stage of the economy.
- **Contraction** (or recession): This phase is generally characterized by increasing unemployment, decreasing economic activity, and declining economic output.
- **Trough**: This is the lowest point in economic activity. The eventual upward direction of the economy following the trough is called a **recovery.**

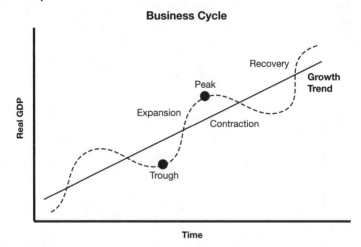

Business Cycle

Although, generally, the phases of the business cycle have not been extended for long periods, there have been periods of prolonged contraction or expansion in U.S. history. A prolonged contraction, or recession, is called a **depression.** A depression is a serious, sustained recession that lasts at least three years and results in a decrease in real GDP of 10 percent or more. The Long Depression from 1873 to 1896, for example, is the longest lasting contraction, surpassing the Great Depression of the 1930s by 22 months. Between 1873 and 1879, 18,000 businesses went bankrupt. The longest period of economic expansion began in July 2009 and continued until March 2020.

Output Gap

When evaluating whether or not the economy is performing well, one measure economists look at is the **output gap**. This is the difference between the economy's **actual output** (what has been achieved in reality) and the **potential output** (how much the economy could ideally produce if it used all its resources, including employees, natural resources, equipment, and technology). This does not mean that unemployment is eradicated or that all capital is being used. Potential output rather involves unemployment at what is called a full-employment rate. This is also considered unemployment's natural rate.

The output gap, like the GDP, can either rise or fall, and both conditions have associated concerns. A positive output gap could occur when output is more than full capacity – for example, if a sector of the economy engages employees in a significant amount of overtime work in order to make production meet demand. This could result in inflationary pressure and often means that the growth phase is ending. On the other hand, a negative output gap, when production is less than the economy could produce at full capacity, would be associated with low employment growth and profits.

Factors that Affect the Business Cycle

Business cycles are inevitable in a market economy, because maintaining a stable balance between aggregate demand and aggregate supply is unrealistic. Producers are always trying to predict future demand. If producers expect demand to increase, they hire more people and increase production. The economy expands. But if they predict incorrectly or if all their competitors also increase production, they will produce more than then can sell. To remain in business, they lay off workers and decrease production. The economy contracts.

Several other factors foster economic fluctuations:

- **Monetary policies:** Ineffective expansion or contraction of the money supply can cause macroeconomic instability. (See Topic 4.6 for more about monetary policy.)

- **Natural events:** Some events, such as droughts or earthquakes, can cause economic hardship for large regions. An event such as a flu pandemic can adversely affect the worldwide economy.

- **Political insecurity:** Business confidence and investments can decline when political factors, such as war, make policies unreliable.

- **Trade barriers:** A reduction in trade barriers tends to promote overall economic growth.

- **Government spending:** An increase in government spending may stimulate the economy, while a decrease can slow it down.

1. In one to three paragraphs, explain what the business cycle is, identify its phases and discuss the concepts of actual output, potential output, and the output gap.

KEY TERMS

recession	trough	actual output
expansion	recovery	potential output
peak	depression	
contraction	output gap	

MULTIPLE-CHOICE QUESTIONS

1. What is the long-term directional trend of the economy?
   (A) cyclical
   (B) upward
   (C) downward
   (D) fluctuating
   (E) flat

2. An output gap is the difference between
   (A) actual and potential output
   (B) full-employment output and potential output
   (C) recessionary output and output during a depression
   (D) a peak and the next trough
   (E) a peak and the next peak

3. What factor or factors determine when a recession becomes a depression?
   (A) the depth of the trough experienced
   (B) the length and severity of the contraction
   (C) what phase of the business cycle it appears in
   (D) the amount of time since the previous recession
   (E) the size of the difference between actual and potential output

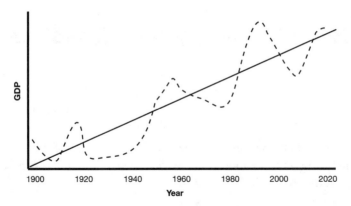

1. For items (a) through (d), draw a point where each scenario would fall on the business cycle graph shown above.

   (a) The Great Depression (Indicate with a letter *a*.)

   (b) The Internet Boom (Indicate with letter *b*.)

   (c) The Great Recession (Indicate with letter *c*.)

   (d) A negative output gap (indicate with letter *d*.)

   (e) In your own words, explain the difference between a positive output gap and a negative output gap.

THINK AS AN ECONOMIST: *DESCRIBE ECONOMIC CONCEPTS*

Economics has a unique set of concepts that provide the foundation for its theories. Being able to accurately describe the key concepts is an essential part of understanding these theories. When trying to describe a concept, consider questions such as these: What is the definition? How does it relate to other concepts? Why is it important in the field of economics?

For example, consider the business cycle. As you read in this topic, the business cycle illustrates the transitions between periods of economic expansion, when people buy more goods and services and the real gross domestic product (GDP) is growing, and contraction, or recession, when production output and purchases decrease. The business cycle is important because understanding it helps government policy makers and individual decision makers interpret variations in economic activity and plan accordingly.

Apply the Skill

Another economic concept that you learned in this topic is the output gap.

1. What is the definition of the output gap?

2. How does full employment relate to the output gap?

3. Why is the concept of the output gap important in the field of economics?

UNIT 2

Long Free-Response Question

1. Country Y, a country that makes cars and computers, is in a recession.

   (a) Draw a correctly labeled production possibilities curve for Country Y. Place cars on the vertical axis and computers on the horizontal axis. Label the recession point *A*.

   (b) The figures below (shown in millions) outlines the country's spending on final goods and services by consumers, businesses, government, and international trade.

   - **Consumption** $600
   - **Investment** $300
   - **Government** $500
   - **Exports** $30
   - **Imports** $100

   (i) Calculate the nominal gross domestic product of Country Y.

   (ii) If Country Y had a closed economy would GDP be higher, lower, or remain the same? Explain.

   (c) The table below shows the number of cars and computers produced in 2018 (which is the base year) and 2019.

	2018 Quantity	2018 Price	2019 Quantity	2019 Price
Cars	10	70	12	80
Computers	6	50	9	60

   Calculate each of the following:

   (i) The nominal GDP in 2018

   (ii) The real GDP in 2019

   (d) The following figures are labor statistics for Country Y.

   - **Population**   100,000
   - **Unemployed**   18,000
   - **Employed**   72,000
   - **Imports**   10,000

   (i) Calculate the rate of unemployment.

   (ii) With the given recession, explain what type of unemployment Country Y is experiencing and why.

   (e) If Country Y experienced unexpected inflation, would banks that offered fixed-rate loans benefit or be disadvantaged? Explain.

UNIT 3

National Income and Price Determination

When you think of income, you probably think of the total amount of money someone earns from various sources during a year. National income is calculated differently. It is the total market value of production in a country's economy during a year, which is usually expressed as the gross domestic product (GDP). As you learned in Unit 2, economic activity fluctuates over time in what is known as the business cycle. These fluctuations affect an economy's output and price level, both in the short run and in the long run.

Economists use the aggregate demand–aggregate supply model to analyze these fluctuations, as well as the impact of spending and production decisions, and the effects of economic policy actions on macroeconomic outcomes. (The term aggregate is used to indicate that all of the goods and services produced by the economy are being taken into account.) In the long run, flexible wages and prices will adjust and unemployment will return to its natural state.

Governments also use fiscal policy to achieve macroeconomic goals. By cutting taxes or increasing government spending, they can stimulate economic growth, while by raising taxes or decreasing government spending they can slow an overactive economy. In this unit, you will learn how economists use the aggregate demand–aggregate supply model to make economic policy decisions.

DEMAND FOR RECLAIMED BARN WOOD CAUSES WAVE OF NEW BARN CONSTRUCTION.

Amy HWANG

CartoonStock.com

Topic Titles and Essential Knowledge

Topic 3.1 Aggregate Demand (AD)

- The aggregate demand (AD) curve describes the relationship between the price level and the quantity of goods and services demanded by households (consumption), firms (investment), government (government spending), and the rest of the world (net exports).

- The negative slope of the AD curve is explained by the real wealth effect, the interest rate effect, and the exchange rate effect.

- Any change in the components of aggregate demand (consumption, investment, government spending, or net exports) that is not due to changes in the price level leads to a shift of the AD curve.

Topic 3.2 Multipliers

- A $1 change to autonomous expenditures leads to further changes in total expenditures and total output.

- The expenditure multiplier quantifies the size of the change in aggregate demand as a result of a change in any of the components of aggregate demand.

- The tax multiplier quantifies the size of the change in aggregate demand as a result of a change in taxes.

- The expenditure multiplier and tax multiplier depend on the marginal propensity to consume.

- The marginal propensity to consume is the change in consumer spending divided by the change in disposable income. The sum of the marginal propensity to consume and marginal propensity to save is equal to one.

Topic 3.3 Short-Run Aggregate Supply (SRAS)

- The short-run aggregate supply (SRAS) curve describes the relationship between the price level and the quantity of goods and services supplied in an economy.

- The SRAS curve is upward-sloping because of sticky wages and prices.

- Any factor that causes production costs to change, such as a change in inflationary expectations, will cause the SRAS curve to shift.

- Moving along the SRAS curve, an increase in the price level is associated with an increase in output, which means employment must correspondingly rise. With the labor force held constant, unemployment will fall. So, there is a short-run trade-off between inflation and unemployment.

Topic 3.4 Long-Run Aggregate Supply (LRAS)

- In the long run all prices and wages are fully flexible, while in the short run some input prices are fixed. A consequence of flexible long-run prices and wages is the lack of a long-run trade-off between inflation and unemployment.

- The LRAS curve corresponds to the production possibilities curve (PPC) because they both represent maximum sustainable capacity. Maximum sustainable capacity is the total output an economic system will produce over a set period of time if all resources are fully employed.

- The LRAS curve is vertical at the full-employment level of output because in the long run wages and prices fully adjust.

Topic 3.5 Equilibrium in the Aggregate Demand–Aggregate Supply (AD–AS) Model

- Short-run equilibrium occurs when the aggregate quantity of output demanded and the aggregate quantity of output supplied are equal—i.e., at the intersection of the AD and SRAS curves.
- Long-run equilibrium occurs when the AD and SRAS curves intersect on the LRAS—i.e., at the full-employment level of real output.
- The short-run equilibrium output can be at the full-employment level of output, above it, or below it, creating positive (i.e., inflationary) or negative (i.e., recessionary) output gaps.

Topic 3.6 Changes in the AD–AS Model in the Short Run

- A positive (negative) shock in AD causes output, employment, and the price level to rise (fall) in the short run.
- A positive (negative) shock in SRAS causes output and employment to rise (fall) and the price level to fall (rise) in the short run.
- Inflation can be caused by changes in aggregate demand (demand-pull) or aggregate supply (cost-push).

Topic 3.7 Long-Run Self-Adjustment

- In the long run, in the absence of government policy actions, flexible wages and prices will adjust to restore full employment and unemployment will revert to its natural rate after a shock to aggregate demand or short-run aggregate supply.
- Shifts in the long-run aggregate supply curve indicate changes in the full-employment level of output and economic growth.

Topic 3.8 Fiscal Policy

- Governments implement fiscal policies to achieve macroeconomic goals, such as full employment.
- The tools of fiscal policy are government spending and taxes/transfers.
- Changes in government spending affect aggregate demand directly, and changes in taxes/transfers affect aggregate demand indirectly.
- The government spending multiplier is greater than the tax multiplier.
- Expansionary or contractionary fiscal policies are used to restore full employment when the economy is in a negative (i.e., recessionary) or positive (i.e., inflationary) output gap.
- Fiscal policy can influence aggregate demand, real output, and the price level.
- The AD–AS model is used to demonstrate the short-run effects of fiscal policy.
- In reality, there are lags to discretionary fiscal policy because of factors such as the time it takes to decide on and implement a policy action.

Topic 3.9 Automatic Stabilizers

- Automatic stabilizers support the economy during recessions and help prevent the economy from being overheated during expansionary periods.
- Tax revenues decrease automatically as GDP falls, preventing consumption and the economy from falling further.
- Tax revenues increase automatically as GDP rises, slowing consumption and preventing the economy from overheating.
- Government policies, institutions, or agencies may also have social service programs whose transfer payments act as automatic stabilizers.

Source: *AP® Macroeconomics Course and Exam Description.* Effective Fall 2019 (College Board).

Aggregate Demand (AD)

"Consumption is the sole end and purpose of all production; and the interest of the producer ought to be attended to, only so far as it may be necessary for promoting that of the consumer."

Scottish political economist Adam Smith, *The Wealth of Nations* (1776)

Essential Question: What is aggregate demand and how is it determined?

The owner of a local shoe store closely monitors which products are selling—and which are not selling—in order to respond to customer demand and current trends. She also needs to minimize the quantity of shoes she has in stock that are not moving off the shelves. This is simple, straightforward supply and demand. If managed well, it can help a shoe store can turn a profit every week, month, and year.

So how are supply and demand measured and managed on a national scale? And not only for shoes—but the total demand for every good or service the economy produces? Aggregate demand is the total amount of demand for all goods and services in an economy. Cars, t-shirts, dry cleaning, fighter jets, pizza delivery—they are all part of the calculation. Economists use this broad calculation to understand how economies work. Businesses, individuals, and governments use it to respond to national and international events that effect the economic future.

What Is Aggregate Demand?

Aggregate demand (AD) is the demand for all finished goods and services at various price levels in a given period of time. This is different from GDP, which measures the total market or monetary value of all the finished goods and services produced in a country in a given period. AD is more interested in how desirable all those GDP goods are in an economy and how much money is spent buying those goods. The way aggregate demand is calculated, however, is the same way GDP is calculated: $AD = C + I + G + X - M$.

- C = consumer spending on goods
- I = investment spending on goods like factories and equipment
- G = government spending on goods and services
- X = exported goods to other countries
- M = imported goods from other countries

AD and GDP are calculated in the same way because they are connected. If demand for certain goods rises, more of those goods will be produced, thus raising the GDP. The reverse is true as well: Less demand means less reason to produce as much of the good or service.

The Aggregate Demand Curve

Aggregate demand is visually represented by the **aggregate demand curve**, which shows the relationship between the desire for aggregate goods and services by consumers, businesses, government, and the rest of the world and the aggregate price level for all goods and services. The vertical Y-axis represents the price level for all the AD goods and services. The horizontal X-axis represents the real GDP, or the total output of goods. The AD curve slopes downward from left to right because aggregate demand increases or decreases as prices increase or decrease. As the price level decreases, more goods will be purchased.

The Aggregate Demand (AD) Curve

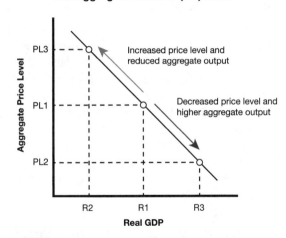

The Difference Between Demand and Aggregate Demand It may seem perfectly reasonable to equate the law of demand, which affects an individual good or service, with aggregate demand. After all, both curves are downward sloping. But they are not the same. The demand curve for an individual product, like a designer handbag, reflects how the demand for the handbag changes based on its price (provided the prices of other goods remain constant). A primary reason the quantity demanded for a designer handbag falls when the price goes up is that consumers decide to spend their money on other goods or services.

The aggregate demand curve, however, is not focused on an individual product. It is concerned with the simultaneous change in pricing for all goods and services. For example, if the sales of a designer handbag drop but consumers purchase more smartphones, it does not necessarily change the total demand for goods and services in the economy. But there are economic elements that will have an impact on the relationship between aggregate price levels and all final goods and services (GDP) created.

The Wealth Effect One reason demand for GDP goods will drop is because the aggregate price of goods rises. When aggregate prices go up, consumers do not have as much buying power as they do with lower prices. For example, imagine that a couple budgets $4,000 in January to spend on furniture for their new house that they will purchase when the house is completed in September. If the aggregate price level goes up by 10 percent between January and September, the couple is able to buy the equivalent of 10 percent less furniture—what they could have bought for $3,600 in January. They might decide to buy less total furniture because their money is not able to buy as much as they wanted, or they might decide to purchase less expensive furniture.

Since the change is to aggregate demand, it means that all other consumers would feel the same effect of the 10-percent aggregate price increase, leading millions and millions of people to reduce their spending on goods and services. The opposite is true as well: Lower aggregate prices result in increased consumer buying power and more demand for goods. The **wealth effect** is what happens to consumer spending when the aggregate price level changes. When the aggregate price level goes up, the aggregate demand curve slopes downward.

The Interest Rate Effect Consumers and businesses—the C and I in the aggregate demand and GDP calculations—make purchasing decisions based not only on price but on the funds they have available. The actual money they have in their accounts or funds that are available to them via loans are primary spending resources for consumers and businesses. The **interest rate effect** refers to the impact that changes in borrowing power has on aggregate demand and aggregate prices. If interest rates go up, consumers and businesses become more hesitant to borrow money for larger purchases (refrigerators, cars, homes, and so on) because their purchasing power is lower, and the total cost will be higher. Conversely, lower interest rates might make businesses and consumers more likely to make investments or bigger purchases because they will get more for their money.

A person shopping for real estate will consider the interest rates available to them before pursuing a purchase. The lower the interest rate for large purchases like homes, the more likely buyers will be able to buy.

The Exchange Rate Effect Aggregate demand can also be affected by the currency exchange rate with other countries. In order for countries with different currencies to do business, they must be able to exchange currencies through a foreign exchange market. If a currency like the U.S. dollar increases in value compared to other currencies, the dollar has **appreciated** in value and gives people who have U.S. dollars stronger buying power to purchase foreign goods. If the U.S. dollar decreases in value compared to other currencies, it has **depreciated** in value and the buying power for foreign goods is lessened. (See Topic 6.2 for more on exchange rates.)

The currency exchange rates have an impact on the demand and price of goods and services in their respective countries. For example, if a new smartphone in the U.S. costs $1,000, while the same phone in Spain costs €1,000, and the exchange rate between dollars and euros is $1 = €1, the phone has the same price. But if the exchange rate is €1.20 = $1, the Spanish smartphone is 20 percent cheaper than the U.S. phone. Similarly, if the exchange rate is €0.80 = $1, the Spanish phone is about 20 percent more expensive than the U.S. phone. The exchange rate's influence on aggregate demand for goods between countries causes decreases and increases depending on how weak or strong the countries' currencies are relative to each other.

What Shifts the Aggregate Demand Curve?

As you have already seen, movement *along* the aggregate demand curve is driven by changes in price level. As prices rise, the aggregate quantity of goods demanded falls. As prices fall, the aggregate quantity of goods demanded rises. But just as with demand in Topic 1.4, certain economic factors can shift the aggregate demand curve left or right, signaling a decrease or increase in the quantity of goods and services demanded at any price level.

Changes in Consumer Spending The level at which consumers spend is dependent, to a significant degree, on their confidence about the future direction of the economy. When consumers expect the economy to remain strong or improve, meaning that their personal finances will likely do the same, they increase spending. This increases the quantity of goods and services demanded at any price level, shifting the AD curve to the right. When consumers foresee a weakening economy, they limit their spending. Aggregate demand decreases and the AD curve shifts to the left.

Changes in wealth, too, change consumer spending. Economy-wide phenomena such as a stock market or real estate boom can increase wealth to the extent that aggregate demand increases. An unexpected event such as the oil embargo of the 1970s that caused oil prices to suddenly increase, or the impact of COVID-19 in 2020 that caused a sharp decline in the stock market, have the opposite effect, decreasing spending and aggregate demand.

Changes in Investment (Business Spending) Confidence about the future of the economy also directly affects investment (spending) by businesses. If businesses expect the economy to remain strong or improve, they generally have high expectations about future revenues from the goods or services they provide. They, in turn, line up investment plans on this basis. Investment takes the shape of building new facilities, upgrading technology, investing in new equipment, and the like. Business investment on this scale increases aggregate demand and shifts the AD curve to the right. Negative expectations about the economic future can have the opposite effect, decreasing aggregate demand and shifting the AD curve to the left.

Changes in Governmental Policies Increases in government spending can shift the aggregate demand curve as well. Many of the better-known "alphabet agencies" of the New Deal during the Great Depression, such as the Civilian Conservation Corps (CCC), the Works Progress Administration (WPA), and the Federal Emergency Relief Administration (FERA), were designed specifically to employ people, putting money in their pockets. Increases in income lead to increases in spending, which lead to increases in aggregate demand. Massive government spending on weapons and supplies for World War II was another example of the government's ability to shift the AD curve.

Governments also influence aggregate demand through tax policy and transfers. Tax cuts are often employed as a tool to put more money in the hands of consumers and businesses, in an effort to boost spending. Government transfers, too, help boost spending. For example, in response to the unemployment and economic stagnation caused by the COVID-19 crisis of 2020, the U.S. government approved direct payments of $1,200 per adult person (and $500 per dependent) for most U.S. citizens. Again, the goal was to encourage spending and thereby increase aggregate demand—or even just keep it from decreasing too drastically.

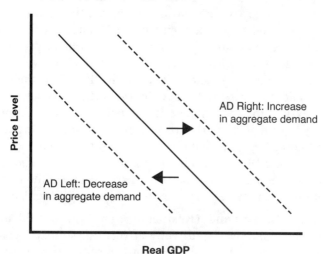

Shifts in Aggregate Demand

ANSWER THE TOPIC ESSENTIAL QUESTION

1. In one to three paragraphs, explain what aggregate demand is and how it is determined.

KEY TERMS

aggregate demand (AD) interest rate effect
aggregate demand curve appreciate
wealth effect depreciate

MULTIPLE-CHOICE QUESTIONS

Questions 1 to 3 refer to the chart below.

Aggregate Demand during the Great Depression

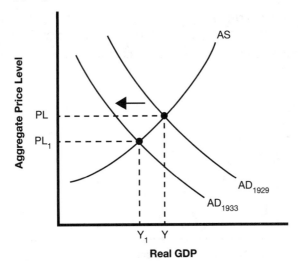

1. Which of the following best describes why aggregate demand shifted left between 1929 and 1933?

   (A) Interest rates for loans dropped quickly.

   (B) Exchange rates for the U.S. dollar depreciated.

   (C) Consumer income dropped severely.

   (D) Inflationary pressures reduced government spending.

   (E) Businesses undertook major investments.

2. How does the leftward shift on the curve reflect the shock to employment during the Depression?

(A) GDP fell because of fear of inflationary price levels.

(B) Rising price levels made it difficult for workers to afford goods.

(C) More people were able to contribute to production of goods.

(D) Rapid growth in unemployment reduced consumer buying power.

(E) Uncertainty about the economy did not affect business hiring.

3. Which would be the most effective way for government action to reduce falling aggregate demand between 1929 and 1933?

(A) Offer businesses low interest loans for investment.

(B) Promote certain goods and services to the buying public.

(C) Create federal jobs to provide work and income for the unemployed.

(D) Stop all imports and purchase only domestic goods and services.

(E) Pass legislation to raise taxes on businesses and the extremely wealthy.

FREE-RESPONSE QUESTIONS

1. Use the graph below to answer all parts of the questions that follow.

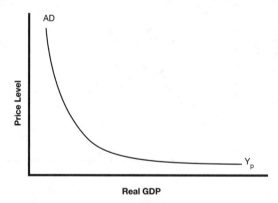

(a) Describe the relationship between price level and real GDP reflected in the graph.

(b) If the U.S. experiences a recessionary period, how will the AD curve shift? Explain your answer.

(c) Suppose that a war between the U.S. and China ensues. The government increases its purchases of military equipment. How will this war impact the aggregate demand in the United States? Explain.

(d) Businesses confidence is on the rise due to a leap in the stock market. How is the aggregate demand curve altered in this situation?

(e) A new tariff is placed on all imported goods. How will the aggregate demand curve be affected? Explain.

THINK AS AN ECONOMIST: *DRAW AN ACCURATELY LABELED VISUAL TO REPRESENT AN ECONOMIC MODEL*

Economists use graphs to display economic behavior, creating models that attempt to show how producers and consumers will behave. One way of showing an economic model is with a demand curve, such as the "The Aggregate Demand (AD) Curve" in this topic.

Economists can also use other kinds of visuals to model economic behavior. For example, a market demand schedule shows the market demand for a product at given prices.

Apply the Skill

Use a two-column chart to show the impact on aggregate demand of each of these economic circumstances. List each change on its own row in the first column. Use an up or down arrow in the second column to indicate whether the particular change will have the effect of increasing or decreasing aggregate demand.

Chart these changes in a nation's economy:

- Banks cut interest rates for consumer loans.
- Unemployment jumps as businesses lay off workers.
- Congress passes a law raising income tax rates across the board.
- International sales of American-made cars increase.
- The inflation rate rises from 1.3 percent to 4.0 percent.

Topic 3.2

Multipliers

"Don't save what is left after spending; spend what is left after saving."

Billionaire investor Warren Buffett (b. 1930)

Essential Question: How do changes in income and taxes effect spending, savings, and the GDP?

Melina was surprised by the $4,000 end-of-year bonus she received from her employer. It was much more than she expected. Melina can spend the money, save it, or do a combination of the two. Now she can afford to replace her old TV with a bigger, more advanced model that she has been eyeing. And she can replace the noisy muffler on her car. Even with these expenditures, she will still have a chunk of her bonus money to add to her savings account. The end of the year turned out much better than Melina expected.

Melina's reward for excellent work does not only affect her. What she does with her bonus money has ripple effects throughout the economy. Buying an expensive new TV means more TVs need to be produced, which means more workers get paid and more electronics supply companies have to sell parts to make that TV. And more shipping companies make money shipping additional products. The workers who make the TV and the parts for the TV continue to receive income—maybe even annual bonuses. Then they can make purchases, which will create demand for the products they buy. The money Melina puts into savings contributes to the bank's ability to lend more money to other borrowers. Melina's benefit has a multiplying effect on the economy, aggregate demand, and the real GDP.

What Is the Multiplier Effect?

A **multiplier** is an economic factor that changes and causes subsequent changes in other associated areas. The **multiplier effect** refers to how an increase (or decrease) in one economic activity causes increases (or decreases) across a range of other related economic activities. The multiplier effect can cause increases in gross domestic product (GDP) that are much larger than the initial change in the economy that started the ripple effect. In the example above, where Melina received unexpected income and spent a portion of it, her purchase of a TV resulted in subsequent economic activity that was worth more than the price of her purchase. When consumers gain new income, as Melina did, they make decisions about how much of the new income they should spend or save.

How they decide to use that new money is what determines the impact of the multiplier effect on the economy.

Marginal Propensity to Consume and Save

The **marginal propensity to consume (MPC)** refers to the percentage of new income a consumer spends on goods and services compared to what they save. Suppose you get a raise that amounts to an extra $200 a month in take-home pay. That is new disposable income. If you spend $160 of that $200—or 80 percent—every month, and save the remaining $40, your marginal propensity to consume is expressed as 0.8 ($160 divided by $200). People commonly use the symbol Δ (delta) to represent a change in a quantity. If ΔC means "change in consumption" and ΔDI means "change in disposable income," the calculation to represent your MPC is:

$$\Delta C / \Delta DI = MPC$$

So, in this example with a $200 increase in income, the MPC is 0.8 ($0.8/1 = 0.8$). As discussed above, spending that $160 in new income is what sets off the multiplier effect. Let us say the $160 is spent on a new dress. The store will spend a percentage of that $160 (saving some of it) to pay employees and bills and order new merchandise. The store workers will spend some of their additional income (and save some) on other goods, as will the manufacturer, and so on and so on.

The MPC is also determined by income level. A household with a higher income will spend a smaller percentage of its new income because many of its wants are already met. Lower income households will have a higher MPC because a higher percentage of their income will be used for immediate concerns.

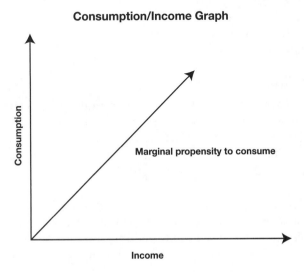

Consumption/Income Graph

The MPC graph slopes upward because as disposable income increases, so does consumption.

What about that unspent new income? It is assumed that the money is saved: Whether it actually is or not—it is simply not spent. That is called the **marginal propensity to save (MPS)** and refers to the percentage of aggregate new income not used for consumption. The MPS and MPC work hand in hand because every amount of new income is considered a whole dollar (whether it is $1 or $100,000). In a calculation where ΔS means "change in savings" and ΔDI means "change in disposable income," your MPS is:

$$\Delta S / \Delta DI = MPS$$

So, in the example of an additional $200 in income, if $160 is spent, $40 is saved. This means the MPS is 0.2 (40/200 = 0.2). Combining the MPC and MPS should always equal 1.

As with the MPC, the MPS is largely determined by household income. Lower income households are usually less able to save a large percentage of new income, whereas higher income households are able to save a larger percentage of new income. Economists use both the MPC and the MPS to help calculate the impact of the multiplier effect on an economy. The higher the MPC is, the higher the multiplier and the greater the increase in total consumption. The higher the MPS is, the more money is saved for future use.

Autonomous Spending and Disposable Income Consumers, businesses, and governments all have autonomous expenditures, which are necessary costs built into operating a home, business, or government. For consumers, rent, utility bills, and food are all items they must expend money on simply to maintain their daily lives. Often, these autonomous expenses do not change drastically over a short period of time, so consumers can budget for these costs.

What is left over after these autonomous expenditures are taken care of is considered **disposable income**. Consumers can either save this income or spend it (MPC or MPS). Regardless of a consumer's total disposable income, the multiplier effect works the same way. Whether someone buys a new microwave or a yacht, the expenditure will ripple through the economy and generate more total GDP than the price of the original product.

The Expenditure Multiplier

An annual bonus or a raise in salary are good examples of how the **expenditure multiplier** (also called the spending multiplier) works for an individual. Melina's $4,000 annual bonus and subsequent MPC makes a small but important contribution to GDP. The multiplier effect can be much bigger and make a greater impact on GDP when a government or business makes a large expenditure.

If the Iowa state government decides to spend $200 million on a new facility for a state university, the initial expenditure will cause a chain reaction through the economy because of all the additional consumption that goes into building the new facility. Everything from buying materials and equipment to paying worker salaries and workers buying lunches at businesses near the construction site involves consumption. All those levels of spending (MPC) create a change in real GDP that is shown by this formula:

Initial expenditure = $200 million
Second level of consumer spending = MPC × $200 million
Third level of consumer spending = MPC² × $200 million
Fourth level of consumer spending = MPC³ × $200 million
(The levels of spending can continue on indefinitely.)
Total increase in real GDP = (1 + MPC + MPC² + MPC³ ....) × $200 million

Each level of MPC is based on what percentage of new income will be spent (rather than saved) by the consumer. If we assume the MPC is 0.8 of each new dollar in disposable income, this table shows how a $200 million state expenditure plays out:

	GDP Increase from Initial Expenditure (in millions)	Total Increase in Real GDP (in millions)
Initial Expenditure	100.00	100.00
2nd level	80.00	180.00
3rd level	64.00	244.00
4th level	51.20	295.20
5th level	40.96	336.16
...	...	...

Based on five levels of consumer MPC, that initial $200 million expenditure by the state of Iowa has already generated $338 million in real GDP—and it will be even more when additional levels of spending are added in. The formula to calculate the expenditure multiplier can be written in two ways. Each formula ends with the same product:

Expenditure multiplier = 1 / (1 − MPC)
Expenditure multiplier = 1 / MPS

The increases in levels of spending and GDP that result are clear indicators of increased aggregate demand.

The Tax Multiplier

Government tax policy can impact aggregate demand and GDP as well, though in a much smaller way than expenditures. The **tax multiplier (TM)** refers to how an increase (or decrease) in taxes impacts spending and GDP. A tax cut increases disposable income; a tax increase decreases disposable income. Households react to a tax decrease differently, just as they do to other increases in income. Overall, lower income households will spend a larger percentage of additional income from taxes whereas higher income households will save more of it.

Say the federal government enacts an across-the-board tax cut of 8 percent that results in a $400 billion increase in disposable income for taxpayers. (This also means the federal government will receive less in revenue to pay its bills.) If we assume the MPC is 0.75 (of every $1), people will spend $300 billion of that tax cut (the other 0.25, or $100 billion, is MPS). The second level of consumer spending would be 0.75 × $300 = $225 billion. The third level will be $169 (225 × 0.75), and so on. The formula for the tax multiplier is:

$$TM = MPC / MPS = MPC / 1\text{-}MPC$$
$$TM = Simple\ tax\ multiplier$$
$$MPC = Marginal\ propensity\ to\ consume$$
$$MPS = Marginal\ propensity\ to\ save$$

One important difference between the tax multiplier and the expenditure multiplier is that people will *not* spend the full $400 billion of the initial tax decrease. They will save more of it. With the expenditure multiplier, the full initial total *is* spent by the government or investing business. This is one of the key reasons that expenditures have a larger impact on aggregate demand and GDP than tax decreases.

ANSWER THE TOPIC ESSENTIAL QUESTION

1. In one to three paragraphs, explain how changes in income and taxes affect spending, savings, and the GDP.

KEY TERMS

multiplier	disposable income
multiplier effect	expenditure multiplier
marginal propensity to consume (MPC)	tax multiplier (TM)
marginal propensity to save (MPS)	

MULTIPLE-CHOICE QUESTIONS

1. If a city of 100,000 people invests $1 billion in a major electrical grid upgrade, what direct outcome will businesses in the city during the upgrade?

(A) Inflation will rise due to increased aggregate demand.

(B) People will likely save more money as a result of increased local business.

(C) Increased income will spur consumption by the city's population.

(D) Disruption to business districts during the upgrade will reduce overall consumption.

(E) Autonomous expenses will rise for local businesses and households.

2. Assume that Jacob spent $20,000 of his disposable income of $30,000 in 2019. If his disposable income increased to $40,000 and his marginal propensity to consume equals 0.8, what did his consumption increase by?

(A) $4,000

(B) $8,000

(C) $9,000

(D) $10,000

(E) $12,000

3. If the marginal propensity to consume is 0.75, the government decreases personal income taxes by $100, real gross domestic product will

(A) increase by $300

(B) decrease by $400

(C) increase by $250

(D) decrease by $160

(E) increase by $1,000

FREE-RESPONSE QUESTIONS

1. Use the graph below to answer all parts of the questions that follow.

Multiplier Effect

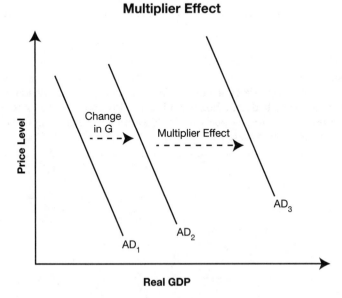

(G = government expenditure)

(a) Describe what causes the shift in aggregate demand between AD_1 and AD_2.

(b) How is the multiplier between AD_2 and AD_3 determined?

(c) Aggregate demand (AD) shifts to the right in this graph. Explain how the change in government expenditure (G) impacts real gross domestic product (GDP).

(d) Both government expenditure and tax cuts affect aggregate demand and GDP. Explain the primary difference in GDP impact between the two expansionary policies.

(e) What effect would an increase in personal income taxes have on AD_3? Explain.

THINK AS AN ECONOMIST: *DETERMINE THE EFFECTS OF AN ECONOMIC CHANGE USING CALCULATIONS*

Economists use quantitative data and calculations to determine the effects of a change in an economic situation. Government economists are no different. They use data and calculations to try to estimate the effects of government policy decisions. Doing so requires them to answer two questions:

- What variable in the situation changed?
- What effect will that change have on economic outcomes?

Of course, when government policy decisions involve the multiplier effect, they have to take into account that the effect of a change extends beyond the initial impact.

Apply the Skill

Suppose you are an economist in the governor's office charged with the task of determining the multiplier effect of a tax cut in the state income tax. Assume that current output in the state due to the tax cut is $11 billion and potential output is $20 billion. Assume that the MPC in the state is 0.75. Calculate the minimum amount of a tax cut that is necessary to close the gap.

Topic 3.3

Short-Run Aggregate Supply (SRAS)

"In boom times companies have high profits. They increase production to satisfy demand for goods. This leads to excess supply. Companies cut prices to compete for customers, leading to lower profits, lay-offs, and economic depression. Eventually lower prices lead to an increase in demand and profits go back up. The economy is a yo-yo."

Niall Kishtainy, *A Little History of Economics* (2017)

Essential Question: How do employment and production costs affect price and supply in the short run?

Jones Smart Supply Company makes hands-free smartphone holders for car dashboards. Jones employs 400 workers and has been growing at a surprising rate for the past four years—especially as more and more states have adopted punitive laws against using smartphones while driving. But this year, with the holiday season approaching, Jones has to pay more than double the amount for a key component of its phone holder due to tariffs on China implemented by the U.S. government. The socket component that makes Jones's holders unique will now cost the company $3 per unit (instead of $1). This higher per-unit cost will markedly cut into Jones's anticipated profit. The company is facing a short-run supply issue. What can Jones do? Lay off workers and save on wages? Raise their prices? Produce fewer hands-free holders? Which option is best?

Short-Run vs. Long-Run

Economists examine how the economy and its producers react to changes differently depending on how much time the producers have to respond. The term **short-run** does not necessarily mean "a short amount of time." It refers to the fact that producers have fixed and variable costs—like wages and contracts—that limit their ability and flexibility to respond to market changes to maintain their profits.

A spike in the price of oil, for example, makes producing almost everything more expensive. Oil is used not only as a raw material to make products such as plastics and many chemicals, but it provides most of the fuel for transporting goods by truck, train, or plane. So, when oil prices increase, producers need to make immediate adjustments if they want to maintain their same level of profitability. Reducing costs for raw materials or wages quickly can be very hard (see explanation of "sticky wages" below). Hiking prices could make products lose their attraction to consumers. Usually, the option that makes the most sense in the short run is to decrease supply, creating what is known as a short-run supply problem.

The term **long-run,** on the other hand, refers to a period of time when all production and costs can be changed. Businesses looking at the long-run have much more flexibility and ability to respond to expected or predicted changes. (Short-run changes do not allow for such broad capabilities in reaction time.) Concerns such as adding more employees or increasing warehousing space can be planned for and inform long-run thinking about where the business will be located. Improvements in production technology that can increase output and lower costs are also long-run considerations.

The Short-Run Aggregate Supply Curve

Short-run aggregate supply (SRAS) refers to the total output (aggregate) of goods and services (GDP) that exist in a period of time when production costs can be considered fixed (and thus not easily and quickly changed). The **short-run aggregate supply curve** shows the positive relationship between an economy's aggregate price level and the total quantity of final goods and services (real GDP) supplied by producers—in the short run. The SRAS curve slopes upward because higher aggregate prices lead to higher profit for every unit produced. If the price for a certain product rises, the producers will produce more products and might need to employ more workers to do so. And as one might expect, a fall in the aggregate price level will result in a decrease in the total quantity of aggregate output (GDP).

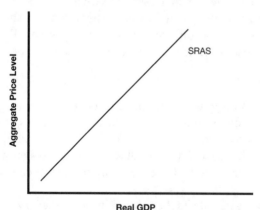

Short-Run Aggregate Supply Curve

The SRAS curve slopes upward because higher demand for products leads to higher profits per product produced.

Nominal and Sticky Wages Businesses determine the **profitability** of their products based on a simple formula:

Price per unit sold – Production costs per unit = Profit per unit

Some production costs are fixed, meaning they cannot be changed for an extended period of time. For many businesses, the largest fixed cost is the amount they pay their employees (wages, salaries, and benefits combined). **Nominal wages** are the dollar amounts paid to employees, and they are not easily changed. Some are set by contracts between workers and management that have to be honored for a specified period of time.

Further, companies know that reducing wages risks losing valuable employees and raising wages risks reducing profits that could go to owners. Companies are also hesitant to change nominal wages because of their effect on employee attitudes.

- If the economy is poor and sales are down, companies do not want to create resentment from employees by cutting wages.

- If the economy is good and demand for labor is high, companies do not want to create high expectations in employees by raising wages

Overall, when nominal wages are slow to rise or fall in response to changes in the economy, they are referred to as **sticky wages**.

Note that sticky wages are not sticky forever. Even contracts and agreements eventually have to be renegotiated and usually the new ones are based on economic conditions. In 2019, the United Auto Workers Union (UAW) and the big three automakers (Ford, GM, and Fiat Chrysler) negotiated a new contract, which changed the wages for employees. From 2014 to 2019, the big three automakers realized increased profits, but workers' wages were stuck at the agreed levels from the previous contract. The UAW was able to negotiate higher wages and higher profit sharing for their union members, though it took a 40-day work stoppage, or strike, against GM to settle the contract dispute with the company. This new contract covered the next four years, which meant that the automakers and UAW agreed what the nominal wages would be regardless of whether the market for automobiles rose or dipped.

Changes in Pricing Pricing, or deciding how much a product costs, is determined in part by the cost of elements that go into producing, marketing, and delivering the product. **Nominal price rigidity**, or price stickiness, refers to prices for goods and services that are fixed or not very flexible. For example, a consumer's phone service plan with a set monthly price for two years can be considered fixed (or rigid). But after two years, that price can change. Luxury brand goods are often priced more rigidly. Instead of dropping their prices to meet reduced demand, these companies will opt to reduce total output and maintain the sticky price. Changes in pricing are usually based on multiple market considerations.

To think through the pricing process, consider a perfectly competitive market, which exists only in theory. It would have certain elements:

- an unlimited number of buyers and sellers

- products that are identical (or can be easily substituted)

- companies that have no power to set prices

For example, if the aggregate price level falls, the price for an individual good (like a hat) falls. But the company's hat production output does not fall by the same amount because the production costs are fixed. So, a drop in hat prices means the profit per hat drops. The best the hat company can do is reduce the quantity of hats they produce in the short run to try to respond to the price drop. However, if the aggregate price level rises, the price for hats rises. Remember, the company's hat production costs remain fixed, so there is no change in output costs for each hat even though the price per unit is rising. In this case, the company would probably increase hat output in the short run.

An imperfectly competitive market is not just a theoretical idea; it is the market producers and consumers encounter every day. It has more realistic elements:

- competition for market share
- a wide variety of products
- prices that can be set by supply and demand or by the producers.

The term *imperfect* refers to the fact that these markets do not react and respond like the ideal, or perfect, market. This means there can be benefits for the consumers and producers, like price competition and improvements in products. There can also be detrimental effects to the market: monopolies (one seller) and oligopolies (few sellers) can develop in imperfect markets and undermine the very idea of competition. Imperfect markets show how the pricing process works differently from a perfectly competitive market.

For example, the hat company can choose to set its own price for their hats based on production costs and their desired profit. If the hats are a hit with consumers and fly off the shelves, the company can increase the price and increase its output, which will increase the profit per unit. Economists refer to this as **pricing power**. But if the aggregate price level falls and the hats stop selling, the company can cut prices and slow production to offset the lost demand and profits. In both situations, the company's production costs remain fixed.

Shifts in the SRAS Curve

As economists know so well, and as you have just read, stickiness occurs because economies do not adjust instantaneously. The SRAS curve shows how businesses respond to such stickiness. The SRAS curve is a graphic example of the relationship between real production and price level. As the price level increases, so does production. When price levels fall, production falls, too.

Movement *along* the SRAS curve occurs as a result of changes in the relationship between aggregate price level and aggregate supply. However, movement *of* the SRAS curve also occurs. This happens when the actions of producers in an economy either increase (rightward shift) or decrease (leftward shift) aggregate supply at *any* price level. Several determinants can cause these shifts.

Changes in Input Cost Input costs are the prices of the resources needed to produce a particular product. These costs include such things as materials, labor, and energy.

An increase in input cost causes the SRAS curve to shift to the left because it makes goods more expensive to produce. This can reduce profits. When an input like the price of energy increases suddenly, for example, it causes a decrease in aggregate supply and has a negative economic impact. Unemployment may rise, inflation can increase, and the economy can contract as production wanes.

On the other hand, the aggregate supply curve shifts rightward when inputs fall and productivity increases. This creates the possibility of lower unemployment, higher output, and lower inflation. When energy prices are low, for example, the economy can expand, and unemployment and inflation can decrease.

Energy prices are not the only key inputs that can shift the SRAS curve. A change in the cost of raw materials used to produce other products, for example, steel, lumber, plastic, or sugar, can also change the quantity of aggregate supply at any price level, thereby shifting the SRAS curve.

Changes in Workplace Productivity Workplace productivity is also an important factor affecting the SRAS curve. In economics, the term productivity is a measure of how much a manufacturer can produce, also known as output, with a given quantity of inputs. Workplace inputs include such things as labor and technology.

When a positive change in inputs, such as the introduction of efficient digital order-processing systems, increases workplace productivity, output increases and the curve shifts to the right. That means at every price level, the aggregate output supply increases. When a change in inputs results in decreased workplace productivity, the curve shifts to the left.

Many things influence productivity, including better management practices, new technology, and sustained labor actions, such as strikes.

Changes in Government Action Governments often intervene in market economies. What they do or do not do can impact the SRAS curve. Governments impact economies through a variety of laws, regulations, taxes, and subsidies. New laws, revised regulations, higher taxes, and lower subsidies, even if they prove worthwhile in the long run, can cause the SRAS curve to shift to the left. The opposite occurs when governments change laws, decrease regulations, lower taxes, and increase subsidies.

Inflationary Expectations Movement along the SRAS curve is also dependent on inflationary expectations. When producers expect inflation to rise, they foresee being able to sell their goods at a higher price. In response, producers will increase supply, causing a shift of the SRAS curve to the right. When deflation is expected, the opposite occurs.

SRAS Curve Shifts

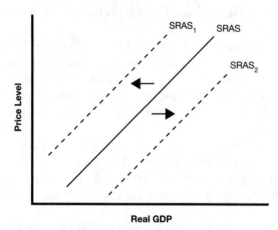

The SRAS curve shifts to the left (SRAS1) when there is a decrease in short-run aggregate supply. The SRAS curve shifts to the right (SRAS2) when there is an increase in short-run aggregate supply.

ANSWER THE TOPIC ESSENTIAL QUESTION

1. In one to three paragraphs, explain how employment and production costs affect price and supply in the short run.

KEY TERMS

short run	short-run aggregate supply	sticky wages
long run	curve	nominal price rigidity
short-run aggregate supply (SRAS)	profitability	pricing power
	nominal wages	

MULTIPLE-CHOICE QUESTIONS

1. If a major disruption of worldwide oil supplies occurred, resulting in 25- to 40-percent higher oil prices, how would it impact the SRAS curve?

(A) The oil crisis would be offset by decreased wages and the SRAS curve would remain stable.

(B) Prices on the SRAS curve would drop due to lack of consumer demand.

(C) The SRAS curve would reflect the cost change by shifting to the left.

(D) Real GDP on the SRAS curve would be unaffected because goods would still be needed.

(E) The SRAS curve would shift to the right due to increased aggregate prices.

2. Which of the following would shift the short-run aggregate supply curve to the right?

(A) An increase in business taxes

(B) A requirement for car manufacturers to retrofit their plants to be able to include air-bags in new cars

(C) New legislation that requires all food and medicines to have nutrition and warning labels

(D) New technology that replaces assembly-line workers with robots

(E) An increase in the price of lumber and steel

3. Which of the following would NOT shift aggregate supply to the right?

(A) A decrease in the price of oil

(B) Government reducing regulations on manufacturing

(C) Government easing requirements for citizenship

(D) Government increasing tax on manufacturers

(E) Farmers receiving a subsidy to raise cattle

FREE-RESPONSE QUESTIONS

1. Use the graph below, which depicts the SRAS during the Depression, to answer all parts of the questions that follow.

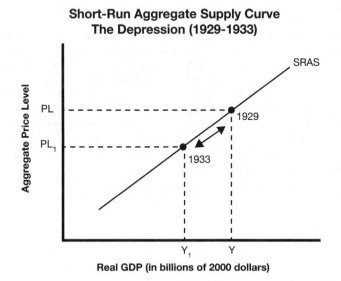

Short-Run Aggregate Supply Curve
The Depression (1929-1933)

(a) Describe what happened to the aggregate price level between 1929 and 1933 and how it impacted consumers.

(b) How did real GDP respond to the change in aggregate price level and why?

(c) Describe how this graph reflects the way deflation impacts an imperfectly competitive market.

(d) What effect did the change in real GDP have on employment numbers?

(e) What might producers have done between 1929 and 1933 to respond to the fall in SRAS?

THINK AS AN ECONOMIST: *DRAW AN ACCURATELY LABELED GRAPH TO REPRESENT AN ECONOMIC MARKET*

The aggregate supply curve generally slopes upward and to the right, as does an individual firm's or the market's supply curve. The rationale is fundamental to the law of supply: Firms are willing to produce more as price increases.

As with a market supply curve, the aggregate supply curve can shift to the left or to the right when economic conditions change, and firms are willing to produce more or less at any given price. In the short run, producers are sensitive to certain changing market conditions. Changes in those conditions can prompt short-run production decisions that affect the aggregate supply curve.

Apply the Skill

One of the factors that affects the aggregate supply curve is cost of materials, which can be affected by trade barriers if the materials are imported. You read earlier in the topic about Jones Smart Supply Company, manufacturer of hands-free smartphone holders for car dashboards. Jones saw the cost of a key component of its product triple due to a tariff imposed by the United States on goods imported from China. Jones Smart Supply was not the only company to see such an increase. Countless other manufacturers saw the prices of their materials go up as well. The tariffs on Chinese goods, then, had an effect on aggregate supply. Draw a graph that shows the general shape of the short-run aggregate supply curve for the United States both before the tariffs (labeled SRAS1) and after the tariff (SRAS2). You do not need to show specific dollar values for the price of GDP figures for output. Just show the basic shape of the two curves and indicate the direction of change.

Topic 3.4

Long-Run Aggregate Supply (LRAS)

"Of course, it is not the employer who pays wages. He only handles the money. It is the product that pays wages and it is the management that arranges the production so that the product may pay the wages."

Henry Ford (1863–1947), founder of Ford Motors and
developer of assembly line production

Essential Question: How does the flexibility of the long run affect pricing and production costs for businesses?

Two companies share the same office complex: Banner Plastics and Feldman Textiles. Banner makes customized industrial fittings for use in large municipal projects like replacing old city water and sewage pipes. Feldman is a textile company that makes customized fabrics for airlines, airports, trains, and buses. When the world price of oil skyrockets due to unrest in the Middle East, Banner Plastics experiences severe impacts. It needs to make quick decisions about reducing output to offset the increase in production costs. Feldman Textiles, on the other hand, is relatively unaffected by the increase in world oil prices. In fact, Feldman is about to invest half a million dollars in a new color-mixing technology that will ultimately save it both labor and dye material costs.

This is the difference between the short run and long run: Banner Plastics is limited because most of their production costs are rigid, or fixed, in the short run, whereas Feldman Textiles is not limited by the short run and has more flexibility to plan for technology changes that will reduce their production costs in the long run.

The Long-Run Aggregate Supply Curve

Recall that in the short run, producers have fixed costs, such as wages and contracts, that limit their ability and flexibility to respond to market changes to maintain their profits. **Long-run aggregate supply (LRAS)**, on the other hand, refers to the timeframe when price levels, wages, and contracts can adjust to the changes in the economy. Nominal wages and aggregate price levels are not sticky in the long run. In fact, in the long run, aggregate price levels have no effect on aggregate output (or real GDP). Feldman Textiles, in the example above, can plan and implement technology upgrades to their production system based on long-run expectations of output and wage costs that will ultimately increase profits and reduce costs. The company is not restricted by short-run fixed costs, and neither is their output.

Despite the fact that they both illustrate the connection between price level and real GDP, the LRAS curve differs from the SRAS curve. The **long-run aggregate supply curve** shows the relationship between aggregate price level and the quantity of aggregate output that would exist if all costs, including nominal wages, were completely flexible. The LRAS curve does not actually curve—it is a vertical line. One reason the LRAS curve is vertical is because changes in aggregate price levels have no effect on aggregate output in the long run.

Imagine that the aggregate price level for goods in an economy falls by 20 percent, and all production costs, including wages, also fall by 20 percent. What would happen to GDP in the long run? Nothing. Profits would drop by 20 percent but so would all of the output costs. So, businesses would maintain their profit margins even with a large reduction in the aggregate price level.

Long-Run Aggregate Supply Curve

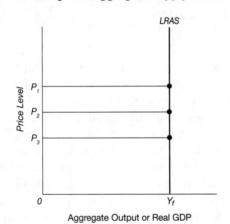

The LRAS curve is a vertical line because it represents an economy's output at full employment (Y_f), so it remains static in a graph.

Full-Employment, or Potential, Output Another reason the LRAS curve is a vertical line is because it represents an economy's **full-employment output** (Y_f). This is also sometimes called maximum sustainable capacity or the **potential output**—level of real GDP if all prices and wages were fully flexible and used efficiently. Think of potential output as the ideal if an economy is working on all cylinders. Of course, potential output is an ideal and can only be estimated, like a prediction of how well the economy could perform. The U.S government's Congressional Budget Office (CBO) estimates the annual potential output for federal budgetary analysis purposes. Because this potential output is an estimate, real GDP will usually fall either below or above the potential output line depending on how well the economy performs.

The difference between the full-employment output and real GDP is called the **output gap**. Between 2000 and 2007, for example, the output gap was fairly consistent, landing just above and just below the full-employment output line. In 2008, when the financial crisis hit the U.S. and world economies, that changed. In the graph on the following page, you can see the large dip in real GDP and the wide output gap that remained through 2013.

Potential Output vs. GDP

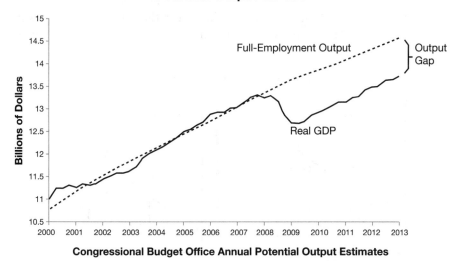

Congressional Budget Office Annual Potential Output Estimates

Full-employment output and real GDP are often closely aligned. The output gap widens greatly in 2008 as a result of the financial crisis.

The vertical line of the LRAS, which represents the economy's potential output, tends to shift to the right—meaning it increases—over time because of long-run factors:

- increases in physical capital
- increases in human capital
- technological progress

Unlike the SRAS curve, the LRAS curve has the benefit of time. It remains a static vertical line because, in the long run, wages and prices fully adjust.

Short-Run to Long-Run Curve Shifts

An economy can be on both the SRAS and LRAS curves simultaneously. This occurs when real GDP and potential output coincide (see the graph above for years 2001, 2005, and 2007 for examples). The economy can be on the SRAS curve during periods when the aggregate output does not match potential output. But the SRAS will shift over time until the economy reaches a point where both curves cross and aggregate output matches potential output. Wages and other production costs have a large effect on these shifts. If the economy's SRAS real GDP is strong and exceeds the LRAS potential output, it means lots of people are working and creating great numbers of goods. (This is akin to maximum sustainable capacity.) This usually means unemployment is low and competition for workers will cause a rise in nominal wages—which shifts the SRAS to the left because now output costs have risen for producers.

The opposite process will cause the SRAS to shift rightward: When the SRAS real GDP is weak and falls short of the LRAS potential output, fewer people are working, and fewer goods are being created. This usually results in a lower need for workers, so unemployment rises, nominal wages fall, and the SRAS curve shifts to the right. Note that when both the leftward and rightward shifts occur, the aggregate price level does not change because it has no effect on aggregate output.

SRAS Shifts and the LRAS Curve

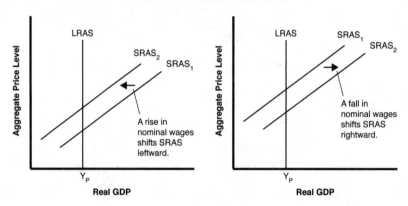

The long-run aggregate supply curve (LRAS)—based on potential output (Y_p)—is unaffected by changes in aggregate price level. The short-run aggregate supply (SRAS) curve shifts in response to real GDP and its relation to potential output.

LRAS and the Production Possibilities Curve The long-run aggregate supply curve and the production possibilities curve (PPC), which you learned about in Topic 1.2, are related because they are two different ways of looking at maximum sustainable capacity in an economy. The LRAS and PPC look at total economic output if all resources are fully employed—but from different perspectives.

COMPARING LRAS CURVES AND PPCS		
Characteristic	**Long-Run Aggregate Supply Curve**	**Production Possibilities Curve**
Assumptions Used to Create	• Assumes all costs, including nominal wages, are completely flexible and efficiently used	• Assumes goods and services production is as efficient as possible
Relationship Portrayed	• Shows relationship between aggregate price level and the aggregate output (real GDP) based on potential output (Y_p)	• Shows the relationship between two possible products based on scarcity and opportunity
Value as a Baseline	• Establishes a baseline for measuring an economy's output (falling below, matching, or exceeding the baseline)	• Establishes a baseline for measuring inefficient, efficient, and unachievable production

The PPC can provide capacity information about two specific products, whereas the LRAS provides capacity information about the total economy. Supply and demand, opportunity, and scarcity are important measures that economists use to understand the complex relationship among prices, wages, and real GDP.

ANSWER THE TOPIC ESSENTIAL QUESTION

1. In one to three paragraphs, explain how the flexibility of the long run affects pricing and production costs for businesses.

KEY TERMS

long-run aggregate supply (LRAS)   potential output
long-run aggregate supply curve   output gap
full-employment output

MULTIPLE-CHOICE QUESTIONS

1. Which best describes a primary reason the LRAS curve is a vertical line in a graph?

   (A) Because it represents where aggregate prices and real GDP intersect

   (B) Because LRAS is tied to production costs, which remain static over time

   (C) Because variations in aggregate price levels have no effect on aggregate output

   (D) Because LRAS is the opposite of SRAS, which curves or slopes based on economic conditions

   (E) Because it represents full unemployment, which is estimated by the CBO

2. Which of the following is a reason the LRAS will shift to the right over time?

   (A) rising commodity costs

   (B) potential output is revised downward

   (C) nominal wage increases

   (D) advances in production technology

   (E) actual GDP matches potential output

3. In what ways are the production possibilities curve and long-run aggregate supply related?

(A) Both show two different products.

(B) Both show the different time periods in an economy.

(C) Both show demand of one product over another.

(D) Both show supply of one product over another.

(E) Both show an economy that is using its resources to its fullest capacity.

FREE-RESPONSE QUESTIONS

1. Use the graph below to answer all parts of the questions that follow.

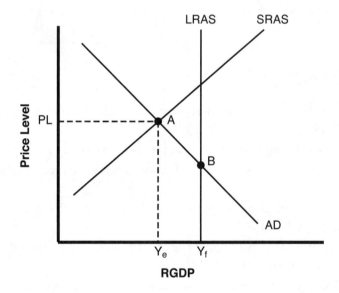

(a) Explain what the long-run aggregate supply curve represents in an economy.

(b) Identify one factor that would create growth, shifting the LRAS curve and explain how that would occur.

(c) Explain the difference between point A and point B.

(d) Explain what point A on the graph would above represent on a production possibilities curve.

(e) Explain what point B on the graph above would represent on a production possibilities curve.

THINK AS AN ECONOMIST: *DESCRIBE ECONOMIC CONCEPTS*

Economics has specialized concepts that economists use to explain economic behavior. To do so, they take these steps:

- Define the concept.
- Explain how the concept relates to other concepts.
- Explain why the concept is important in the field of economics.

For example, economists define the multiplier effect as the way an increase (or decrease) in one economic activity causes increases (or decreases) across a range of other related economic activities. The multiplier effect is related to gross domestic product (GDP) because increased consumer purchasing causes increases in GDP. This is important because it helps explain the benefits of income growth to an economy.

Apply the Skill

Economists use the long-run aggregate supply curve to explain the long-term effects of producers' decision-making about how much to produce. Define the concept and explain both how it relates to potential output and why it is an important concept.

Topic 3.5

Equilibrium in the AD-AS Model

"The equilibrium between supply and demand is achieved only through a reaction against the upsetting of the equilibrium."

British economist David Harvey, *The Limits to Capital* (1982)

Essential Question: How does the AD-AS model reflect the economic fluctuations and production decisions that affect prices and GDP?

Running a small retail business is complicated. Managing employees and carrying out the necessary day-to-day tasks are only part of the process. Understanding clients' needs, predicting trends, managing inventory, keeping on top of the supply chain, reacting to changes in nominal costs and competitive prices, ensuring product orders are shipped on time and material orders arrive in time—it can be an exhausting balancing act to keep a business afloat. And the goal is always to have your supply match your demand at a good price to have a successful business.

Now imagine trying to get a handle on a national economy with very similar variables and influences—but multiplied by millions of businesses. Even understanding such a complex system is a prodigious challenge. As you have learned, economists use a variety of tools and measurements to try to understand the actions and reactions of an economy. The aggregate demand-aggregate supply model is one of the essential tools used to understand the complicated fluctuations in an economy.

Equilibrium and the AD-AS Model

In previous topics in this unit, you have encountered aggregate demand (total demand for goods and services in an economy) and aggregate supply (total output of goods and services in an economy). The **aggregate demand-aggregate supply model** (AD-AS) combines aggregate demand data with aggregate supply data. This allows economists and analysts to get an overview of an economy by bringing together the key elements that affect it. Demand, long- and short-run supply, prices, unemployment, and real GDP all coincide in the AD-AS model. One can learn a lot about what has happened and what may happen by analyzing this fundamental economic tool.

The word *equilibrium* refers to when two or more things are in balance. In economics, **equilibrium** has a more specific definition: It is when market supply and demand are balanced and prices are stable. This is not an easy or usual state for an economy to attain, and even when economic equilibrium does occur, it is fleeting. In simple supply and demand terms, there are actions consumers and producers take that push the economy toward equilibrium. If there is a shortage of goods, prices will rise; if there is a surplus of goods, prices will drop. From the macroeconomic point of view, however, the AD-AS model tells a more complicated story of the economy, with both long-run and short-run implications.

Short-Run Macroeconomic Equilibrium

When an economy is at a point of **short-run macroeconomic equilibrium**, it means the amount of aggregate output supplied by producers equals the aggregate demand by consumers, businesses, and governments. (This is marked on a graph with E_{SR}). This would indicate that an economy's price levels are stable, with no major cost shifts to require short-run adjustments for producers. This is called **short-run equilibrium aggregate price level** and is represented on a graph by P_E. This also indicates that employment is stable, and unemployment is low because demand must be met consistently. This is called **short-run equilibrium aggregate output** and appears on a graph as Y_E.

The AD-AS Model

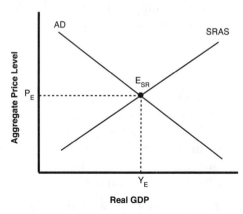

Where the aggregate demand (AD) and short-run aggregate supply (SRAS) curves intersect is considered the equilibrium point (usually noted with E_{SR}). The total aggregate output (GDP) demanded by consumers and businesses is equal to the output supplied. The P_E line marks the short-run aggregate price level and the Y_E marks the short-run equilibrium level of aggregate output.

The AD-AS model will reflect market fluctuations just like the supply and demand model you learned about earlier. (See Topics 1.4 and 1.5.) If the aggregate price level is above the equilibrium point, the aggregate output supplied by producers exceeds demand for goods—which leads to a drop in the aggregate price level in an attempt to maintain equilibrium. The opposite holds if the aggregate price level is below the equilibrium point: there is not enough aggregate supply to meet demand and prices will rise.

Take the release of a new tech product such as a smartphone, for example. The XeTek company releases a new style of smartphone with innovative features and a very affordable price. It is a huge hit and consumers buy the new phone in droves. Because the demand for the product exceeds XeTek's supply, the price will rise. That is just one company experiencing supply and demand disequilibrium. The AD-AS model looks at the aggregate numbers for an entire economy.

Note that both aggregate output and aggregate prices trend upward. Very few years in the past century experienced a fall in aggregate price level.

AD-AS Disequilibrium

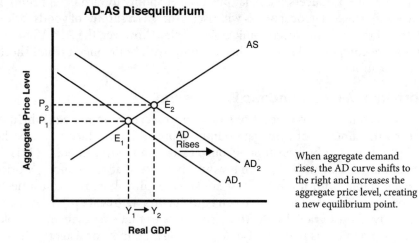

When aggregate demand rises, the AD curve shifts to the right and increases the aggregate price level, creating a new equilibrium point.

Long-run macroeconomic equilibrium occurs when the short-run aggregate macroeconomic equilibrium intersects with the long-run aggregate supply curve—essentially equaling potential output and full employment. Long-run macroeconomic equilibrium assumes the passage of time so that the economy is on both the LRAS and SRAS curves.

Short-Run Output Gaps

Recall that an economy can be on the short-run and/or long-run at varying times. Short-run aggregate output fluctuates more frequently based on economic activity. It can be at, above, or below the full-employment level of output. When aggregate demand and pricing shift in the short-run, there can be **output gaps**—differences between actual and potential output—that are reflected in relation to the LRAS, or an economy's potential output.

Inflationary Gap When aggregate demand for goods and services is greater than aggregate supply, the economy has an **inflationary gap**. This can develop when economic production levels are high due to low unemployment and more consumer disposable income, robust trade with other countries, or government purchases. Aggregate demand (AD) increases and the AD curve shifts to the right, resulting in higher aggregate price levels and aggregate output (GDP). Employment and nominal wages rise. This new aggregate output level exceeds the LRAS curve, creating the inflationary gap. In the long-run, aggregate supply, demand, output, and price levels will self-correct and move toward long-run macroeconomic equilibrium.

Recessionary Gap When an economy is operating below full employment equilibrium it has a **recessionary gap**. Because demand is down, unemployment will rise and prices will drop. Producers responding to this recessionary gap will make changes in production costs, wait until they can adjust the sticky nominal wages, and ultimately increase output. Over time, the SRAS curve will begin to shift back to the right until it again reaches the equilibrium point where the SRAS and LRAS curves intersect with a new AD point.

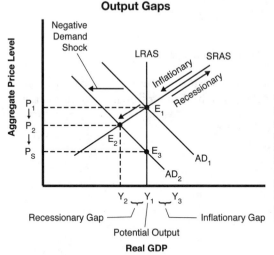

Output Gaps

This graph depicts what happens to aggregate supply, demand, output, and price levels in the short- and long-run when there is a recessionary gap. Note that an inflationary gap (indicated as Y_3 on the horizontal axis) would be represented by the same source lines (LRAS, SRAS, AD) but all moving in the opposite direction (rightward instead of leftward).

ANSWER THE TOPIC ESSENTIAL QUESTION

1. In one to three paragraphs, explain how the AD-AS model is used as a tool to reflect economic fluctuations and production decisions that affect prices and GDP.

KEY TERMS

aggregate demand
aggregate supply
aggregate demand-aggregate supply
model (AD-AS)
equilibrium

short-run macroeconomic equilibrium
short-run equilibrium aggregate price level
short-run equilibrium aggregate output
long-run macroeconomic equilibrium
output gap

MULTIPLE-CHOICE QUESTIONS

1. Which must be at the same levels to attain short-run macroeconomic equilibrium?
   (A) real GDP and potential output
   (B) the SRAS curve and the LRAS curve
   (C) aggregate output and demand for goods and services
   (D) price levels and aggregate output
   (E) aggregate supply and potential price levels

2. If price level is above long-run equilibrium, what must happen to help price levels return to long-run equilibrium?

(A) Real GDP must decrease in the short run.

(B) Long-run supply estimates must reduce.

(C) Production costs must be adjusted upward.

(D) Tax rates must be increased to reduce AD.

(E) Tax rates must be decreased to increase AD.

3. Assuming an economy is in a recession, if the aggregate supply curve increases (shifts to the right), which of the following would occur?

	Price Level	Real Output
(A)	Increase	Decrease
(B)	Increase	Remain the same
(C)	Decrease	Remain the same
(D)	Decrease	Increase
(E)	Decrease	Decrease

FREE-RESPONSE QUESTIONS

1. Assume the federal government institutes a large stimulus program for infrastructure repair. Use the graph below to answer all parts of the questions that follow.

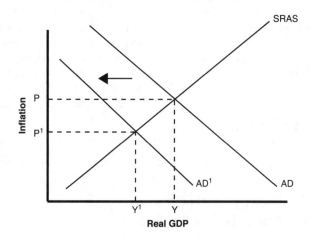

Demand Shock and AD-AS Model

(a) In what direction would this stimulus shift aggregate demand? Explain.

(b) What would the effect of the above shift have on real output and price level?

(c) How would employment be affected by this stimulus program?

(d) What might be a potential long-run pitfall of this stimulus program?

(e) Assume a devastating crash of the stock market occurred. How would the economy respond to such a massive negative demand shock? Draw a graph (or use the one above) that shows the shifts in aggregate demand, real GDP, aggregate pricing, and the short-run aggregate supply curve. Remember to use arrows to indicate these changes.

 THINK AS AN ECONOMIST: *DRAW AN ACCURATELY LABELED GRAPH TO REPRESENT AN ECONOMIC MARKET*

The aggregate supply curve generally slopes upward and to the right, as does an individual firm's or the market's supply curve. The rationale is fundamental to the law of supply—firms are willing to produce more as price increases.

As you know, the aggregate demand and aggregate supply curves can shift in response to economic conditions. These shifts happen in the short run. In the long run, both AD and AS tend toward a new equilibrium point.

Apply the Skill

Study the graph below. Write a brief explanation of what dynamic is taking place and what the three arrows on the graph represent.

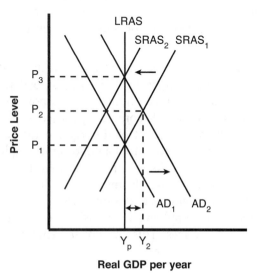

Changes in the AD-AS Model in the Short Run

"Supply and demand always uses prices and profits to signal to producers what society required. Thus producers, in search of profit, produce what society requires—in the correct quantity and at a competitive price."

Scottish economist Adam Smith, *The Wealth of Nations* (1776)

Essential Question: How do shocks to supply and demand impact employment, prices, and output in the short run?

Whenever a major world event takes place, economies around the globe experience effects and respond to such large events. Devastating earthquakes, terrorist attacks, technological innovations, a crisis in the oil market, even major government spending plans can all cause shocks to economies. How a shock impacts an economy depends on the state of the economy when the shock occurs. There can be demand shocks and supply shocks, and both of these can be either negative or positive. Whichever way they break, shocks to an economic system result in short-run consequences.

Aggregate Demand Shocks

An **aggregate demand shock** is an unforeseen event or occurrence that causes an increase or decrease in demand for goods and services. It can be either positive or negative.

Positive Demand Shock An increase in aggregate demand, represented by a shift of the aggregate demand curve to the right, is a **positive demand shock**. In the late 1990s, a technology revolution spurred a positive demand shock. The rise of the Internet and portable computing caused a spike in demand for related goods and services. The effect of this rippled through the economy, resulting in rising prices, increased output, and lower unemployment.

Some positive demand shocks are intentional by the government as a response to an economic downturn. Examples include large government tax cuts and sudden decreases in interest rates on loans.

Producers respond by supplying more, which often requires increased hiring and paying higher wages. This can create general economic growth, although it can also lead to inflation.

Negative Demand Shock A decrease in aggregate demand, represented by a shift of the aggregate demand curve to the left, is a **negative demand shock.** Examples include events that cause enough fear or uncertainty among consumers that they decide to purchase less and save more and events that reduce employment. For example, a high-profile terrorist attack can cause a decline in aggregate demand. In 2020, to slow the spread of the COVID-19 outbreak, people stayed at home, dramatically reducing their overall consumption. Some acted out of uncertainty, but many had to cut back on expenditures because they had lost their income.

Producers have to make choices about how to respond to the decrease in demand. Because nominal wages are sticky, production costs are primarily reduced by decreasing output, which can lead to a decrease in prices, too.

Changes in the AD-AS Model in the Short-Run

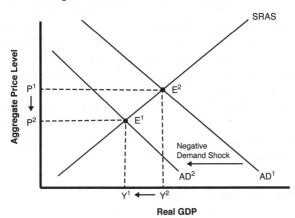

The negative demand shock shifts the aggregate demand (AD) curve to the left. This leads to a decrease in both aggregate prices and aggregate output.

Short-Run Aggregate Supply Shock

A **supply shock** is when something unforeseen quickly and dramatically changes product supply levels. Like demand shocks, supply shocks can be positive or negative. A **positive supply shock** creates increased aggregate supply; a **negative supply shock** results in lower aggregate supply. But unlike demand shocks, supply shocks cause aggregate output (GDP) and aggregate price levels to move in opposite directions—no matter whether the shock is positive or negative.

Positive Supply Shock A positive supply shock, like the tech boom in the United States in the late 1990s, is distinguished by a number of economic shifts:

- Production costs decrease.

- Output quantities increase.

- Aggregate price levels adjust downward.

This kind of supply shock shifts the SRAS curve to the right. Employment rises as well because producers generally need more workers to increase supply.

Negative Supply Shock A negative supply shock, such as a hurricane or earthquake or the economic crisis in 2008, affects the short run in the opposite direction:

- Production costs increase.

- Output quantities decrease.

- Aggregate price levels adjust upward.

This supply shock shifts the SRAS curve to the left. Unemployment can also rise because supply decreases (though sticky nominal wages and contracts mitigate severe drops in unemployment). Historically, shocks to the AS model tend to be negative.

Stagflation One form of negative supply shock has a special name: **stagflation**. This occurs when inflation meets decreasing aggregate output (stagnation + inflation). Unemployment also rises. This is a particularly difficult negative shock for an economy or government to respond to. The most recent experience of stagflation hit the U.S. economy hard in 1973. Middle East oil-producing countries put an embargo, or ban, in place for many Western nations like the United States. This sudden supply shock—oil prices increased about 400 percent in a few months—exploded the global price of oil, which increased the costs to produce and transport goods and services. Aggregate output began to decrease, but aggregate prices began to rise. Add an increase in unemployment from producer layoffs, and you can see how stagflation becomes a very difficult downward spiral (or curve shift) to turn around.

Changes in the AD-AS Model in the Short-Run/Stagflation

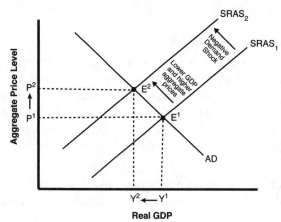

Stagflation means aggregate output falls and aggregate price levels increase. Unemployment also rises when this occurs.

Types of Inflation

Inflation measures the rate at which the aggregate price levels in an economy increase over time. Economists gauge inflation because it's an indication of consumer purchasing power. Some inflation is believed to be needed to contribute to economic growth. There are, however, different forms of inflation.

Demand-Pull Inflation This occurs when aggregate prices rise in response to a supply shortage. This is the most common and well-known cause of inflation. It is common on a microeconomic level: a hot new product comes out, consumers go crazy for it, it becomes hard to get, and the price goes up.

At the macroeconomic level, several widespread developments in an economy can cause demand-pull inflation:

- **Economic growth** Confident consumers spend more money and use more debt.

- **Export surge** If the value of exports increases relative to the value of imports, more money will be entering the domestic economy.

- **Government spending** More federal spending on big projects means more goods and services demand.

- **Inflation expectations** If inflation is expected to rise, companies may hike up prices and consumers may make major purchases before prices rise.

- **More money in the system** If governments increase the money supply but output cannot keep up with demand, prices will increase.

An example of demand-pull inflation would be if the U.S. government instituted a special tax-credit incentive to get people to buy electric cars and the program was a massive success. If automakers could not keep up with the extreme demand, the price of the most popular models would spike, resulting in higher aggregate prices for the cars.

One of the most famous and extreme examples of demand-pull inflation occurred in Germany after World War I ended in 1918. Production collapsed in the postwar economy, and the government, saddled with enormous debts, responded by printing more and more money. This combination—so much cash and so few available goods—produced not just regular inflation, but hyperinflation. For a while, the price of common items doubled every 3.7 days. Bundles of the worthless currency were used as building blocks by children and as kindling for making fires.

Cost-Push Inflation This is a supply issue that results in higher prices for consumers. Unlike demand-pull inflation, cost-push inflation occurs when the cost of materials and wages increases. The higher costs for production reduce aggregate supply even though demand for goods remains constant, so the higher production costs get passed on to consumers. There are a variety of supply changes that can cause cost-push inflation:

- The cost of raw materials increases.

- Wages and associated labor costs increase.

- Natural hazards affect production facilities.

- Changes in government regulations occur.

All of these cause production cost increases to which producers respond with price increases in order to maintain profitability. An example of a material cost increase is when coffee prices spiked between 2001 and 2006. The aggregate price per pound rose from 50 cents to $1.60, so coffee retailers passed along the cost increase to their customers. In 2009, Japan was hit by a magnitude 9 earthquake and tsunami that devastated cities where large semiconductor production plants were located. Japan accounted for 20 percent of the world's semiconductor supply. Because so many facilities were damaged—and semiconductor supply dropped—the price for electronics such as smartphones, TVs, medical equipment, and even washing machines increased.

Source: Library of Congress

Gas line in the 1970s caused by the shortage of oil and rising gas prices as a result of the OPEC embargo.

A dramatic example of cost-push inflation occurred in the 1970s when the Organization of Petroleum Exporting Countries (OPEC), an oil-producing cartel of member nations, imposed an oil embargo on the United States and other Western countries. Despite the fact that there was no increase in demand, the supply restrictions caused oil prices to quadruple. Gas prices skyrocketed, jumping by 37 percent in 1973 alone, and consumers waited in long lines to fill their cars' tanks. In an attempt to shorten lines and head off panic buying, some U.S. states enacted odd-even rationing. Vehicles with license plates ending in an odd number could only buy gas on odd-numbered days.

1. In one to three paragraphs, explain how positive and negative shocks to both supply and demand impact employment, prices, and output in the short run.

KEY TERMS

aggregate demand shock
positive demand shock
negative demand shock

negative supply shock
positive supply shock
stagflation

MULTIPLE-CHOICE QUESTIONS

1. If there is a positive demand shock, which best describes how aggregate price levels react?

   (A) Aggregate price levels will remain generally static.

   (B) Aggregate price levels are not affected by demand shocks.

   (C) Aggregate price levels will likely rise due to scarcity.

   (D) Aggregate price levels respond based only on supply levels.

   (E) Aggregate price levels will drop due to much higher demand.

2. Which does NOT contribute to demand-pull inflation?

   (A) Growth in GDP

   (B) Increased exports

   (C) Expectation of rising prices

   (D) Increase in workers' wages

   (E) Federal spending programs

3. A supply shock, such as a severe drought, would lead to

   (A) a decrease in price level and an increase in employment

   (B) a decrease in price level and an increase in unemployment

   (C) an increase in price level and an increase in employment

   (D) an increase in price level and an increase in unemployment

   (E) an increase in price level and an increase in real wages

1. Use the graph below to answer all parts of the questions that follow. For these questions, one does not build upon the others.

LRAS and the AD-AS Model

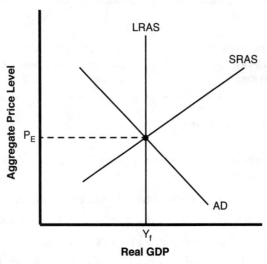

(a) What would be the short-run effect of a negative shock like the government passing a large increase in the minimum wage?

(b) If a solar panel company can no longer import necessary materials from China because of a trade war, what kind of inflation would likely occur? How will that affect the aggregate price levels?

(c) Draw a graph that represents the effect the trade war would have on this economy.

(d) How would the graph change if the federal government implements measures such as a large tax increase and a severe cut in non-military spending?

(e) Assume farmers across the world experience remarkably moderate temperatures and ideal precipitation. The yield on the four primary crops—corn, rice, wheat, and potatoes—is nearly 50 percent higher than customary and anticipated. What will be the short-run effect on aggregate price levels and aggregate output?

Economists can demonstrate the effects of a change by using accurately labeled graphs. Two common types of graphs used to display data are bar graphs and line graphs. Each type is better suited to displaying particular kinds of data.

- Bar graphs are best suited to comparing data points at specific points in time or in different locations.
- Line graphs are useful for showing trends over time.

Each type of graph plots data against the horizontal x-axis and the vertical y-axis. With a bar graph, the y-axis is typically the quantity being measured. The x-axis is used to plot the different points in time or places being compared. With a line graph, the y-axis is the quantity measured, and the x-axis is the period of time covered by the graph. A simple bar graph might look like this:

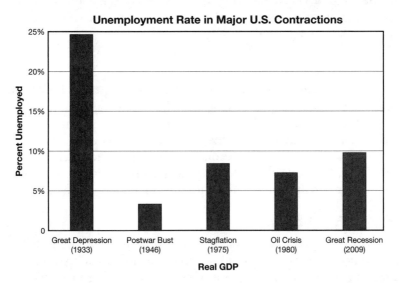

For an example of a line graph, see the graph showing changes in the components of the Consumer Price Index (CPI) from 2000 to 2017 in Topic 2.5.

Apply the Skill

The chart below shows the inflation rate each year in the 1970s. Use the data to construct a graph that emphasizes the change over time.

1970	1971	1972	1973	1974	1975	1976	1977	1978	1979
5.6%	3.3%	3.4%	8.7%	12.3%	6.9%	5.8%	6.7%	9.0%	13.3%

Topic 3.7

Long-Run Self-Adjustment

"This long run is a misleading guide to current affairs. In the long run we are all dead. Economists set themselves too easy, too useless a task if in tempestuous seasons they can only tell us that when the storm is past the ocean is flat again."

British economist John Maynard Keynes, *A Tract on Monetary Reform* (1923)

Essential Question: In the long run, how does the economy adjust to supply and demand shocks in order to return to full employment and economic growth?

Problems that were urgent and seemed devastating often look much less daunting after time has passed. Consumers, businesses, and governments keep an eye on the long run, but it's the more immediate, short-run problems and obstacles that generally demand the greatest attention and effort. The same applies to how people behave in economic situations: they focus on the short run. As Keynes famously noted, the long-run view is not always useful in helping people in their dynamic interaction with the immediacy of the economy.

Long-Run Equilibrium

Recall that the long run assumes a passage of time. Some economists suggest a decade or more needs to pass for long-run corrections to take place. **Long-run equilibrium** occurs when the point of short-run equilibrium intersects with the long-run aggregate supply curve. This means short-run aggregate output is equal to potential output (the LRAS line on graphs). In the long run, the economy is self-correcting, and shifts in the long-run aggregate supply curve indicate changes in the full-employment level of output and economic growth over time.

When short-run demand shocks occur, the long run reflects the outcomes of those shocks based on how consumers, businesses, and governments responded. Wages, prices, and employment levels will adjust to their natural rates after a short-run aggregate demand or supply shock passes.

LRAS and Aggregate Demand Shocks Unlike the short-run perspective, in the long run, all elements of production and its costs (materials, labor) are variable. Aggregate demand and GDP are essentially the same. The vertical **long-run aggregate supply** (LRAS) curve on a graph is a straight line because changes in aggregate price levels have no effect on aggregate output in the long run. And the LRAS curve represents the economy's potential output—the GDP level if all prices and wages were fully flexible, resources were used efficiently, and the economy was at full employment output.

So, what happens to the LRAS curve when there is a positive aggregate demand shock—for example, an unexpected decrease in interest rates by the Federal Reserve? The aggregate demand (AD) will shift to the right because of increased demand, and the SRAS curve will shift to the left because supply cannot keep pace with demand in the short run. Aggregate demand (AD) will shift to the right in response to increased demand from the increased government expenditures. Price levels will rise, and GDP will exceed potential output—the LRAS curve—and create an inflationary gap.

The inflationary gap results in higher real GDP and higher price levels and would decrease unemployment below the natural rate of unemployment. The higher price levels reduce the real wages of workers who begin to demand higher nominal wages to offset the higher prices. This increases the costs of production, shifting the SRAS to the left, reducing the real GDP back to the LRAS and increasing unemployment back to the natural rate of unemployment. At this point long-run equilibrium is restored.

LRAS and Positive Demand Shock

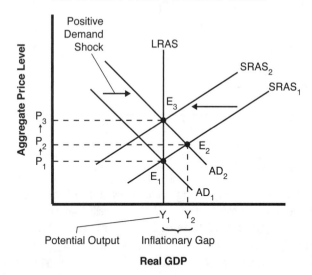

A positive aggregate demand shock shifts SRAS and AD in opposite directions and exceeds potential output (GDP). This inflationary gap will eventually self-correct, and potential output, AD, and SRAS will meet LRAS for a new equilibrium point.

If a negative demand shock occurs, something like a pandemic or a terror attack, the opposite of what's depicted in the graph will happen. Aggregate output and prices will fall in the short-run. Unemployment will rise as well. This is called a recessionary gap, and GDP falls short of the LRAS, or potential output. But this will self-correct over time. Real GDP, employment, and price levels will adjust back to a new LRAS point to attain equilibrium.

LRAS and Aggregate Supply Shocks More time and study is given to aggregate demand shocks than aggregate supply shocks because supply shocks that affect the entire economy are comparatively rare. But when supply shocks hit, they tend to be harsh, especially regarding employment numbers.

- In 1973, the Arab-Israeli War resulted in an oil embargo initiated by OPEC (the Organization of Petroleum Exporting Countries) against countries OPEC believed supported Israel. This, in turn, led to an increase in oil prices and an unemployment rate near 10 percent.

- In 1979, the Iranian revolution and hostage crisis resulted in another decrease in oil supply. This and the fear of further supply interruptions spiked oil prices again; unemployment neared 12 percent.

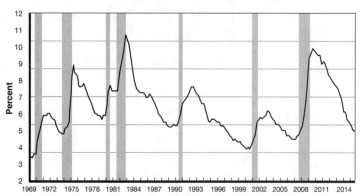

U.S. Unemployment 1970-2014

Shaded areas indicate U.S recessions

The grey shaded areas indicate recessionary periods. In each recessionary period, unemployment tends to rise slightly. Note the spike in unemployment that immediately followed a supply shock to the economy in 1973 and 1979.

The 2008 financial and housing crises were a combination of both supply and demand shocks, but you can see that the recessionary effect of an aggregate supply shock has a more devastating effect on unemployment than short-run aggregate demand shocks. There are a few damaging things happening at once with a supply shock: aggregate output is falling, unemployment is rising, and prices are going up.

Policy makers can use fiscal and monetary policies to try to get aggregate demand back on track (see Topics 3.8, 4.6, and 5.1). But there are fewer policy options to shift the short-run aggregate supply curve to its original position. Increasing government stimulus to increase aggregate demand and slow down rising unemployment will reduce aggregate output at the risk of causing inflation. Decreasing stimulus to reduce aggregate demand may rein in inflation, but it risks causing higher unemployment. Like all economic decisions, either option offers a tradeoff.

1. In one to three paragraphs, explain how the long run adjusts to supply and demand shocks in order to return to full employment and economic growth.

KEY TERMS

long-run equilibrium   long-run aggregate supply

MULTIPLE-CHOICE QUESTIONS

1. Assuming a negative supply shock, in which of the following ways could the economy self-adjust and be restored to full employment?

   (A) The government could decrease spending.

   (B) The federal reserve could lower interest rates.

   (C) The government could institute new regulations for manufacturers.

   (D) Citizens could accept lower wages.

   (E) Citizens could ask for higher wages.

2. How do supply shocks differ from demand shocks regarding GDP and price levels?

   (A) Demand shocks cause prices and GDP to decrease sharply.

   (B) Demand shocks affect prices and GDP in opposite directions.

   (C) Supply shocks only impact prices and not GDP.

   (D) Supply shocks move prices and GDP in opposite directions.

   (E) Supply shocks cause prices and GDP to drop severely.

3. What do shifts in the long-run aggregate supply curve indicate?

   (A) Economic growth

   (B) Falling price levels

   (C) Rising producer costs

   (D) Stable nominal wages

   (E) GDP fluctuations over time

1. Assume there has been a negative demand shock to the economy. Use the graph below to answer all parts of the questions that follow.

Negative Demand Shock and the LRAS

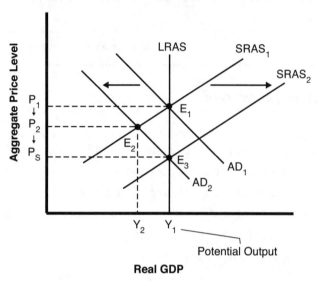

(a) What does the shift from AD_1 to AD_2 signify?

(b) What happens to employment numbers when aggregate demand shifts due to a negative demand shock?

(c) What is the short-run impact of lower aggregate demand on price levels? Explain.

(d) Describe what must happen once a recessionary gap occurs for the SRAS curve to shift rightward to establish a new equilibrium point (E_3 in the graph).

(e) Assume there is a *positive* demand shock to the economy. Re-label this graph to show how AD and SRAS shift and how prices are affected. (Be sure to denote which way curves shift and mark the equilibrium points.)

THINK AS AN ECONOMIST: *DETERMINE THE OUTCOME OF AN ECONOMIC SITUATION USING ECONOMIC MODELS*

Economists use models to analyze markets and explain the outcomes of economic situations. For example, economists note that market forces push a market toward equilibrium. When disequilibrium occurs, producers and consumers change their behavior until supply and demand meet at the market price again. This is true both on the microeconomic level, regarding individual firms and industries, and on the macroeconomic level, in terms of aggregate supply and demand.

Apply the Skill

Economists identify two reasons that disequilibrium occurs in the aggregate demand-aggregate supply (AD-AS) model. They are demand shocks and supply shocks. In 2020, the U.S. economy was jolted by the economic ramifications of the COVID-19, or coronavirus, pandemic. Mayors and state governors ordered the forced closing of most places of business except those providing essential services. Employers had to send most or all of their employees to work at home—when such work was possible. Economic life for many Americans and U.S. firms came to a virtual standstill.

What kind of shock to the economy was the COVID-19 pandemic? Was it a positive or negative demand shock or a positive or negative supply shock? Identify the type and explain your reasoning based on the AD-AS model.

Fiscal Policy

"The great thing about fiscal policy is that it has a direct impact and does not require you to bind the hands of future policy makers."

American economist and Nobel Laureate Paul Krugman (May 2012)

Essential Question: How do government fiscal policies involving spending and taxation affect demand, GDP, and employment?

The biggest players in a nation's economy are the consumers and businesses that purchase and produce goods and services. The next biggest player is the federal government, which can impact the economy positively or negatively through laws, regulations, taxes, spending, and adjustments to the money supply. Sharp disagreements over government economic policies fuel political debates. Since the beginning of modern industrialization in the mid-18th century, governments have played an important role in economies, and the role has generally expanded. It is through fiscal policies that governments respond to developments in the national economy.

Government Fiscal Policies

Fiscal policy refers to the changes in spending and taxes governments make to affect overall spending. Modern fiscal policy was greatly influenced by British economist John Maynard Keynes, whose ideas about government evolved in the early 1900s and then sharpened in reaction to the Great Depression of the 1930s. Before Keynes, most economists believed that economies were self-correcting. The Great Depression proved to many that a hands-off approach was not sufficient. Or, even if in theory the economy would correct in the long run, the short-term suffering in unemployment and reduced consumption was not a good tradeoff.

Keynes believed governments could help stabilize an economy by implementing fiscal policies based primarily on spending and taxation that reduced dramatic ups and downs. The usefulness of his ideas was demonstrated by the New Deal legislation passed under President Franklin Delano Roosevelt in the United States and by similar efforts in other countries. They became more influential in Europe and the United States after World War II, when these regions experienced almost three decades of economic growth.

Some fiscal policies are ways the government handles complicated needs and services for the public—national defense and social insurance, for example—that do not necessarily involve a return of goods and services. Other fiscal policies are meant to be a stimulus to the economy. In 2009, after the 2008 financial crisis known as the "Great Recession," the economy was reeling and unemployment was approaching 10 percent. The Obama administration's American Recovery Act of 2009 was an $800 billion stimulus package that spent money to create jobs and provided tax relief for citizens and businesses. By the end of 2009, GDP was on the uptick. In 2010, unemployment stopped rising and began to slowly drop.

Taxation and Expenditures Governments collect taxes to pay for the goods and services that citizens want. About half of all government revenue goes directly to state and local governments. These taxes vary from place to place but often include income taxes, sales taxes, and property taxes. Many people pay more in these taxes than they pay to the federal government.

The other half of government revenue goes to the federal government, mostly in one of three forms:

- personal income taxes
- corporate profit taxes
- social insurance fees for programs such as Social Security, Medicare, and Medicaid

In some statistics, payments for social insurance programs are not figured as part of taxes. These fees are dedicated to particular programs, so they are not available for general expenditures. Most people pay more for these programs than they pay in federal income taxes.

Federal spending falls into two broad categories:

- **Mandatory spending/transfers** These are programs that must be paid for with no goods or services in return. This is the biggest chunk of the total federal spending (62 percent in 2018). These include **social insurance** programs such as Social Security, Medicare, and Medicaid. These are also called **entitlements**, though the name is misleading as taxpayers pay into these programs via social insurance fees throughout their working life.

- **Discretionary spending** This spending results from legislation or policies that are not mandatory. Discretionary spending makes up 31 percent of 2018 federal spending. Every year, Congress must approve and decide discretionary spending limits on national defense, education, highway funds, aid to foreign countries, and so on.

Fiscal Policy as Stimulus

Economies run in cycles. They grow and expand with low unemployment, high wages, and a lot of buying power for consumers and businesses. Economies also contract, when unemployment rises, GDP dips, and wages and prices stagnate or fall. Fiscal policy is intended to moderate downturns in the economy (like recessions) and aid in continuing expansion.

Changes in government spending have a direct effect on aggregate demand and purchasing. If the federal government spends billions on a national highway improvement program, GDP will rise and unemployment will begin to fall because of the increased short-run demand. If the government makes a change in tax policy—like an across-the-board cut in federal income tax—it will also impact aggregate demand, but not as directly and as successfully as spending does.

There is always a lag associated with discretionary stimulus spending by governments because once Congress approves a program, it takes some time to implement the policies and allow the effects of the stimulus to take effect. But as you can see in the AD-AS model graph, an influx of federal money increases demand for goods, which increases the quantity supplied of goods needed and causes a rise in price levels. As you might expect, unemployment will drop because more workers are needed.

Federal Stimulus and the AD-AS Model

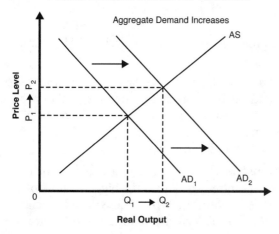

Though there may be a lag between when a federal stimulus plan is enacted by Congress and when its effects are realized in the economy, fiscal stimulus spending generates an increase in aggregate demand.

Multiplier Effect and Fiscal Stimulus Policy One reason fiscal spending and transfer policies are so effective is because of the multiplier effect (covered in Topic 3.2). Recall that when governments spend money on goods and services, a chain reaction throughout the economy is created. Depending on peoples' marginal propensity to consume (MPC) and marginal propensity to save (MPS), every dollar of stimulus will lead to a certain amount of additional spending. For example, if the multiplier is 2, it means for every $1 of federal spending, an additional $2 dollars will be spent—which increases demand and GDP.

Imagine a $50 billion federal program to replace lead water pipes running to homes and businesses. People want to replace these pipes because they can cause lead poisoning, which particularly harms young children. With a multiplier of 2, that initial federal outlay will end up increasing real GDP by $100 billion because of the multiplier effect. As the table below shows, the first round of initial federal spending is $50 billion—that reflects the direct purchases of goods and services by the government. That money allows workers to buy more goods and services—everything from lunch to equipment to new clothes to entertainment. Each subsequent round of spending by consumers and businesses adds more to the total effect on GDP. Because consumers will save some portion of their increased income (MPS), the effect of the stimulus is lower with each round of spending. But in this case, it ultimately results in double the initial amount spent by the federal government—which fuels GDP and economic growth.

Spending Effect on Real GDP	$50 Billion in Federal Purchases for Lead Pipe Replacement Program
1st round	$50.0 billion
2nd round	$25.0 billion
3rd round	$12.5 billion
....	....
....	....
Eventual effect	$100.0 billion

Multiplier Effect and Taxes and Transfers Everyone knows what taxes are. A transfer payment is money transferred to citizens with no good or service in return. Social Security, Medicare, and Medicaid are examples of transfer payments. When governments make changes in taxes or transfer payments, the multiplier effect still applies. However, the tax/transfer multiplier's impact on GDP and the aggregate demand curve is much less than the spending multiplier's. Tax stimulus is cutting tax rates or offering tax rebates or incentives for certain kinds of purchases and investments.

In the previous example of the $50 billion federal program to replace lead water pipes, imagine that the government uses that money to make transfer payments to households instead of actually paying to replace the old lead pipes. People will save (MPS) more of that transferred money and use it to pay bills or debts. The chain reaction that stimulus spending causes, fueling demand and the GDP, is much smaller with transfers and tax incentives. So, each subsequent round, as the graph shows, makes a much smaller impact on demand. That initial $50 billion maxes out at the initial amount.

Transfer Effect on Real GDP	$50 Billion Increase in Federal Transfer Payments
1st round	$25.00 billion
2nd round	$12.50 billion
3rd round	$6.25 billion
....	....
....	....
Eventual effect	$50.00 billion

Expansionary and Contractionary Fiscal Policy

Two of the main purposes behind government fiscal policies are to combat recessions and inflation. If there is a recessionary gap (aggregate output falling below potential output) or an inflationary gap (aggregate output exceeding potential output), fiscal policy can shift the aggregate demand curve to get back to potential output equilibrium.

During a recession, **expansionary fiscal policy** is employed when potential output is not being met. The goal is to increase aggregate demand to close the gap between actual GDP and potential GDP. Expansionary policies include these three approaches:

- increase government purchasing of goods and services (often called stimulus spending)
- increase government transfers to households
- decrease taxes

The idea is that if people have more disposable income to spend, they will buy more goods and thus increase aggregate demand, which increases aggregate output and gets the economy closer to potential output (or full employment output). This was the Obama administration's fiscal policy approach to the 2008 financial crisis. Increased government spending is the most direct and effective of the three approaches.

Expansionary Fiscal Policy

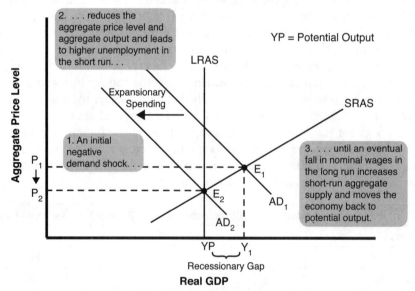

Expansionary fiscal policy attempts to shift aggregate demand rightward to close the recessionary gap between real GDP and potential output.

To address inflationary gaps, policy makers employ **contractionary fiscal policy**. The goal of this fiscal policy is to decrease aggregate demand to close the gap between actual GDP and potential GDP. Contractionary policies include these three approaches:

- decrease government spending on goods and services
- decrease government transfers to households
- increase taxes

The idea with contractionary fiscal policy is that if the government and consumers and businesses spend less, there will be less aggregate demand, which will eventually decrease aggregate output and gets the economy closer to potential output. Reducing government spending is the most direct and effective of the three approaches. During the Vietnam War in the 1960s, President Lyndon Johnson passed a temporary 10 percent tax increase to try to deal with rising inflation. Contractionary responses such as raising taxes are rarely used in the United States as there are other policies, such as actions by the Federal Reserve, that can be used to greater effect. Tax increases are also deeply unpopular with voters, making them equally as unpopular as they are with legislators.

Contractionary Fiscal Policy

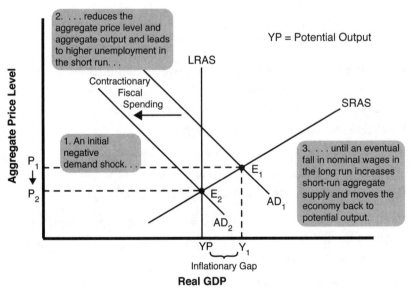

Contractionary fiscal policy attempts to shift aggregate demand leftward to close the inflationary gap between real GDP and potential output.

1. In one to three paragraphs, explain how government fiscal policies involving spending and taxation affect demand, GDP, and employment.

KEY TERMS

fiscal policy

discretionary policies

mandatory spending

transfers

social insurance (entitlements)

multiplier effect

expansionary fiscal policy

contractionary fiscal policy

MULTIPLE-CHOICE QUESTIONS

1. When governments increase spending on goods and services, which indicator is the spending intended to directly affect?

   (A) Nominal wages

   (B) Short-run aggregate supply

   (C) Aggregate demand

   (D) Output potential

   (E) Aggregate price levels

2. Which type of fiscal policy might the government institute to respond to an inflationary gap in the economy?

   (A) Hike import taxes on all foreign goods

   (B) Raise the national minimum wage

   (C) Increase federal spending on goods and services

   (D) Increase personal and corporate taxes

   (E) Freeze all mandatory and discretionary spending

3. To eliminate a recessionary gap, the government is most likely to do which of the following?

   (A) Increase interest rates

   (B) Decrease government spending

   (C) Decrease taxes

   (D) Increase taxes

   (E) Decrease transfer payments

1. Assume the graph below shows the economy of Freedonia. Answer all parts of the questions that follow.

SRAS and Fiscal Policy

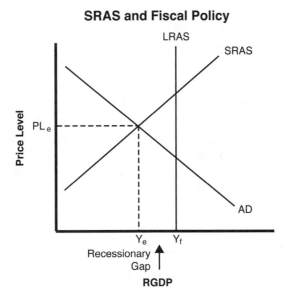

(a) Which kind of GDP gap is Freedonia experiencing? Explain.

(b) Which kind of fiscal policy—expansionary or contractionary— would shift the economy to potential output (Y_f)? What are some policies they could employ to close this gap?

(c) Assume the marginal propensity to consume is 0.8, the equilibrium level of GDP is $200 billion and potential GDP is $260 billion. Calculate the change in government spending necessary to bring about full employment.

(d) Explain what should happen to employment numbers when the gap is closed and why.

(e) Draw a graph that represents the shifts in aggregate demand (AD), short-run aggregate supply (SRAS), and price levels when the government's fiscal policy to close the gap is implemented. Label the AD and SRAS curves appropriately and indicate the direction of the shifts with arrows.

Government economists use economic models to analyze situations and explain what actions policy makers should take. To do so, they take these steps:

- Identify the specific economic conditions and describe the likely short-term future conditions.

- Use an economic model to recommend policy actions and explain the impacts these policies will have on economic conditions.

For example, in an inflationary period, government economists will identify whether demand-pull or cost-push inflation is taking place. They will predict whether the inflation rate will continue to rise absent any changes in the economy and how long that rise will take place. Suppose they identify the cause as increased energy costs. They may recommend that the government release some of the strategic oil reserve to increase the supply of oil and put a price cap on oil. These actions would be intended to bring energy prices down.

Apply the Skill

The graph below shows the impact on the Aggregate Demand-Aggregate Supply model resulting from a drop in aggregate demand.

AD-AS Disequilibrium

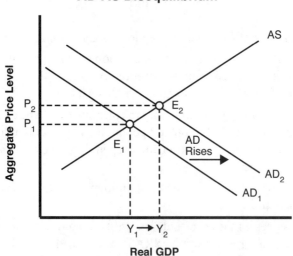

You are a government economist. Recommend the correct fiscal policy for the government to use, choosing among these three options:

- Increase or reduce government purchasing of goods and services.
- Increase or decrease government transfers to households.
- Cut or increase taxes.

Explain what policy—or policies—you recommend and what effect you think they will have on the economy.

The Great Recession began in December 2007 and ended, officially, in June 2009. This recession was responsible for an estimated $4 trillion contraction in U.S. GDP. Though the recession is largely thought to have started in the United States, many other countries around the world felt its effects, and some entered their own recessionary periods.

Keynesian Response to the Great Recession Keynesian economics dictates that governments, during a recession, should use fiscal policy actions such as tax breaks and increased government spending to increase aggregate demand and encourage economic growth.

This was the strategy employed by the Bush and Obama administrations. According to Miguel Faria-e-Castro, an economist at the Federal Reserve, Congress authorized increases to discretionary spending from 2007 to 2009 of $1.2 trillion per year. Faria-e-Castro stated, "New programs ranged from financial assistance for large banks and car manufacturers to tax rebates for low-income households and also included funding for public projects, such as highway construction." The purpose of these fiscal policies was to increase confidence in markets again and get people and businesses spending again.

Expansionary Austerity and the Great Recession On the other hand, some governments, particularly in Europe, decided to implement another type of fiscal policy known as expansionary austerity. Proponents of this policy believe that by cutting government spending and reducing deficits, governments provide the means for economies in recession to return to economic growth.

Economists such as Harvard's Alberto Alesina believe that spending cuts, for example, were often "associated with economic expansions rather than recessions." The reasoning is that spending cuts created confidence among consumers and businesses alike and that the positive effect on private consumption and investment outweigh the negative effect of reduced government spending.

Which Approach Is Better or More Effective? According to economist Paul Krugman, the "doctrine of expansionary austerity . . . brutally failed the reality test; instead, the evidence pointed overwhelmingly to the continued existence of something very like the old-fashioned Keynesian multiplier."

However, Tim Worstall, a fellow at the Adam Smith Institute in London, points to parallels in the historical evidence of Britain's use of expansionary austerity during the Great Depression and the Great Recession. Worstall, referring to the Great Depression, stated, "Britain's experience in the 1930s was very, very different from the American one. Yes, there was the same sort of financial crash, then the collapse in world trade, then the European banking systems fell over and so on. So, much the same as conditions in 2008 and 2009 then. But Britain's recovery was entirely unlike that of the U.S. Britain came off the gold standard in 1931 and two years later output (GDP) was above pre-crisis levels. And the government had been cutting spending the whole while."

Automatic Stabilizers

"Power has only one duty—to secure the social welfare of the People."
Benjamin Disraeli, British prime minister and author (1804–1881)

Essential Question: How do automatic stabilizers moderate business cycles and impact aggregate demand and GDP?

Economists disagree on how actively the government should respond to economic changes in general or to a specific economic change. However, creating mechanisms that respond without special government action can help even out the ups and downs in an economy. Since these variations occur consistently, individuals and businesses can plan for them.

What Are Automatic Stabilizers?

Automatic stabilizers are fiscal policies that help moderate fluctuations in an economy and occur without special government action. They are set up by legislation and can be adjusted the same way, but once in place, they happen on their own. When the economy starts to decline, they help stimulate the economy by putting more money in the hands of consumers. When the economy starts to overheat, they can help slow it down. The U.S. government uses several automatic stabilizers, including these:

- a progressive income tax structure
- unemployment insurance
- the Supplemental Nutrition Assistance Program
- Medicaid

Progressive Income Tax Structure Adjusting **income tax** rates is one of the primary automatic stabilizers used to moderate swings in the economy. The multiplier effect (see Topic 3.2) is not as productive with tax cuts as it is with federal stimulus spending. But tax cuts do help, which is why they are used as stabilizers. A **progressive taxation** system is one in which as income increases so does the percentage of tax paid. For example, people might pay no tax on the first $20,000 they earn, 10 percent tax on the next $80,000 they earn, and 20 percent on any money they earn beyond that. In the United States, the federal income tax is progressive. In contrast, some states have a flat-rate income tax in which everyone pays the same rate regardless of total income. Some taxes are regressive, ones in which people with lower incomes pay a higher percentage of their income in taxes than do people with higher incomes. Sales taxes are generally regressive because lower income people spend a higher percentage of their income than do wealthier individuals.

Automatic Stabilizers Response During Overheating Economy

■ Social benefits and taxes can act as automatic stabilizers

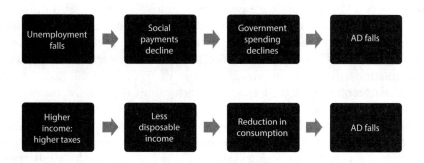

The kind of automatic stabilizer that kicks in depends on the shift that is occurring in the economy. You can see how both types of fiscal policies ultimately impact aggregate demand (AD).

During a recession—a negative demand shock—taxation as a stabilizer automatically reduces the percentage of taxes from personal income as the personal income falls. By leaving more money in people's pockets as disposable income, people will be able to buy more goods and thus support a healthy aggregate demand and real GDP. (This also applies to business and corporate taxes.)

Recessions are the most common economic condition for which taxation automatic stabilizers are important. They promote recovery. However, during very severe downturns, the government often reinforces the changes promoted by the stabilizers with additional actions. For example, when the Great Recession began during the winter of 2007–2008, automatic stabilizers began to counter it immediately. Then, the Federal Reserve quickly began to increase the supply of money in the economy. In February 2009, Congress passed and the president signed the American Recovery Act, which further countered the recession by boosting aggregate demand. The combination of automatic stabilizers and actions by the government reversed the economic decline by the end of 2009, starting a period of sustained growth that continued until 2020.

Unemployment Insurance Unemployment is one of the key indicators of an economy's health, so it stands to reason that a program like **unemployment insurance** is used as an automatic stabilizer. Unemployment insurance gives newly unemployed workers some money—about half their salary—to get by until they can find a new job. The Federal Unemployment Tax Act (FUTA) was passed in 1939 while the country was still trying to recover from the Great

Depression. FUTA is a federal program that works with the states to provide people monetary benefits when they lose their jobs through no fault of their own. All states have to meet the FUTA federal guidelines for this program, so there are some differences depending on where one lives, but the purpose of the program is the same everywhere.

Employers pay a certain amount quarterly to their state's unemployment insurance fund. The amount paid into the unemployment insurance fund is based on a percentage of employee salaries, but the maximum an employer must pay is $420 per employee per year. Employees who are laid off or lose their jobs must file an application with their state's unemployment bureau. Unemployed workers are then paid weekly for up to 26 weeks. Unemployment insurance can be extended for additional weeks under certain circumstances and situations. For example, in 2009, part of the American Recovery Act extended unemployment insurance benefits for some recipients up to 99 weeks.

In a recessionary period when unemployment rises and workers have less (or no) disposable income, an automatic stabilizer like unemployment insurance reduces the impact of rising unemployment on a troubled economy. Unemployed workers making half of their usual salary still need to pay their bills and can still make purchases, which helps buoy aggregate demand and real GDP.

Supplemental Nutrition Assistance Program Commonly known as the "food stamp" program, the **Supplemental Nutrition Assistance Program** (SNAP) gives vouchers (transfers) to low-income households below the FPL to buy food. These transfers are usually made electronically to a state or federal welfare benefits card monthly or weekly (depending on the state).

The calculation to determine how much SNAP money a person or family receives each month is rather complicated. According to recent U.S. Department of Agriculture data, an individual can receive approximately $150–$190 per month from SNAP (that's $5–$6.33 a day); a family of four can receive $465–$650 monthly (that's $15.50–$21.66 daily for four people). As of 2019, approximately one in every eight Americans used the SNAP program. The majority of SNAP benefits go to elderly people, disabled individuals, and families with children.

There are limits on the kinds of food recipients can spend SNAP money on. Healthy foods (fruits, vegetables, meat and fish, dairy, breads and cereals) are allowed, as are some limited types of snack foods and soda. SNAP accounts cannot be used to buy alcohol, tobacco, prescription drugs, fast food, and a variety of household items.

Medicaid The public health insurance program **Medicaid** funds health care for individuals or families with low or no income. Signed into law in 1965 by President Lyndon Johnson, it is a jointly funded program between states and the federal government. Because it is administered by the states, Medicaid coverage can differ quite a bit depending on which state you live in. In 2017, just under one in every four Americans received coverage through Medicaid, and the program cost $593 billion.

For some citizens, if they did not have Medicaid, they would have no medical insurance at all. Along with the popular Medicare program (which is different, primarily providing health care for those aged 65 and older), it is another jointly administered program.

Two in every five recipients of Medicaid are children—the largest subgroup of American beneficiaries of this program. Medicaid also covers people with disabilities. Eligibility for Medicaid is determined using the Federal Poverty Line. The Affordable Care Act, sometimes referred to as Obamacare, was passed in 2010, and it expanded the coverage and eligibility for Medicaid for states that chose to adopt the new provision. Thirty-six states adopted the new ACA Medicaid program, which by 2017 had reduced the percentage of uninsured in the United States from 16 percent to 9 percent.

Projected and Actual Medicaid Spending

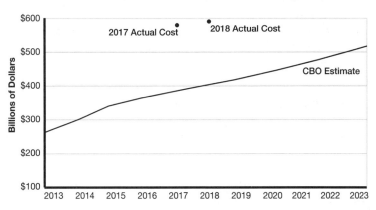

The Congressional Budget Office (CBO) annually makes 10-year projections on Medicaid spending in outlying years based on current budget planning. This is the CBO's projection for Medicaid spending from 2013 through 2023. You can see that the projections for 2017 and 2018 were off by about $200 billion each year. Some of this difference can be attributed to the aging U.S. population. Since approximately 2005, the Baby Boomer generation has been moving beyond 60 years old, when medical needs and the cost of health care increase for most people.

Like unemployment insurance and the SNAP program, Medicaid is an automatic stabilizer. These transfer payment programs tend to go up in use and cost when the economy is contracting (such as during a recession), and the use and cost fall when the economy is expanding. Combined, they help to moderate fluctuations in an economy—especially negative fluctuations—and attempt to maintain aggregate demand and real GDP.

Government Transfers Automatic stabilizers such as food stamps and Medicaid serve the same purpose as tax cuts and unemployment insurance— to cushion the impact of a negative (or positive) shock to the economy. Recall that **government transfers** are payments to individuals with no goods or services provided in return. Most social service programs—sometimes called welfare programs—are joint efforts by states and the federal government. They are paid for by taxes at the state and federal levels. Anyone receiving welfare benefits must have income below the **Federal Poverty Line**. The FPL differs for individuals and families. In 2019, the FPL was

- $12,490 for an individual
- $16,910 for a two-person household
- $25,750 for a family of four

For perspective on the federal poverty level, consider this: an individual with a full-time job working 40 hours a week at $10 per hour—about $3 more per hour than the federal minimum wage in 2020—would make $20,000 for an entire year. A family of four with one full-time employed worker who made $15 per hour—that's double the federal minimum wage—would make $30,000 a year. Neither of these examples would have been eligible for welfare benefits according to the Federal Poverty Line. As of 2018, 50 percent of American workers made less than $30,000 a year.

But in a recessionary period, both the examples above would likely be at risk of falling below the FPL, at which point they would be eligible to receive social service program benefits.

ANSWER THE TOPIC ESSENTIAL QUESTION

1. In one to three paragraphs, explain how automatic stabilizers moderate business cycles and impact aggregate demand and GDP.

KEY TERMS

automatic stabilizers
income tax
progressive taxation
unemployment insurance

Supplemental Nutrition Assistance Program (SNAP)
Medicaid
government transfers
federal poverty line

---

1. What is the primary purpose of automatic stabilizers as fiscal policy?

(A) To replace direct cash payments with vouchers

(B) To moderate fluctuations in the economy

(C) To increase the unemployment rate

(D) To raise income taxes on those with the most income

(E) To keep aggregate prices stable

2. Why are government transfers more effective than tax cuts as automatic stabilizers?

(A) Tax cuts only happen when annual taxes are filed.

(B) Transfers have a greater multiplier effect.

(C) Tax cuts are not tied to the federal poverty level.

(D) Transfers cost less than tax cuts.

(E) Transfers do not adhere to the federal poverty level.

3. Who most directly funds the unemployment insurance system?

(A) All employees

(B) The federal government

(C) All employers

(D) Individual states

(E) Employers who wrongfully fire workers

FREE-RESPONSE QUESTIONS

1. Answer all parts of the questions that follow.

SRAS and Fiscal Policy

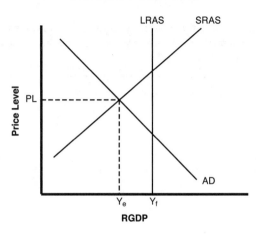

(a) The graph depicts the beginning of a recession. Explain what will happen to the aggregate supply curve as the recession worsens.

(b) Identify one automatic stabilizer that would work to correct the recession and explain how it would ease the recession.

(c) What effect would the automatic stabilizer you identified in part (b) have on the above graph?

(d) Draw a graph that represents an inflationary economy and describe how automatic stabilizers should mitigate the changes in aggregate demand (AD) and price levels. Label the AD curve appropriately and indicate whether the price level increases, decreases, or remains the same.

(e) Identify one automatic stabilizer that would work to correct the inflationary economy you drew on the graph in part (d).

THINK AS AN ECONOMIST: *DESCRIBE ECONOMIC PRINCIPLES*

Certain economic principles underlie economic policy. Being able to accurately explain these principles is an essential part of understanding economic thought. To describe an economic principle, answer these questions about it:

- What does the principle mean?
- When and how is it applied to economic behavior?

For example, economists apply the principle that economic decision makers—whether individuals or firms—make decisions on the margin. That is, economic actors decide whether to continue to consume or produce one additional unit based on whether the additional benefit gained from doing so is more than the additional cost of that increase. For example, a consumer stops purchasing slices of pizza when the discomfort from eating another slice outweighs the cost of purchasing it.

Apply the Skill

Another economic principle is the creation of automatic stabilizers to impact aggregate demand. Explain how automatic stabilizers work and why they have a beneficial impact on aggregate demand.

UNIT 3

Long Free-Response Question

1. Assume that Curuguay, a country that makes capital goods and consumer goods, is operating at below full employment.

    (a) Using a correctly labeled graph of aggregate demand, aggregate supply, and long-run aggregate supply, show each of the following:

        (i) Long run aggregate supply labeled Y_f.

        (ii) The current output and price level labeled as Y_1 and PL_1 respectively.

    (b) Assume the recessionary gap in Curuguay is $120 billion and the marginal propensity to consume is 0.75.

        (i) Calculate the minimum increase in government spending necessary to bring about full employment.

        (ii) If the government decided to decrease personal taxes instead, would the change required to bring about full employment be greater than or smaller than the increase in spending you calculated in question (b) (i)?

        (iii) Explain your answer to question (b) (ii).

    (c) If it is assumed that the government takes no discretionary policy action to correct the gap,

        (i) Will short-run aggregate supply increase, decrease, or stay the same?

        (ii) Explain your answer to question (c) (i).

        (iii) Illustrate the change you identified here in question (c) on the graph you created in question (a). Label the new equilibrium price PL_2.

    (d) Draw a correctly labeled production possibilities curve based on the change you identified in question (c). Label the Y axis *capital goods* and the X axis *consumer goods*. Label the original point of the economy point A and the point that represents the change in fiscal policy point B.

    (e) The government of Curuguay creates a law that enables immigrants to receive their citizenship much more easily. Will the long-run aggregate supply curve increase, decrease, or remain the same?

UNIT 4

Financial Sector

The financial sector is made up of thousands of institutions that move the economy's scarce resources from savers to borrowers. The sector is made up of entities such as banks, credit unions, investment companies, credit card companies, consumer-finance companies, and insurance companies. Financial assets include not only money but also bank deposits, stocks, bonds, and mutual funds that can be easily converted to cash.

People, businesses, and institutions save and borrow money for many reasons. The money that savers deposit in banks expands as those institutions lend it to borrowers, who in turn, deposit it. Banks then lend those deposits, which borrowers also deposit. This process goes on many times, essentially expanding the amount of money in the nation's monetary system.

Central banks like the U.S. Federal Reserve use monetary policy to achieve macroeconomic goals, such as controlling inflation. They have several tools to accomplish these ends, including increasing or decreasing the money supply and setting interest rates that will affect the rates banks pay savers and the rates they charge borrowers.

In this unit, you will learn about financial assets, interest rates, how the financial sector works, and how monetary policy affects the economy.

Topic Titles and Essential Knowledge

Topic 4.1 Financial Assets

- The most liquid forms of money are cash and demand deposits.
- Other financial assets people can hold in place of the most liquid forms of money include bonds (interest-bearing assets) and stocks (equity).

- The price of previously issued bonds and interest rates on bonds are inversely related.
- The opportunity cost of holding money is the interest that could have been earned from holding other financial assets such as bonds.

Topic 4.2 Nominal vs. Real Interest Rates
- A nominal interest rate is the rate of interest paid for a loan, unadjusted for inflation.
- Lenders and borrowers establish nominal interest rates as the sum of their expected real interest rate and expected inflation.
- A real interest rate can be calculated in hindsight by subtracting the actual inflation rate from the nominal interest rate.

Topic 4.3 Definition, Measurement, and Functions of Money
- Money is any asset that is accepted as a means of payment.
- Money serves as a medium of exchange, unit of account, and store of value.
- The money supply is measured using monetary aggregates designated as M1 and M2.
- The monetary base (often labeled as M0 or MB) includes currency in circulation and bank reserves.

Topic 4.4 Banking and the Expansion of the Money Supply
- Depository institutions (such as commercial banks) organize their assets and liabilities on balance sheets.
- Depository institutions operate using fractional reserve banking.
- Banks' reserves are divided into required reserves and excess reserves.
- Excess reserves are the basis of expansion of the money supply by the banking system.
- The money multiplier is the ratio of the money supply to the monetary base.
- The size of expansion of the money supply depends on the money multiplier.
- The maximum value of the money multiplier can be calculated as the reciprocal of the required reserve ratio.
- The amount predicted by the simple money multiplier may be overstated because it does not take into account a bank's desire to hold excess reserves or the public holding more currency.

Topic 4.5 The Money Market
- The demand for money shows the inverse relationship between the nominal interest rate and the quantity of money people want to hold.
- Given a monetary base determined by a country's central bank, money supply is independent of the nominal interest rate.
- In the money market, equilibrium is achieved when the nominal interest rate is such that the quantities demanded and supplied of money are equal.
- Disequilibrium nominal interest rates create surpluses and shortages in the money market. Market forces drive nominal interest rates toward equilibrium.
- Factors that shift the demand for money, such as changes in the price level, and supply of money, such as monetary policy, change the equilibrium nominal interest rate.

Topic 4.6 Monetary Policy

- Central banks implement monetary policies to achieve macroeconomic goals, such as price stability.
- The tools of monetary policy include open-market operations, the required reserve ratio, and the discount rate. The most frequently used monetary policy tool is open-market operations.
- When the central bank conducts an open-market purchase (sale), reserves increase (decrease), thereby increasing (decreasing) the monetary base.
- The effect of an open-market purchase (sale) on the money supply is greater than the effect on the monetary base because of the money multiplier.
- Many central banks carry out policy to hit a target range for an overnight interbank lending rate. (In the United States, this is the federal funds rate.)
- Central banks can influence the nominal interest rate in the short run by changing the money supply, which in turn will affect investment and consumption.
- Expansionary or contractionary monetary policies are used to restore full employment when the economy is in a negative (i.e., recessionary) or positive (i.e., inflationary) output gap.
- Monetary policy can influence aggregate demand, real output, the price level, and interest rates.
- A money market model and/or the AD–AS model are used to demonstrate the short-run effects of monetary policy.
- In reality, there are lags to monetary policy caused by the time it takes to recognize a problem in the economy and the time it takes the economy to adjust to the policy action.

Topic 4.7 The Loanable Funds Market

- The loanable funds market describes the behavior of savers and borrowers.
- The demand for loanable funds shows the inverse relationship between real interest rates and the quantity demanded of loanable funds.
- The supply of loanable funds shows the positive relationship between real interest rates and the quantity supplied of loanable funds.
- In the absence of international borrowing and lending, national savings is the sum of public savings and private savings.
- For an open economy, investment equals national savings plus net capital inflow.
- In the loanable funds market, equilibrium is achieved when the real interest rate is such that the quantities demanded and supplied of loanable funds are equal.
- Disequilibrium real interest rates create surpluses and shortages in the loanable funds market. Market forces drive real interest rates toward equilibrium.
- The loanable funds market can be used to show the effects of government spending, taxes, and borrowing on interest rates.
- Factors that shift the demand (such as an investment tax credit) and supply (such as changes in saving behavior) of loanable funds change the equilibrium interest rate and the equilibrium quantity of funds.

Source: *AP® Macroeconomics Course and Exam Description.* Effective Fall 2019 (College Board).

Topic 4.1

Financial Assets

The one thing I will tell you is the worst investment you can have is cash. . . . Cash is going to become worthless over time. But good businesses are going to become worth more over time.

Warren Buffett, speaking at Columbia University, November 12, 2009

Essential Question: What are financial assets, and what is meant by "the opportunity cost of money"?

As billionaire investor Warren Buffett points out, under normal circumstances, cash *is* worth less over time. The value of a dollar has dropped significantly since 1913, when the Consumer Price Index began measuring inflation by comparing the prices of a basket of goods and services every month. By 1920, the value of a dollar was only about half what it was in 1913, largely as a result of inflation during World War I. Today's dollar buys less than 4 percent of what a 1913 dollar bought, meaning it takes $25 to buy what $1 bought in 1913. And a dollar today buys only half of what a dollar could buy in 1990. But there are ways of investing money to keep up with inflation or even build wealth.

What Are Financial Assets?

An **asset** is any resource of value that can be converted into cash. There are several ways of classifying assets—real, intangible, and financial; tangible and intangible; liquid and nonliquid.

- Real assets are physical things like real estate, land, fine art and antiques, precious metals, and commodities such as soybeans or oil.

- Intangible assets are property that is not physical, like intellectual property, which includes patents for inventions, trademarks for company logos, and copyrights for songs.

- Financial assets consist of things like currency and investments in stocks and bonds.

Financial assets get their value from a contractual claim or ownership claim. For example, currency is just paper with a value printed on it, but that value is backed by the federal government. The most common financial assets are cash and bank deposits such as checking and savings accounts. These are sometimes referred to as **demand deposits** because they can be withdrawn as desired. Most savings accounts and many checking accounts pay interest, in this case, money paid by a financial institution to depositors. Interest is usually expressed in terms of an annual percentage rate.

Banks also offer money market accounts, which pay market interest rates but limit the number of transactions that may be made during a period of time, as well as term deposits such as certificates of deposit (CDs). Term deposits usually pay a higher rate of interest than savings accounts, but an investor's money is tied up for a length of time that may range from three months to five years.

Financial assets also include certain types of investment accounts, such as stocks, bonds, and mutual funds. Stocks are equity, meaning investors who buy stocks become part owners of a company and share in its profits and losses. Investors may hold stocks indefinitely or sell them to other investors. Governments and companies issue interest-bearing assets called bonds to raise money. The holder of the bond is a lender, and the bond indicates how much has been lent, what the interest rate is, and when it will be redeemed, or bought back. Mutual funds are organizations that sell shares to the public and use the proceeds to purchase a portfolio of stocks or bonds, or both.

Liquid and NonLiquid Assets The word **liquidity** refers to the ease with which assets can be converted to cash, which can then be used for paying bills, purchasing goods or services, or any of the other things that cash is used for. The most liquid accounts are those that can be most easily converted, such as checking and savings accounts. The more liquid the asset, the lower the return on investment (ROI). Money held as cash has no ROI. Checking and savings accounts are quite liquid, so they provide their holders with a low interest rate. Therefore, they have a low ROI. Term deposits are less liquid, so they usually have higher interest rates and ROIs.

Because they are readily traded, securities are considered liquid. **Securities** are investments traded on the secondary market, also known as the stock market. They include equities, bonds, and derivatives. Equity securities are ownership shares in a corporation. They include stocks and mutual funds. Bonds, as previously discussed, are long-term loans to a corporation or government entity. Derivatives are financial contracts that derive their value from underlying assets. They are often used for commodities such as gold, oil, or gasoline.

Although they have value, real assets and most intangible assets are considered nonliquid because they cannot be quickly converted into cash.

Risk Financial **risk** is the danger of losing money. It can apply to individuals, businesses, government entities, and the financial market. Individuals face risk when they make decisions that affect their ability to earn money or pay their debts. Businesses face risks that their cash flow will not be adequate to meet their obligations. Governments face risk when they are unable to control inflation. Financial markets face risks due to changes in the market interest rate, defaults by sectors or large corporations, or other macroeconomic forces.

As you might expect, there are many forms of financial risk.

- **Credit risk** This is the danger associated with lending money. If the borrower defaults or is unable to repay the loan, investors experience decreased income from loan repayments as well as lost principal and interest.

- **Liquidity risk** This may involve securities or assets that cannot be sold or bought fast enough to cut losses. Investing in real estate involves more liquidity risk than investing in a mutual fund.

- **Speculative risk** Most financial investments, such as the purchase of stock, involve speculative risk, since share values may go down, resulting in a loss.

- **Foreign investment risk** Investments made by people in one country of assets in another country take many kinds of risks. Among these are variations in market operations, higher investment costs, and political volatility, including nationalization of industries. One of the most common risks in this category comes from changes in currency exchange rates. For example, as the value of U.S. dollars as measured in Mexican pesos changes, the value of an investment made by someone in the United States of an asset in Mexico also changes constantly.

Bank accounts are essentially risk-free. Most bank accounts—including checking, savings, money market, NOW, and CDs—are insured up to $250,000 by the Federal Deposit Insurance Corporation (FDIC).

Bonds and Interest Rates

A bond is a promise by a corporation or government to repay a specified sum of money (the face value, or principal, of the loan) at the end of a specific number of years, along with fixed annual interest. A bond's maturity date is the date at which the issuer of the bond promises to redeem it at its face value. For example, an investor who pays $500 in 2020 for a 10-year bond with a face value of $1,000 can expect to receive $1,000 in 2030.

TYPES OF BONDS		
Type	**Description**	**Level of Risk**
Treasury bonds ("Treasuries")	The U.S. government issues Treasury bonds such as savings bonds to fund government activities or to pay off debt.	Lowest: Because they are backed by the "full faith and credit" of the U.S. government, they carry almost no risk at all. The only risk is if Congress decides to not repay the money the government has borrowed.
Agency bonds	U.S. government agencies such as Fannie Mae and Freddie Mac issue bonds to provide assistance to home buyers and others.	Low: Though issued by the federal government, these bonds do not have the government's "full faith and credit" guarantee.

TYPES OF BONDS		
Type	**Description**	**Level of Risk**
Municipal bonds ("Munis")	State and municipal governments issue bonds to finance special projects or other governmental necessities. Cities may issue municipal bonds to fund new buildings to house schools or libraries, for example.	Low: State and municipal governments can tax people to repay loans, but laws often limit how much they can borrow.
Corporate bonds	Corporations issue bonds to finance expansions or other activities. These bonds are fully taxable but pay a higher rate of interest than government bonds.	Highest: Corporations sometimes lose so much money they can't repay investors fully.

Interest Rates Interest is the cost of borrowing money as well as the profit depositors receive from a bank for the use of their money. Banks make their money by lending the money that depositors entrust to them. The rate of interest they charge on **loans,** the money they lend, is significantly higher than the interest they pay depositors. The difference between what a bank pays to depositors and what it charges borrowers covers its costs of operation and provides it a profit. For example, during a time of low interest rates, a bank might pay 1 percent on savings accounts. It might charge 4 percent for a home mortgage loan and 20 percent on credit card purchases.

A bond is essentially a loan. The interest a bond's issuer pays over the term of a security is referred to as its coupon rate. The issuer makes these interest payments according to a predetermined schedule, which may be semi-annual, annual, or when the bond matures. A bond's interest rate is based on the prevailing market interest rate at the time the bond is issued. Once the bond has been issued, if the prevailing interest rate rises, the value of the bond decreases, and if it falls, the value of the bond increases. In other words, a bond's value varies inversely with interest rates.

Rate of Return The percentage **rate of return,** or yield, varies from one type of savings or investment to another. The rate of interest in a savings account depends on the bank, the type of account, and when it is opened. Securities offer the possibility of earning more money than savings accounts, but the rate of return may rise or fall along with the fortunes of the company that issued the stocks or bonds.

Investors who buy bonds at face value and hold them to maturity earn the interest rate that was set when the bond was issued. However, if they purchase previously issued bonds on the secondary market, the return they earn from interest may be higher or lower than the bond's coupon rate. This effective rate of return is called yield to maturity.

If market interest rates go up, the bond's price will fall if the investor decides to sell it. When interest rates fall, investors prefer to hold in their portfolios previously issued bonds with higher interest rates rather than purchase newly issued bonds with lower rates. As a result of increased demand, the price of previously issued bonds rises.

The Cost of Money Interest rates reflect the cost of money. When you deposit money into a savings account, the interest you receive is the payment from the bank to use your money. When you borrow money, the interest rate you pay is what you are spending to get the use of someone else's money.

Money has a **time value**, a consideration of how the value of money changes over time because of factors such as inflation and interest earned. In general, a dollar today is worth more than a dollar in the future.

The opportunity cost of holding money depends on the rate of interest that could be earned by investing it in other financial assets such as bonds. Between 2009 and 2019, the U.S. inflation rate hovered around 2 percent. The average interest rate for savings accounts was very low by historic standards, often less than 1 percent. So, money placed in a savings account lost value, but not as much as money kept under a mattress.

The best CD rates paid around 2 percent interest, meaning that money placed in a CD would more or less hold its value against inflation. U.S. Treasury bonds paid an average interest rate of 2.5 percent, while interest rates on riskier corporate bonds averaged 3.1 percent. The average stock market return was almost 9.5 percent before inflation. When inflation is considered, the actual increase in value was around 7.5 percent. However, investing in stocks was risky. By one measure, stocks decreased in value by one-third in the single year 2008.

ANSWER THE TOPIC ESSENTIAL QUESTION

1. In one to three paragraphs, discuss financial assets and the opportunity cost of money.

KEY TERMS

asset	risk
demand deposit	loans
liquidity	rate of return
securities	time value

MULTIPLE-CHOICE QUESTIONS

1. Which of the following assets would be most liquid?

   (A) Fine art

   (B) Antiques

   (C) Real estate

   (D) Commodities such as oil

   (E) Stock in a corporation

2. One example of financial assets that can be withdrawn at will are
   (A) nonliquid assets
   (B) interest rates
   (C) municipal bonds
   (D) demand deposits
   (E) corporate bonds

3. When the prevailing market interest rate drops, one effect on previously issued bonds is that
   (A) their interest rate also drops
   (B) their interest rate rises
   (C) their value also drops
   (D) their value rises
   (E) their value is unaffected

FREE-RESPONSE QUESTIONS

1. For each of the following assets, briefly describe the relation between risk and rate of return.
   (a) Savings account
   (b) Certificate of deposit
   (c) Corporate bond
   (d) Treasury bond
   (e) Stock in a corporation

To describe the similarities and differences betweeen economic concepts, economists address these questions:

- What characteristics do the concepts share?
- What characteristics differentiate the concepts?
- Why do the concepts have these differences?

An asset is any resource of value that can be converted into cash. The majority of assets for financial institutions are financial assets—typically the loans they issue to individuals and businesses. These are assets to financial institutions because they represent promises by the borrowers to repay the loan over time. Liabilities are financial debts or obligations that are settled over time. To financial institutions, demand deposits are liabilities because the institutions have an obligation to return to depositors their money when requested.

Apply the Skill

Individuals and businesses have assets and liabilities as well. Identify the similarities and differences between the assets and liabilities of a business and those of a financial institution. Explain why these two entities differ in how they view demand deposits and loans.

Topic 4.2

Nominal vs. Real Interest Rates

Money costs too much.

Ralph Waldo Emerson, *The Conduct of Life,* 1855

Essential Question: How do interest rates provide a measure of the price of money that is borrowed or saved?

It's strange to think that money has a cost. But those who provide capital to others do so in order to make a profit. Interest rates are the cost of money, and they are the avenue through which banks and other lending institutions attempt to make a profit on their transactions. The cost of money—interest rates—can be measured in different ways.

Interest and Inflation

As you learned in the previous topic, banks pay depositors interest on most accounts. They then use the money deposited to make loans, charging more interest on the loans than they pay for the use of depositors' money. The difference between the amount a bank collects and the amount it pays out enables it to generate a profit.

A loan is money lent by one party to another with the understanding that it will be repaid at a future date, along with a fee for its use. The amount of the original loan is the principal, and the additional fees added to that are the interest. Interest is typically expressed as an annual percentage rate (APR).

Interest Financial institutions such as banks and credit unions, corporations, and governments all issue loans so that they can earn interest on them. If lenders believe that a period of inflation is approaching, they can protect themselves against the loss of purchasing power of their loan by charging a higher rate of interest than they would have if there were no inflation.

Conversely, if deflation occurs—that is, if the Consumer Price Index drops—interest rates go down. Deflation occurs in times of economic crisis, such as recession or depression, and is indicated by a negative inflation rate. People start to keep hold of their money, putting off major purchases because they expect prices to continue to drop. At times, interest can become negative. In effect, the lender is paying the borrower to take a loan. In 2014, the European Central Bank, a bank supported by the governments of most countries in Europe, introduced negative interest rates as a way to stimulate borrowing and spending.

Interest rates affect the economic decisions of individuals, businesses, and governments. Most people take into account the cost of borrowing when they make major purchasing decisions, such as whether to buy a car. Similarly, business firms thinking of replacing equipment or expanding their operations compare the cost of financing those moves with the return on the same funds if they were placed in interest-bearing investments. Such decisions affect the nation's economic well-being.

Inflation The U.S. inflation rate is based on the Consumer Price Index (CPI), which measures the average change in prices of a "basket" of goods and services over a period of time. The CPI helps determine cost-of-living increases in salaries and Social Security benefits, among other things. It also helps the Federal Reserve determine whether it needs to modify economic policies, including interest rates.

As you learned in the previous topic, the trend is for prices to rise over time, which means that the buying power of a dollar drops. For example, a cup of coffee that cost $0.25 in 1970 would have cost $1.00 in 2000 and $1.59 in 2019.

The following graph shows the average U.S. inflation rates from 1960 to 2018. The period between 1965 and 1982 is known as the Great Inflation. It led economists to rethink the policies of central banks such as the Federal Reserve. Since the mid-1990s, the rate of inflation has been fairly low.

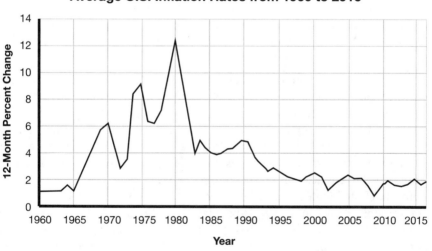

Average U.S. Inflation Rates from 1960 to 2016

Source: U.S. Bureau of Labor Statistics

How Interest Rates Are Set

Lenders and borrowers use their expected real interest rate and the expected rate of inflation to establish nominal interest rates. Three forces determine those rates in the United States:

- **The Federal Reserve System (Fed).** The Fed sets the Fed funds rate and the prime rate. The Fed funds rate is the interest rate banks charge each other to lend Federal Reserve funds overnight. The prime rate is what banks charge their best customers. It is usually above the Fed funds rate but slightly below the average variable interest rate, which fluctuates over time as market interest rates change.

- **The U.S. Treasury.** The U.S. Treasury borrows money for the U.S. government by selling fixed-income investments for various term lengths. Treasury bills mature in 4 weeks to a year. Treasury notes mature in 2 years to 10 years. Treasury bonds mature in 30 years. The Treasury also issues Treasury Inflation-Protected Securities (TIPS) for terms of 5, 10, and 30 years. These are similar to Treasury bonds, but the Treasury increases their value if inflation increases.

- **The financial industry.** Banks are usually free to set the interest rates for deposits and loans. However, banks have to take into account their competition, as well as Federal Reserve rates and other factors, such as stock market performance and expected levels of inflation.

The Federal Reserve System, known as "the Fed," was established in 1913. It acts as the central bank for the United States. The Fed is headquartered in Washington, D.C., which is where its seven-member board of governors meets. The Federal Reserve also operates 12 regional banks based in major cities across the country. The Fed has a number of important functions, including setting and implementing the country's monetary policy, regulating banks, and maintaining the stability of the U.S. financial system. It is a powerful institution, and its ability to influence interest rates as described above is an outgrowth of this power. (For more on the Fed, see Topic 4.6.)

Nominal vs. Real Interest Rates The percentage return that is advertised for bank deposits, loans, or bonds is usually referred to as the annual percentage rate, or APR. The APR is a **nominal interest rate,** one that does not take into account inflation, compounding, and other factors. Banks use the nominal interest rate when they describe their loans, as do financial advisers when they describe investments. The Fed funds rate (also called the Federal funds rate) mentioned above is also a nominal interest rate.

In the United States, the Federal Reserve System sets short-term nominal interest rates. Banks and other financial institutions base the interest they charge on those rates. The Fed may decide to keep nominal rates low to spur economic activity, since low interest rates encourage consumers and businesses to take on more debt and spend more. This was the case following the recession of 2008, when the Fed dropped its Fed funds rate to between 0 percent and 0.25 percent until December 2015.

As you have already learned, interest rates must exceed the rate of inflation, or the returns on investments will lose buying power. The **real interest rate** can be calculated in hindsight by adjusting the nominal interest rate for inflation. It gives borrowers a better idea of the actual cost of borrowing and lenders a better idea of the actual yield on the loans they make. In other words, it shows the true interest rate of loans and bonds.

To determine the real interest rate, subtract the rate of inflation from the nominal interest rate:

Real interest rate = Nominal interest rate – Rate of inflation

Thus, if the nominal interest rate on a loan is 5 percent and the rate of inflation is 2 percent, the real interest rate is 3 percent. Normally, because of inflation, the nominal interest rate will be higher than the real interest rate. However, if the inflation rate is 0, the nominal interest rate is also the real interest rate.

In the case of deflation, the real interest rate is actually higher than the nominal rate. For example, the U.S. economy entered a period of deflation between March and October 2009, reaching a low of –2.1 percent in July, and the Fed funds interest rate was 0.16 percent, which would result in a real interest rate of 2.26 percent:

$$2.26\% = 0.16\% - (-2.1\%) = 0.16\% + 2.1\%$$

Real interest rates are considered predictive when the actual inflation rate is unknown, which is the case when a loan is actually being taken out or a bond is being purchased. In other words, interest rates are based on the best estimate of what the rate of inflation will be during the period of the loan or bond. Lenders and investors can estimate their real rate of return by comparing the yields of Treasury bonds and TIPS that have the same maturity, subtracting the rate of return of the bond from that of the TIPS, which estimates the rate of inflation. Because they are interested in making money, lenders and investors tend to be more interested in real interest rates than nominal interest rates. The World Bank has a web page that publishes the real interest rates for most countries.

Real Interest Rates for the United States, 1960–2020

Source: World Bank

ANSWER THE TOPIC ESSENTIAL QUESTION

1. In one to three paragraphs, explain how interest rates provide a measure of the price of money that is borrowed or saved.

KEY TERMS

nominal interest rate   real interest rate

MULTIPLE-CHOICE QUESTIONS

1. How do banks make most of their money?
   (A) By charging depositors interest on their savings accounts
   (B) By selling stocks and bonds
   (C) By investing in U.S. Treasury notes
   (D) By charging interest on loans they issue
   (E) By lending money to other banks overnight

2. Who sets short-term nominal interest rates in the United States?
   (A) The president
   (B) The World Bank
   (C) The Federal Reserve
   (D) The banking industry
   (E) The Consumer Price Index

3. If the nominal interest rate is 7 percent and the rate of inflation is 4 percent, what is the real interest rate?
   (A) −28 percent
   (B) −11 percent
   (C) −3 percent
   (D)   3 percent
   (E) 11 percent

1. Use the following scenario to answer all parts of the free-response questions below.

   Bank A is offering fixed-rate loans at a 5 percent nominal interest rate. The actual inflation rate is 4 percent.

   (a) Calculate the real interest rate.

   (b) Assuming there is no inflation, explain the relationship between the nominal and real interest rates.

   (c) Assume that Jacob takes out a loan from Bank A. Who gains from this transaction: the bank, Jacob, or neither? Explain.

   (d) What is the difference between the Fed funds rate and the prime rate?

   (e) Assume the inflation rate increased to 5 percent. Who gains from this increase? Explain.

THINK AS AN ECONOMIST: *DESCRIBE ECONOMIC PRINCIPLES*

Economists use economic principles to explain economic decision-making or to analyze economic performance. Being able to accurately explain these principles demonstrates an understanding of economics. To describe an economic principle, answer these questions about it:

- What does the principle mean?
- Why is it a useful economic idea?

One principle is the utility of using baseline standards to analyze economic measures in order to better understand economic conditions. For example, while GDP measures the total value in money of all the goods produced in a year by a country, that measure has limitations when comparing one country's output to another's because it does not control for the size of the countries. Per capita GDP allows such comparison, as it divides GDP by population. It effectively states output per person, which controls for size and thus more-effectively measures each country's productivity.

Apply the Skill

This lesson discussed the difference between nominal and real interest rates. What economic principle is demonstrated by this difference between these two concepts? Why is this principle useful? Give an example of how financial institutions would apply this principle.

Definition, Measurement, and Functions of Money

Our entire monetary system is based on trust. . . . Rather like the fairy Tinkerbell in Peter Pan, who is kept alive because the audience claps to affirm its belief in her existence, it is our faith that keeps the system going.

Philip Coggan, "Trust (not Money) Makes the World Go Round,"
OECD Forum, 2014

Essential Question: What are the functions and measures of money?

When people think of money, they usually think of cash, whether they actually handle it or not. Everything people buy has a price expressed in dollars and cents, the legal tender in the United States. However, employers often pay by direct deposit into employees' banks or credit unions, and many businesses no longer accept checks. Some don't even accept cash, and there are those who think that it's time to do away with cash altogether. Today's consumers seem to prefer the ease of paying with credit or debit cards or their smartphones. The possibility of a future cashless economy seems much more plausible than it ever did.

What Is Money?

Money is anything that most people are willing to accept in payment for goods and services. The word *salary* comes from *sal*, the Latin word for salt, because Roman soldiers were often paid their wages in salt rather than money. In Mexico, the Aztecs used cacao beans as money. In colonial North America, ferry operators accepted fur pelts as payment for taking people and goods across rivers.

A Brief History of Money Because it was durable and easy to carry, metallic money became popular thousands of years ago. The Egyptians began to use one of the earliest forms of metallic money, in the form of rings, around 2500 BCE. About 400 years later, the Chinese began using gold cubes as money. The Lydians, a people who lived in what is now Turkey, minted the first metal coins around 600 BCE. From there coins spread to Greece, Rome, the Byzantine Empire, and the rest of Europe.

The Chinese invented paper money in the 7th century CE. The Italian traveler Marco Polo reported use of it in the late 1200s. During the late Middle

Ages, European merchants and travelers exchanged their gold coins for goldsmiths' receipts to protect themselves from highway robbers. The receipts could be exchanged for coins by goldsmiths in other cities. In time, such receipts came to be used as money without being changed to coins. The first European banknotes were issued in 1661, and by the 1690s, the Massachusetts Bay Company began printing paper money in what is now the United States.

The Functions of Money Money serves a number of purposes. It provides a medium of exchange, a unit of account, and a store of value.

- A **medium of exchange** is something that buyers give to sellers when they purchase goods and services. When you buy a pair of jeans, for example, you give the store money, and the store gives you the jeans.

- A **unit of account** provides a convenient standard for expressing the values of different items. For example, $60 might buy one video game or 10 sub sandwiches, but no one would say the price of a video game is 10 subs, or the price of a sub is one-tenth of a video game.

- Because people can save it for future use, money is considered a **store of value.** The restaurant owner who accepts money today for a sub sandwich can hold the money and buy another good or service at a future time.

The Kinds of Money The most obvious kind of money is cash, or currency. **Currency** is the money used in a particular country as a medium of exchange for goods and services, especially paper money but also including coins. In the United States, currency is issued by the federal government. All U.S. currency is legal tender, meaning that it must be accepted in payment for debts. The unit of currency used in the United States is the dollar, while most European nations use the euro, and Japan uses the yen. A **monetary unit** is the basic form of currency in a country and may be issued in various denominations that are multiples (such as $1, $5, $10, $20, etc.) or fractions (1¢, 5¢, 10¢, 25¢, etc.) of the basic unit.

Whatever commodity or definitions a society uses for its money is its monetary standard. Money that gets its value from the substance it is made of is called **commodity money.** As you read earlier, salt and cacao beans were historical forms of commodity money. Coins were minted from metals that were worth the value displayed on the coin.

In contrast, **representative money** has little or no value in itself. Rather, its value comes from the commodity it represents, such as a precious metal. By the mid-1800s, in order to facilitate international trade, many countries used paper currency. Most countries adopted the **gold standard,** which guaranteed that governments would redeem paper money for gold. At times, the United States allowed people to trade in their paper money for either gold or silver. However, the gold standard had many problems. One of these was a lack of flexibility, which led to economic instability. As a country's population and economy grew, it needed more currency in circulation. Expanding the quantity of currency was difficult when money was tied to gold. During World War I, countries began moving off the gold standard so they could print more money to help pay military expenses. Today, no country uses the gold standard.

Source: Public domain, U.S. Treasury

The U.S. Treasury issued gold certificates like this one that could be exchanged for gold coins.

Today, most of the currency in circulation is neither commodity nor representative money. It is **fiat money,** which means that its value is based on the confidence people have in the government that issues it. In the United States, paper money is issued by the Federal Reserve System and backed by the U.S. government.

However, paper currency and coins represent only about one-tenth of the total money in circulation. Most transactions are paid for using financial instruments like credit and debit cards or checks.

In recent years, people have developed money that exists only in digital form. These cryptocurrencies, like any other forms of money, have value only to the extent they are accepted by people. One challenge for cryptocurrencies to gain acceptance is to develop trust. Like any online transactions, cryptocurrencies are subject to hacking and theft.

Measuring the Money Supply

The **money supply** is the total amount of money—cash, coins, and balances in bank accounts—in circulation. Economists closely monitor the money supply and its rate of flow—that is, the number of times it changes hands. However, determining the rate of flow is difficult. It is more challenging because economists use several definitions when discussing the money supply.

The money supply includes assets that households and businesses can use to make payments or to hold as short-term investments. Because some forms of money can be used immediately to make purchases while others might take a few days to convert to cash, there are several ways of measuring the money supply, based on the size of accounts and the liquidity each type of money has in the economy. Three of the many ways to measure the money supply are particularly important:

- **M0:** More commonly known as the **monetary base** (and sometimes referred to as MB), this is a measure of all the currency in circulation and deposits kept by banks and other depository institutions in their accounts at the Federal Reserve. (Depository institutions are institutions that get their funds through deposits by the public. They include savings banks, credit unions, and savings and loan associations as well as commercial banks.)

- **M1:** This is a measure of currency held by the public or in fully liquid demand deposits, such as checking accounts, at depository institutions. It does not include currency at the U.S. Treasury, Federal Reserve Banks, and in vaults of depository institutions. When economists and others discuss the money supply, they are usually referring to M1.

- **M2:** This measure includes M1 plus savings accounts (which are not normally used to make purchases or pay bills), money market deposit accounts, certificates of deposit (CDs) in amounts of less than $100,000, and certain other bank reserves that are less easily converted to cash than those included in M1.

M0 and M1 are sometimes referred to as "narrow money," meaning physical money—coins and paper currency—that is readily available for commercial transactions. Funds in the monetary base are held in both M1 and M2, which are the two monetary aggregates most commonly used to measure the money supply.

Estimates of the money supply provide important information that helps the government set economic policies. In recent decades, however, economists have reconsidered long-held views about the relationships among money supply, inflation, and gross domestic product growth. For example, economists believed that a rapid expansion of the money supply would cause inflation. Then, to help end the Great Recession of 2008, the Federal Reserve doubled the money supply and yet inflation remained very low. Events such as this led economists to reevaluate their ideas about how the economy operates. Topic 4.6 will examine monetary policy in more detail.

ANSWER THE TOPIC ESSENTIAL QUESTION

1. In one to three paragraphs, explain the functions of money and how economists measure it.

MULTIPLE-CHOICE QUESTIONS

1. Which of the following is an example of money as a unit of account?

    (A) A monthly credit card statement

    (B) A money market account

    (C) A checking account

    (D) Pricing of items in a grocery store

    (E) Direct deposit

2. Which of the following best describes fiat money?

    (A) Money that is backed by a commodity such as gold

    (B) Money that is backed by the government that issued it

    (C) U.S. dollars held in foreign financial institutions

    (D) Money that is held in demand deposits

    (E) Money that is not included in the M1 or M2 money supplies

3. Money held by the public that includes demand deposits and currency is measured as

    (A) M1

    (B) M2

    (C) M0

    (D) Fiat money

    (E) Commodity money

---

1. Use the following scenario to answer all parts of the following questions:

   Diego opens a new checking account in Bank A with $5,000.

   (a) If Diego uses the debit card that accompanies this account, what function of money does his transaction serve?

   (b) Diego decides to deposit as much as he can into this account after his initial deposit to purchase a car. What function is his money serving? Explain.

   (c) Diego sees an advertisement for the car he wants for $8,000. In this scenario, money is serving which purpose? Explain.

   (d) Diego writes a check against his account for the car. Which measurement of money will he be using for this purchase?

   (e) After the purchase of his car, Diego has $2,000 left over, $1,000 of which he decides to put into a certificate of deposit. What measurement of money is his $1,000 CD a part of?

THINK AS AN ECONOMIST: *IDENTIFY AN ECONOMIC CONCEPT ILLUSTRATED BY AN EXAMPLE*

Economists analyze the behaviors of economic actors. They must have the ability to identify the economic concepts or principles illustrated by particular actions. By doing so, they have a conceptual framework for understanding the action.

For example, economists observe financial institutions raising interest rates in the face of rising inflation. They recognize this as lenders attempting to maximize their real interest rates. The action demonstrates the firms' acting on their incentive to make profits.

Apply the Skill

Read the description of a series of transactions below. Identify the component of the money supply that is illustrated by each transaction.

First State Bank grants a loan to Acme Enterprises to fund a new construction project. The bank electronically transfers $100,000 to Acme. Acme's treasurer writes a check to All-Pro Construction to cover the first month of construction work on the project. After two weeks of construction work, All-Pro issues payroll checks to its five workers. Harry, who is one of those workers, has 10 percent of his wages automatically deposited in a money market account. Acme makes its first monthly payment on its loan to First State Bank. The bank places 10 percent of that money in its reserve account with the regional Federal Reserve Bank.

Modern Money It is estimated that $1.5 trillion of U.S. physical currency is in circulation worldwide. In 2018, the U.S. economy alone was measured at almost $21 trillion. Clearly, physical currency alone cannot account for the volume of the U.S. economy. Therefore, a virtual currency is widely used and accepted as money. This virtual currency is not only commonly used but is also accepted as an official medium of exchange by the U.S. government.

Cryptocurrency However, virtual dollars were not the only electronic money exchanged. The desire for financial anonymity was the driving reason for American cryptographer David Chaum to devise a form of electronic money he called "ecash." The concept evolved, and early forms of "cryptocurrency" were born. These early forms of cryptocurrency provided a means for parties to exchange bank notes through a set of encrypted keys. This allowed the cryptocurrency to be untraceable by banks or governments. Bitcoin, created in 2009, was the first and best-known cryptocurrency. Eventually other forms of cryptocurrency were created.

The Case for Cryptocurrency as Money According to Clem Chambers, author of the book *Trading Cryptocurrencies: A Beginner's Guide*, cryptocurrencies are, in fact, money. He says that cryptocurrencies are "an excellent means of exchange." He also says cryptocurrencies are as much a store of wealth as any other currency, despite the fact that they have been very volatile. This just makes them similar to currencies of countries that experience high rates of inflation. Lastly, Chambers argues that cryptocurrencies are widely used as a unit of account.

Chambers wrote in *Forbes* magazine, "Again it is self-evident that you can use bitcoin as a unit of account. Every one of the 500-plus crypto exchanges use crypto as a unit of account. The blockchain that is the underlying technology is by definition a 'ledger.' Crypto is by definition a token and by design encapsulated on a ledger."

Cryptocurrencies Are Not Money The argument against cryptocurrencies as money largely lies in the notion that they lack one of money's important traits: reliability. The fact that cryptocurrencies are not backed by a government or a national bank means that widespread use of cryptocurrencies has been hampered by a lack of trust.

The perception of cryptocurrencies as being volatile and unreliable stems from what economic historian Barry Eichengreen calls "high information costs." This means that fiat money has an advantage over cryptocurrency because there is a single issuer (the government) who is credible and creditworthy. Therefore, Eichengreen says that "the only reliable way of creating a stable-value digital currency is for the central bank to issue it." Of course, this would defeat the original purpose of cryptocurrency, to provide anonymity to sender and recipient. But Eichengreen and other economists believe that a cryptocurrency is not money until a government says it is.

Banking and the Expansion
of the Money Supply

Mobile has become the primary way in which millions of our customers interact with us daily. Customers have higher expectations of their interactions with us. They expect it to be easy for them to cross channels.

Brett Pitts, former executive vice president and group head of digital
at Wells Fargo, quoted in "Digital Strategy: Does Your Bank Have One?" (2016)

Essential Question: What role does the banking system play in the expansion of the money supply?

According to the Federal Reserve, on January 8, 2020, there was $1.75 trillion in U.S. currency in circulation, but the total M2 money supply was more than $15.5 trillion. How can the total money supply be nearly nine times as large as the total amount of currency in existence? The answer to that question lies in the ability of banks to expand the supply of money. But that is only a small part of what banks do. Today's banks offer so many services that they have been likened to "financial supermarkets." And, like brick-and-mortar supermarkets, they have had to go digital to compete.

Types of Depository Institutions

Banks are financial institutions licensed by either the federal or a state government to receive deposits and make loans. Broadly speaking, the term *bank* encompasses a variety of **depository institutions** that hold funds or securities for depositors. Banks that directly serve the public fall into three categories: commercial banks, thrift institutions (or "thrifts"), and credit unions.

Commercial Banks With more than $17 trillion in assets as of January 2020, **commercial banks** are the nation's most important financial institutions. Like other businesses, banks may be privately owned and operated or owned by stockholders and managed by boards of directors. Commercial banks work directly with the public, offering a variety of services. One reason that commercial banks dominate the banking sector is that, unlike thrifts, they offer a full range of services to businesses. Another reason for their dominance is the high profits they make from business loans.

Thrift Institutions The original purpose of thrift institutions was to help people buy homes. They could accept customer deposits and make mortgages. Today, they are generally small community-based institutions. Often thrifts are mutual companies, meaning they are owned by their account holders. As a result, they generally pay higher interest than banks on their customers' savings. They are restricted by law in their services to businesses. They must invest 65 percent of their assets in residential mortgages and consumer loans and can lend only up to 20 percent of their assets for commercial loans.

There are two major types of thrift institutions. The first, mutual savings banks, were established in 1816 to serve low-income families, generating profits for their members. Most of them were located in the Mid-Atlantic and northeast regions of the United States. The federal government first chartered **savings and loan associations** (S&Ls) during the Great Depression to provide affordable mortgages for middle-class home buyers. By 1965, there were more than 6,000 S&Ls in the United States, but in the 1970s they were struggling. In an effort to address the challenges of a stagnant economy, Congress deregulated S&Ls, leading to widespread fraud and mismanagement. Between 1986 and 1995, nearly a third of the remaining 3,234 S&Ls in the United States failed. By the end of 2018, there were only 691 federally insured S&Ls left.

Credit Unions Originally, membership in **credit unions** was limited to people who shared a common bond—that is, they worked for the same company or in the same industry or lived in the same community. Today, credit unions allow the general public to join. Credit unions are often grouped with thrifts, but since they are nonprofit organizations, they have two distinct advantages:

1. They are exempt from corporate income tax.

2. They need to generate only enough earnings to fund day-to-day operations, allowing them to pay higher interest on deposits and charge less for loans and ATM fees.

The Business of Banking

The primary function of banks is to accept deposits and lend funds. **Deposits** are sums of money placed in a bank account. People making deposits receive interest on their money. Banks offer several types of accounts, although the most common are checking and savings accounts. Most deposits in checking and savings accounts (demand deposits) and in certificates of deposit (CDs) are insured up to $250,000 by the federal government, either through the Federal Deposit Insurance Corporation (FDIC) for banks and thrifts or through the NCUA (National Credit Union Administration) for credit unions. Before deposit insurance was created in the 1930s, putting money in a bank was risky. If the bank went broke, as they often did, depositors could lose all of their savings.

Depository Accounts As you have seen, checking accounts are considered cash because they are completely liquid. The name came from the fact that customers wrote and signed paper **checks** directing their bank to pay a specified amount of money from their checking account to a particular person or entity. Today, electronic payments often take the place of physical checks. Customers can use debit cards like credit cards or checks to pay for purchases in person or online or to withdraw cash from an **ATM,** or automatic teller machine. Instead of cash, checks, or debit cards, many people pay for purchases using smartphone apps.

Another option for making payments electronically is **electronic funds transfer** (EFT). EFT allows bills to be paid by moving funds from one account to another account at the same bank or a different one. Employers use EFT for direct deposit of paychecks into their employees' accounts, and many people authorize automatic payments for utilities, credit cards, and other recurring bills.

Banks offer several types of savings accounts, most of which pay interest on deposits. Money market accounts and certificates of deposit (CDs) usually pay more interest than basic savings accounts. Depending on the type of account and the amount of money involved, however, cash withdrawals may not be available on demand. **Withdrawals** are sums of money withdrawn, or taken out of an account, either at a bank or an ATM.

Loans and Other Services Banks make most of their money by using depositors' money to make loans and charging a higher rate of interest than they pay on depositors' accounts. Many loans are secured, meaning that borrowers pledge assets as collateral in case they default, or fail to repay. Unsecured personal loans usually have a higher rate of interest than loans that are secured by collateral. With a secured loan, the bank holds a car title as collateral until an automobile loan is paid off, or the title to a house until a mortgage is paid off. Small business loans may be secured by the business owner's personal property. Larger commercial loans also usually require that the business post collateral.

In addition to accepting deposits and making loans, banks offer a variety of financial services. These include issuing credit cards, selling money orders and bank drafts, exchanging foreign currency, and renting safe-deposit boxes for the storage of important documents and other valuables. Many banks offer investment services or maintain trust departments to help their customers manage their wealth.

Reading a Balance Sheet

As discussed in Topic 4.1, everything of value that a business owns is an asset, and everything it owes is a liability. In addition to its real estate and equipment, a bank owns the loans and investments it makes; these are its assets. Bank deposits, on the other hand, belong to the customers who deposited them, and therefore are liabilities. A financial statement that summarizes assets, liabilities, and net worth is known as a **balance sheet.** The table on the following page shows the balance sheet of Capital City National Bank at the end of January 2020.

Capital City National Bank Balance Sheet, January 31, 2020			
Assets		**Liabilities and Net Worth**	
Cash in vault	$ 1,500,000	Total deposits	$34,500,000
Reserve account	2,500,000	Net worth	5,000,000
Loans	25,750,000	**Total**	$39,500,000
Securities	8,500,000		
Other assets	1,250,000		
Total	$39,500,000		

Assets The assets of Capital City National Bank totaled $39,500,000:

- **Cash in vault.** Banks' vaults hold the bulk of their cash (although during business hours some of that cash is in the tellers' drawers), securities, and other valuables. Cash in vault refers to the amount of paper currency and coins the bank has on hand and fluctuates from day to day.

- **Reserve account.** The Federal Reserve System requires banks with more than $16.3 million in deposits to reserve a percentage of their total deposits. Banks keep most of their reserves in accounts at a district Federal Reserve Bank, where they earn interest. Capital City has $2.5 million in its reserve account. Taken with the $1.5 million cash in its vaults, the bank held a total of $4 million in reserves.

- **Loans.** Loans are considered assets because they are owned by the bank and represent debts payable to the bank. Banks earn most of their profits from the interest on consumer and business loans. Capital City had $25.75 million in loans on January 31.

- **Securities.** Rather than allow funds for which they have no borrowers to lie idle, banks invest those sums in relatively safe interest-bearing securities, such as government bonds. Capital City's investments totaled $8.5 million.

- **Other assets.** Capital City's other assets include its building, fixtures, and equipment, including ATMs.

Liabilities and Net Worth In a balance sheet, the sum of the liabilities and net worth equals the sum of the assets; in other words, assets and liabilities should balance each other.

- **Deposits.** A bank's principal obligations are its deposits. They are considered a liability because they represent funds owed to the bank's depositors. City Capital's deposits totaled $34.5 million.

- **Net worth.** The difference between a bank's assets and its liabilities is its net worth. Capital City's net worth was $5 million.

The Federal Reserve System and the Money Supply

A nation's central bank is responsible for regulating member banks. The **Federal Reserve System,** or "the Fed," is the central bank of the United States. Congress founded it in 1913 to promote a safe and stable monetary and financial system. In addition to a governing board in Washington, D.C., there are 12 regional Federal Reserve Banks, each of which is responsible for a geographic area of the United States. (For a complete treatment of the tools that the Federal Reserve uses to conduct monetary policy, see Topic 4.6.)

Reserve Requirements The Fed regulates and supervises the nation's banking institutions. One of the chief ways the Fed does this is by setting the **reserve requirement**, the percentage of its deposits a bank must hold in reserve, either as cash or in deposits with Federal Reserve Banks. The higher the reserve requirement, the less money a bank has to lend on which to make a profit. For this reason, small banks—those with demand deposits totaling less than $16.9 million—are exempted from this requirement.

The Fed updates the reserve requirement regularly, raising the deposit level that is subject to different ratios. As of January 2020, banks with demand deposits between $16.9 million and $127.5 million were required to reserve 3 percent of those deposits. Banks with more than $127.5 million in demand deposits must reserve 10 percent of those deposits. This percentage is the **reserve ratio.** Since even a small change in the reserve ratio causes a significant change in the monetary system, the Fed very rarely changes this number. Any amount over a bank's required reserves, is considered **excess reserves.**

How Banks Create Money Banks expand the money supply by making loans. The Fed requires that they operate on a **fractional reserve banking** system, which means they hold a portion of their depositors' money in reserve. Anything above the required reserves is available to make loans. If a bank's reserve requirement is 10 percent, the bank can lend 90 percent of its total deposits. If Customer A deposits $10,000, the bank needs to keep $1,000 in reserve but can lend $9,000 to Customer B. When Customer B deposits the $9,000 in her checking account, the bank must keep $900 in reserve but can lend $8,100. Each time money is deposited and a new loan is made, money is created. The progress of the original $10,000 through the banking system is shown in the table on the following page.

Progress of $10,000 through the Banking System

Bank	Deposits	Required Reserves	Loan
First	$10,000.00	$1,000.00	$9,000.00
Second	9,000.00	$900.00	8,100.00
Third	8,100.00	810.00	7,290.00
Fourth	7,290.00	729.00	6,561.00
Fifth	6,561.00	656.10	5,904.90
Sixth	5,904.90	590.49	5,314.41
Seventh	5,314.41	531.44	4,782.97
Eighth	4,782.97	478.30	4,304.67
Ninth	4,304.67	430.47	3,874.20
Tenth	3,874.20	387.42	3,486.78
Subtotal	$65,132.15	$6,513.22	$58,618.93
Sum of remaining banks	34,867.85	3,486.78	31,381.07
Total	$100,000.00	$10,000.00	$90,000.00

While it may seem that the creation of money could go on forever, that is not the case. If you were to laboriously add all the possible deposits and loans, eventually you would find that the original $10,000 deposit grows to $100,000 in deposits, thus expanding the money supply tenfold. The amount of money banks generate with each dollar is called the **money multiplier.** The money multiplier is the reciprocal of the reserve ratio:

1/Reserve ratio

For banks with the highest reserve requirement of 10 percent, the money multiplier would be 1/0.10 = 10. For smaller banks with a 3-percent reserve requirement, banks can lend 97 percent of their deposits, and the money multiplier is 33.33 (1/0.03 = 33.33). The actual amount of money created is actually less than the money multiplier predicts, since banks may wish to keep excess reserves and borrowers may not deposit all the money they receive.

ANSWER THE TOPIC ESSENTIAL QUESTION

1. In one to three paragraphs, explain the role of the banking system in the expansion of the money supply.

depository institutions
commercial banks
savings and loan associations
credit unions
deposits
checks
ATM
electronic funds transfer

withdrawals
balance sheet
Federal Reserve System
reserve requirement
reserve ratio
excess reserves
fractional reserve banking
money multiplier

MULTIPLE-CHOICE QUESTIONS

1. The money multiplier is
   (A) the amount of money generated on the balance sheet
   (B) the amount of loans that can be called in on a balance sheet
   (C) the way in which one finds the dollar amount eventually generated by loans given
   (D) the way in which money is measured
   (E) the percentage banks must hold in reserve

2. Which of the following represents a bank's largest liability?
   (A) Loans
   (B) Reserve requirement
   (C) Excess reserves
   (D) Demand deposits
   (E) Securities

3. Which of the following is true of the Fed's reserve requirements?
   (A) Larger banks have a smaller reserve requirement than do smaller banks.
   (B) A bank's required reserves are based on the total value of its deposits.
   (C) A bank's required reserves are based on the value of its demand deposits.
   (D) Banks must deposit all of their reserve funds in their regional Federal Reserve Bank.
   (E) There is no reserve requirement for banks with less than $50 million in demand deposits.

1. Use the following balance sheet to answer all parts of the questions that follow:

Seaside Bank			
Assets		**Liabilities**	
Required Reserves	$10,000	Demand deposits	$100,000
Excess Reserves	$90,000	Owners' equity	$80,000
Loans	$50,000		
Other assets	$30,000		
Total	$180,000	**Total**	$180,000

(a) Based on the above balance sheet, calculate the required reserve ratio.

(b) Suppose the Federal Reserve purchases $2,000 worth of bonds from the above bank. Explain what will change in each of the following?

   (i) Excess reserves

   (ii) Demand deposits

(c) If Pat deposits $2,000 into her checking account, what is the immediate effect on the M1 measure of the money supply?

(d) Calculate the new required and excess reserves due to Pat's deposit after the Federal Reserve bond purchase.

THINK AS AN ECONOMIST: *DETERMINE THE EFFECTS OF AN ECONOMIC CHANGE USING CALCULATIONS*

Economists use quantitative data and calculations to determine the effects of a change in an economic situation. Government economists do the same to try to estimate the effects of government policy decisions. Doing so requires them to answer two questions:

- What variable in the situation changed?
- What effect will that change have on economic outcomes?

When considering the reserve ratio, the effect of a change extends beyond one point.

Apply the Skill

Suppose you are an economist at the Federal Reserve asked to calculate the impact of a possible reduction in the reserve ratio from 4 percent to 3 percent. Assume that $3.5 trillion worth of deposits will be affected by this change. What is the money multiplier at the current 4 percent reserve ratio? What would the money multiplier be under the 3 percent ratio? What is the maximum amount that the money supply will change as a result of this ratio adjustment?

Topic 4.5

The Money Market

Up to a point it is worthwhile to sacrifice a certain amount of interest for the convenience of liquidity. But, given that the rate of interest is never negative, why should anyone prefer to hold his wealth in a form which yields little or no interest to holding it in a form which yields interest?

John Maynard Keynes, *The General Theory of Employment, Interest, and Money* (1936)

Essential Question: How do the demand for and supply of money determine the equilibrium nominal interest rate and influence the value of other financial assets?

As discussed in the previous topics, **liquidity** refers to the ease with which financial assets can be converted to money to spend. The English economist John Maynard Keynes developed a theory on liquidity preference—how people choose to divide their resources between highly liquid forms, particularly cash, and less liquid forms such as bonds. This was part of his larger attempt to understand how the demand for and supply of money influence nominal interest rates.

The Demand for Money

As you have learned, money is a major financial asset. Two functions of money help explain the demand for money:

1. It functions as a medium of exchange, allowing people to purchase goods or services.

2. It functions as a store of value, allowing it to be saved for future use.

The phrase "the demand for money" refers to how much of their assets people choose to hold in some form of easily obtainable money rather than in less liquid assets. He also described three reasons or motives for holding money:

- "The transactions motive" (also known as "the transactions demand for money") refers to the money people hold as cash or in liquid demand deposits such as checking accounts to pay for goods and services they need on a regular basis. This motive is directly related to the level of income.

- "The precautionary motive" (also known as "the precautionary demand for money") refers to money people may hold in less liquid form, such as a savings account, where it will be ready for future contingencies, such as health care expenses or automobile maintenance, that they want to be prepared for.
- "The speculative motive" (also known as the **speculative demand for money** or "asset demand") refers to money people hold in stocks, bonds, and other securities that will earn them interest. These are considered speculative because their value may rise or fall.

In order to focus on the issue of how people make choices, assume that people have only two ways to hold financial assets: in checking accounts or as bonds. Assets in a checking account are highly liquid, while bonds are less liquid. While there is generally an expectation that money invested in bonds will be tied up until they mature, bonds can be converted to cash, although the seller might need to pay a penalty for doing so before maturity.

Other Determinants of the Demand for Money

Liquidity is important, but it does not tell the whole story of how people decide how to allocate their resources. Several other factors also help determine the demand for money.

Level of Income and Real GDP As the total of all incomes in an economy increase, people demand more money, and as total incomes fall, people demand less money. As real gross domestic product (GDP) increases, so do incomes, resulting in a greater demand for money throughout the economy. (Real GDP is the GDP adjusted for inflation.)

Price Level The price level refers to the buying power of money. In the United States, the most common measure of price level is the Consumer Price Index (CPI), which is calculated by measuring changes in the prices of a basket of consumer goods and services. An increase in the price level is referred to as inflation; a decrease is known as deflation. When there is an increase in the price level, there is a corresponding increase in the demand for money. When there is a decrease in the price level, the demand for money also decreases.

Expectations The speculative demand for money is based on bond prices. When people expect bond prices to fall, they sell, thus increasing the demand for money. When people expect bond prices to rise, they buy, which reduces the demand for money. The expectation that bond prices are going to rise or fall actually causes them to do so.

Transfer Costs If the cost of transferring funds between money and nonmoney deposits becomes more expensive, customers tend to make fewer transfers, which increases the quantity of money they demand. If transfer costs decline, the demand for money tends to fall. New technology has made it easier and less expensive for people to convert their wealth into money, so today, people tend to invest more of their money than the did in the past.

Preferences As with other kinds of demand, preferences play a part in the demand for money. Some people like to keep a large amount of money available, while others prefer to invest as much as possible. People's attitudes about the trade-off between risk and yield also affect the demand for money. Some people prefer safe options for storing their money, such as insured deposit accounts but with lower interest, while others prefer to invest their money in bonds with higher yields but with more risk that the bond's issuer may default.

Interest Rates and the Demand for Money

The quantity of money that people hold varies inversely with the nominal interest rates they can earn from other financial assets, such as bonds.

- If people think interest rates are low, they have less incentive to invest in bonds than to hold money, so the demand for money increases.
- If people view interest rates as high, bonds become more attractive, and the demand for money decreases.

The demand curve for money shows the quantity of money demanded at each interest rate. It slopes downward from the left to the right, reflecting the inverse relationship between the quantity of money demanded and the interest rate.

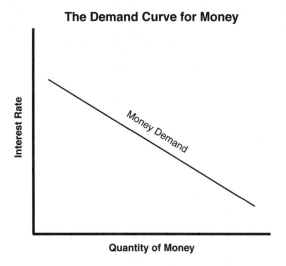

The Demand Curve for Money

The law of demand applies to the relationship between interest rates and the quantity of money demanded. If holding bonds is the alternative to holding money, then nominal interest rates are the price of holding money. As with other goods and services, an increase in this price results in a decrease in the quantity demanded. When there is an increase in the demand for money, the demand curve shifts to the right, reflecting an increase in the quantity of money demanded at any interest rate r, as shown in the paired graphs "Changes in the Demand for or Supply of Money" on page 205. Conversely, a drop in the demand for money would shift the demand curve to the left.

The Money Supply

Central banks are financial institutions that control a country's **monetary supply.** They do this through the production and distribution of money. In the United States, the central bank is the Federal Reserve Bank (Fed), which controls the money supply chiefly through its Federal Open Market Committee (FOMC). The Fed has three basic tools for influencing the supply of money:

- It can buy and sell U.S. Treasury notes, bills, and bonds as a way to directly affect how much money people have for other purchases.

- It can raise or lower the reserve requirements on deposits, which influences how much money banks have available for loans.

- It can raise or lower the discount rate, which is the interest rate the Fed charges for loans of 24 hours or less that its regional banks make to financial institutions to prevent funding shortfalls. Raising the discount rate makes loans to banks more expensive, which signals a reduced money supply and higher overall interest rates. Conversely, lowering the discount rate signals an expanded money supply and lower overall interest rates.

Equilibrium and Disequilibrium in the Money Market

The **money market** is the interaction between the demand for money and the money supply. It is in equilibrium when the nominal interest rate is such that the quantity of money demanded equals the quantity of money supplied. This is referred to as the equilibrium nominal interest rate. In Figure 2, the money demand curve is labeled D, the money supply is the vertical line S, and the equilibrium nominal interest rate is r.

Money Market Equilibrium

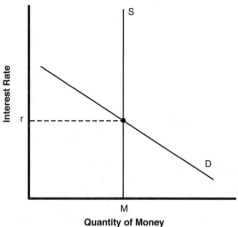

Disequilibrium occurs when there is either a change in demand for money or in the money supply. When that occurs, nominal interest rates create a surplus or shortage in the money market. Market forces cause nominal interest rates to adjust until the quantity of money people want to hold is equal to the amount of money that exists. When the nominal interest rate is above equilibrium, people reduce the amount of money they hold, and when the nominal interest rate is below equilibrium, they increase the amount of money they hold.

Changes in the Demand for Money According to Keynes's theory of liquidity preference, the nominal interest rate adjusts to balance the supply of and demand for money. People may choose to hold more or less money at each nominal interest rate due to changes in any of the five determinants listed above, such as a change in real GDP, the price level, or expectations. If the demand for money decreases, there will be an increase in the demand for bonds, causing the money demand curve to shift to the left and a corresponding drop in the nominal interest rate. An increase in the demand for money will have the opposite effect: The money demand curve will shift to the right, and the resulting higher nominal interest rate will lead to a lower quantity invested.

Changes in the Money Supply If the market for money is in equilibrium and the Fed changes the money supply when there are no changes in any of the determinants of money demand, a corresponding change in the demand for money and in nominal interest rates will occur. The Fed increases the money supply by buying government bonds.

When this happens, the money it pays for the bonds is typically deposited in banks, adding to bank reserves. Then the nominal interest rate must fall to restore equilibrium. Lower interest rates stimulate investment. Bond prices rise, causing nominal interest rates to fall and an increase in the quantity of money people demand.

When the Fed sells government bonds, the money it receives for them is withdrawn from the banking system, and bank reserves fall. Bond prices fall, causing nominal interest rates to rise and a decrease in the demand for money. The changes in bank reserves that result from the buying or selling of bonds change the quantity of money in the economy.

Changes in the Demand for or Supply of Money

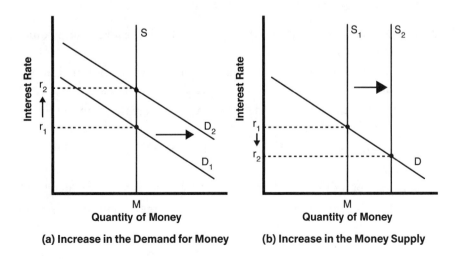

(a) Increase in the Demand for Money   (b) Increase in the Money Supply

In graph (a), an increase in the demand for money, from D_1 to D_2, results in a rise in the equilibrium nominal interest rate, from r_1 to r_2. In graph (b), an increase in the money supply, from S_1 to S_2, results in a fall in the equilibrium nominal interest rate, from r_1 to r_2.

ANSWER THE TOPIC ESSENTIAL QUESTION

1. In one to three paragraphs, explain how the demand for and supply of money determine the equilibrium nominal interest rate and influence the value of other financial assets.

KEY TERMS

liquidity
speculative demand for money

monetary supply
money market

MULTIPLE-CHOICE QUESTIONS

1. According to Keynes, the three motives for holding money are
   (A) the transactions motive, the precautionary motive, and the speculative motive
   (B) the transactions motive, the precautionary motive, and the profit motive
   (C) the transactions motive, the profit motive, and the speculative motive
   (D) the preference motive, the profit motive, and the speculative motive
   (E) the preference motive, the precautionary motive, and the speculative motive

2. As a country comes out of a recession and the price level and income levels increase,
   (A) the demand for money increases, which increases nominal interest rates
   (B) the demand for money decreases, which increases nominal interest rates
   (C) the supply of money increases, which decreases nominal interest rates
   (D) the supply of money decreases, which increases nominal interest rates
   (E) there is a simultaneous increase in the money supply and decrease in money demand

3. What happens when the Federal Reserve buys bonds?
   (A) The transaction demand for money increases, and the supply of money decreases.
   (B) The transaction demand for money decreases, and the supply of money decreases.
   (C) The supply of money decreases, and nominal interest rates decrease.
   (D) The money supply decreases, and nominal interest rates increase.
   (E) The money supply decreases, and nominal interest rates decrease.

FREE-RESPONSE QUESTIONS

(a) Briefly explain the speculative demand for money.
(b) How does the real gross domestic product (GDP) affect the demand for money?
(c) What is price level, and how does it affect the demand for money?
(d) What part do expectations play in the demand for money?
(e) Describe two changes that can lead to disequilibrium in the money market.

THINK AS AN ECONOMIST: *DRAW AN ACCURATELY LABELED GRAPH TO REPRESENT AN ECONOMIC MARKET*

The supply of and demand for money react to market forces in similar ways to the supply of and demand for goods or services. The demand for money responds inversely to changes in the interest rate—the price of money. The supply of money responds to monetary policy set by the Federal Reserve.

Economists use supply-demand curves to display the interaction of these two forces to find the equilibrium price of money. They can also use these curves to show changes in supply and demand that occur.

Apply the Skill

Consider the following situation. Supply (S) of and demand (D) for money establish the equilibrium nominal interest rate (r) for the quantity of money (M). Suddenly the economy enters a downturn, with employers laying off workers and unemployment rising from 4.3 to 6.7 percent. In the face of these economic troubles, consumer spending falls and the demand for money drops lower (D1). Create a supply and demand curve for money showing the original situation described and new market conditions resulting from the change in demand. Label the new demand curve D1 and the new nominal interest rate r1. Assume no change in the money supply. Label the curves, relevant points, and axes correctly. Include arrows showing the direction of change.

Topic 4.6

Monetary Policy

He who controls the money supply of a nation controls the nation.

Attributed to U.S. President James Garfield, 1881

Essential Question: What are the short-run effects of monetary policy on macroeconomic outcomes?

When President George W. Bush nominated him to chair the Federal Reserve Board, Ben Bernanke had no idea that within a year of taking over, the country would be blindsided by a major financial crisis. The Great Recession lasted from December 2007 to June 2009. The Fed implemented aggressive and unprecedented monetary policies to prevent greater damage to the economy. In spite of this, unemployment rose from 5 percent at the end of 2007 to a high of 10 percent in October 2009, and it did not fall back to 5 percent until 2015. However, the Fed's policies likely helped keep the Great Recession from becoming something as damaging as the Great Depression of the 1930s.

What Is Monetary Policy?

A nation's **monetary policy** consists of the actions and communications its central bank takes to manage the nation's money supply and interest rates. There are three major monetary policy objectives:

- To promote maximum employment
- To promote stable prices by controlling inflation
- To promote moderate long-term interest rates

What Is a Central Bank? A **central bank** is the financial institution authorized to produce and distribute money and credit for a nation and to conduct its monetary policy. It does this by managing the level of short-term interest rates and influencing the overall availability and cost of credit in the economy. Monetary policy indirectly affects longer-term interest rates, currency exchange rates, and the prices of stocks, bonds, and other assets. As a result, monetary policy influences a nation's household spending, business investment, production, employment, and prices. The Federal Reserve System, or Fed, is the central bank of the United States. Other central banks include the European Central Bank, the Bank of England, the Bank of Japan, and the Bank of Canada.

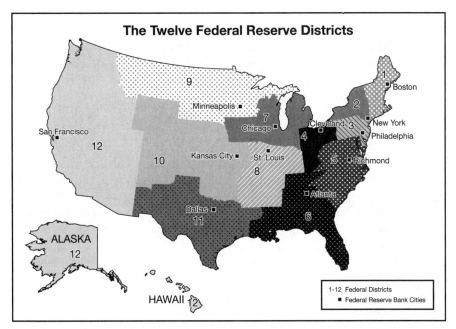

The Twelve Federal Reserve Districts

Source: Federal Reserve Bank of San Francisco

The Tools of Monetary Policy

When interest rates are low, people can more easily afford to buy homes, and businesses are more likely to expand. When interest rates are high, individuals and companies are less likely to borrow and spend. Central banks try to limit the harmful effects of inflation and recession. In times of economic downturn or recession, a central bank will want to adopt an **expansionary policy** to increase the money supply and lower interest rates, thus spurring economic growth. Conversely, in times of inflation it will put into effect a **contractionary policy,** decreasing the money supply and causing interest rates to rise, with the intention of slowing economic growth.

Central banks do this by using their monetary tools to increase or decrease interest rates. The tools of monetary policy used by the Federal Reserve include open-market operations, the required reserve ratio, and the discount rate. The monetary policy tool most frequently used is open-market operations.

Open-Market Operations A central bank can influence the nominal interest rate in the short run by changing the money supply, which in turn will affect investment and consumption. In **open-market operations**, a central bank sells or buys government bonds in the open market to change the money supply. In the United States, the branch of the Federal Reserve that determines the nation's monetary policy is the Federal Open Market Committee (FOMC). The FOMC normally meets eight times a year to discuss whether to maintain or change the current policy. It changes the money supply by either buying or selling government securities such as U.S. Treasury bills to control the supply of money in the economy.

During a recession, the Fed tries to spur growth by increasing the money supply. Conversely, it tries to curb inflation by shrinking the money supply. As you learned in Topic 4.5, the Fed can increase the money supply by buying back securities from the nation's largest security dealers and banks, or it can decrease the money supply by selling securities. When it does so, the equilibrium nominal interest rate either falls or rises.

When an open-market purchase takes place, the Fed is buying, and the public—in this case, a bank or a security dealer—is selling. The Fed gives the seller of the securities a check, which the seller then deposits in the bank, resulting in an automatic increase in the bank's reserve balance with the Fed. The bank can use these new reserves to make additional loans, thus increasing the money supply.

When the bank makes additional loans, the people receiving those loans get the money deposited in their accounts, further expanding the money supply. As you learned in Topic 4.4, this process is referred to as the money multiplier effect. As you will recall, the money multiplier is determined by dividing 1 by a bank's reserve ratio. If it is a large bank with a reserve ratio of 10 percent, the money multiplier is 10, meaning that for every $1,000 deposited, the money supply can expand by $10,000.

Another policy many central banks carry out is to set a target range for the overnight interbank lending rate. In the United States, the FOMC accomplishes this by setting the target **federal funds rate** every six weeks at its regular meetings. Federal funds are the balances that banks maintain in their accounts at their Federal Reserve Bank, and the federal funds rate, or fed funds rate, is the interest that banks charge one another for overnight loans of federal funds. Banks, credit unions, and other lenders base the interest rates they charge their customers on the federal funds rate. An increase in the fed funds rate results in an increase in interest rates on consumer loans, mortgages, and other credit vehicles. Conversely, a decrease in the fed funds rate results in a decrease in those interest rates.

Required Reserve Ratio The central bank also sets requirements for the nation's banking industry, such as the amount of cash a bank must keep on reserve. A major part of a bank's income comes from the interest it earns on the loans it makes using its depositors' money. However, it must also keep enough cash on hand to take care of day-to-day transactions such as withdrawals. Small private banks are sometimes exempted from reserve requirements since they hold only a small percentage of the total assets of a banking system.

Most banks cannot lend all of the money in depositors' accounts but must keep a percentage of those deposits on reserve. In the United States, the Federal Reserve Board of Governors sets this percentage, or reserve ratio. When the Fed increases the reserve ratio, banks' lending ability is reduced. When reserve ratios are reduced, the opposite happens.

In Topic 4.4, you learned that with a reserve ratio of 10 percent, a deposit of $10,000 could lead to an expansion of deposits totaling $100,000 as the deposit traveled through the banking system. This is because of the money multiplier effect. With a reserve ratio of 20 percent, the same $10,000 deposit could be expanded to only $50,000 in deposits, whereas with a reserve ratio of 5 percent it could be expanded to $200,000.

As you can see, the effect of a change in reserve requirements on the banking system as a whole can be quite dramatic. During periods of expansion, when resources are fully employed and prices are moving into inflationary levels, the central bank can move against these trends by increasing the reserve ratio. During recessions the central bank can reduce the reserve ratio, enabling banks to make more loans. By making more loans, the banks can, in turn, add to the money supply and aggregate demand.

Discount Rate Another monetary policy tool of central banks is known as the **discount rate** or rediscount rate. The discount rate is the interest rate charged by a central bank for loans of reserve funds to commercial banks and other financial institutions. When their reserves get low, member banks can replenish them with loans from the central bank. In the United States, this is the Federal Reserve Bank that services their district. Since banks are in business to earn a profit, they must charge their loan customers something more than this rate.

The amount of money that the public borrows is affected by prevailing interest rates. As the cost of loans increases, borrowing decreases. The Fed can use its power of increasing or decreasing the discount rate to affect the volume of loans and the quantity of money in circulation and credit available. The discount rate is usually a percentage point above the federal funds rate, and it is normally changed whenever the FOMC changes the fed funds rate.

The Fed may increase the discount rate to tighten up on credit and slow the growth of the money supply, as it did during the mild inflation of the early 1990s. A slower growth of the money supply, in turn, puts downward pressure on prices and inflation. During recessions like the one that hit the United States between 2007 and 2009, the Fed can choose to reduce the discount rate. As banks follow suit by reducing their interest charges, business and consumer loans increase. This in turn leads to increased business activity, consumer spending, and employment.

The graph on the following page illustrates the relationship between different interest rates, specifically the effect of changes in the federal funds rate and the discount rate on the prime rate and credit card interest rates. The prime rate is the interest rate that commercial banks charge corporations whose credit rating is so high that there is virtually no risk of loss. It also affects all other interest rates. The credit card rate represents the average interest charged on unpaid credit card balances. Notice that the fed funds rate hovered near 0 percent during the economic recovery that followed the Great Recession.

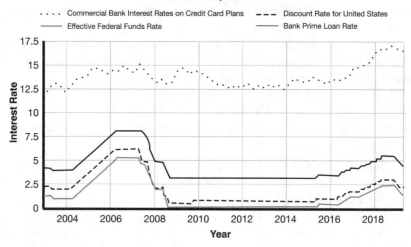

Interest Rates, 2003-2019

· · · · Commercial Bank Interest Rates on Credit Card Plans   − − − Discount Rate for United States

—— Effective Federal Funds Rate   —— Bank Prime Loan Rate

Source: Federal Reserve Bank of St. Louis

The Effects of Monetary Policy

In the short run, monetary policy influences aggregate demand, real output, the price level, employment, and interest rates—either directly by adjusting interest rates or indirectly by adjusting the money supply. The following graphs show some of the short-run economic effects of an increase to the money supply.

Short-Run Effects of Changes to the Money Supply

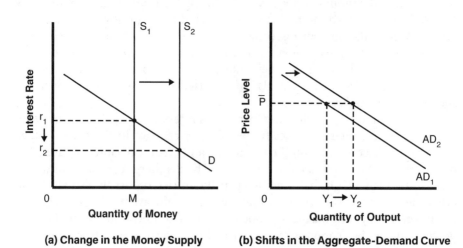

(a) Change in the Money Supply   **(b) Shifts in the Aggregate-Demand Curve**

In graph (a), an increase in the money supply, from S_1 to S_2, results in a drop in the equilibrium nominal interest rate, from r_1 to r_2. Graph (b) shows the resultant shift of the short-run aggregate demand curve to the right, from AD_1 to AD_2, as the quantity of goods and services demanded at a given price level increases from PL_1 to PL_2 and the output from Y_e back to Y_f. A decrease in the money supply would have the opposite effect, shifting the short-run aggregate demand curve to the left and leading to a decreased demand for goods and services at a given price.

During economic downturns or periods of inflation, central banks like the Federal Reserve use expansionary or contractionary monetary policies to stabilize the economy and promote full employment.

Expansionary Monetary Policy Central banks use expansionary monetary policy to lower unemployment and avoid recession while stimulating economic growth. Because it is difficult to catch the contractionary phase of the business cycle in time, expansionary policy usually is not set until after a recession has begun. The Fed has several options available to stimulate the economy:

- **Buy securities.** The Fed buys Treasury notes and other securities, giving banks more money to lend and expanding the money supply. Interest rates drop, making loans less expensive. This boosts spending.

- **Lower the discount rate.** The FOMC may also lower the fed funds rate, which also results in a lower discount rate. This also causes interest rates to drop and boosts spending.

- **Lower reserve requirements.** The Fed rarely lowers the reserve requirement, even though this immediately increases the money supply.

When the Federal Reserve engages in expansionary monetary policy, the money supply increases, which decreases the interest rate. When the interest rate decreases, interest-sensitive spending in the form of business investment and consumption increase, thereby increasing aggregate demand. When aggregate demand increases, price level and real GDP increase as well.

Contractionary Monetary Policy In an inflationary economy, with prices increasing at an unacceptable rate, central banks adopt a contractionary monetary policy. This policy slows the rate of increase in the money supply to something less than the increase in the GDP and reduces aggregate demand. The Fed has several options available to bring inflation under control:

- **Sell securities.** By selling Treasury bills, bonds, and notes to the public, the Federal Reserve System receives the payments from the sales of these securities. The sales reduce bank reserves, the lending ability of the banking system, and the money supply.

- **Raise the discount rate.** By raising the discount rate, the Fed charges local banks more to borrow from the Federal Reserve System. The banks then raise the interest rates they charge their customers. Higher interest rates discourage borrowing, slow the growth of the money supply, and reduce aggregate demand and prices.

- **Increase reserve requirements.** By requiring that local banks hold a larger portion of their deposits on reserve, the Fed reduces banks' lending ability, along with the money supply.

When the Federal Reserve engages in contractionary monetary policy, the money supply decreases, which increases the interest rate. When the interest rate decreases, interest-sensitive spending in the form of business investment and consumption decrease, thereby decreasing aggregate demand. When aggregate demand decreases, price level and real GDP decrease.

Monetary Policy Limitations

The Fed has monetary tools to regulate the economy. How well the Fed can achieve its goals depends on a number of factors.

Forecasting and Timing Difficulties The success of monetary policy depends on how quickly and accurately the Fed recognizes and responds to economic trends. Although economists can describe in general terms how well or how poorly the economy is doing, it is impossible to predict possible problems in the economy with certainty. This makes it difficult for the Fed to know exactly how much to raise or lower interest rates or increase or decrease the money supply. There are numerous time lags, initially between recognizing a problem and adjusting monetary policies, then between making those adjustments and seeing the impact they have on the business community. In retrospect, it may turn out that changes were too early or too late, too extreme or not extreme enough, or perhaps not even necessary.

The Business Cycle Monetary policy is least effective at either end of the business cycle. During the recessionary phase, the Fed will lower interest rates. However, this may not be enough to allay fears created by job layoffs and business failures, and spending may remain at low levels in spite of the reduced cost of loans.

Similarly, as the business cycle climbs toward the upper reaches of expansion, the effectiveness of monetary policy wanes. Then the Fed may increase interest rates to discourage loans, slow the growth of the money supply, and lower prices. But as long as business prospects are good, firms will continue to borrow and expand, believing that increased sales will more than offset the higher cost of money. As a result, prices will continue to rise in spite of the Fed's efforts to reverse the trend.

New Banking Laws In the mid-20th century, most people placed the bulk of their savings in regular savings accounts, and the interest offered by savings institutions was limited by law. In the 1980s, however, Congress removed those limits and repealed the prohibition against the payment of interest on demand deposits. As a result of deregulation, banks became more competitive, but they also became less responsive to shifts in Fed policies. For example, in the days before deregulation, the Fed could tell banks to reduce the interest rates they paid on deposits as a way of discouraging savings and encouraging consumption. Today, however, bankers can ignore such suggestions if they think it would be more profitable to do otherwise.

The Global Economy One result of globalization is that individuals and governments in foreign countries hold many more U.S. dollars than they once did. Even though those holdings are abroad, they still have an effect on prices in the United States, and those prices directly affect the level of economic activity. While the Fed has a great deal of control over the money supply in the United States, it is limited in its ability to regulate dollars in foreign hands, which lessens its ability to regulate the value of the dollar, price levels, and the business cycle.

ANSWER THE TOPIC ESSENTIAL QUESTION

1. In one to three paragraphs, describe the short-run effects of monetary policy on macroeconomic outcomes.

KEY TERMS

monetary policy	open-market operations
central bank	federal funds rate
expansionary policy	discount rate
contractionary policy	

MULTIPLE-CHOICE QUESTIONS

1. Which of the following best describes the discount rate?

   (A) It is the interest rate set by the Fed for overnight interbank lending.

   (B) It is the interest rate charged by a central bank for loans of reserve funds.

   (C) It is the interest rate commercial banks charge their best corporate customers.

   (D) It is the percentage of a bank's deposits that must be held in reserve.

   (E) It is the amount by which the money supply expands as a result of the money multiplier.

2. If the reserve ratio is 5 percent, how much could an initial deposit of $10,000 grow to as a result of the money multiplier?

   (A) $20,000

   (B) $40,000

   (C) $100,000

   (D) $200,000

   (E) $400,000

3. Which of the following is a short-run effect of an increase in the money supply?

(A) Interest rates increase.

(B) Demand for money increases.

(C) Price level increases.

(D) Aggregate demand for goods and services increases.

(E) Aggregate demand for goods and services decreases.

FREE-RESPONSE QUESTIONS

(a) How does the federal funds rate differ from the discount rate?

(b) Identify and briefly explain the three tools that the Federal Reserve has it its disposal.

(c) Assume the United States is experiencing a recession. What open market operation could the Federal Reserve engage in to ease the burden of the recession?

(d) Create a graph that shows the effect of the above monetary policy action on the money market.

(e) Briefly explain the effect of expansionary monetary policy on employment.

THINK AS AN ECONOMIST: *USE ECONOMIC PRINCIPLES TO EXPLAIN HOW TO ACHIEVE A SPECIFIC OUTCOME*

Economists use economic principles to explain what decisions economic actors should make. To do this, they do the following:

- Identify what specific economic behaviors are taking place in a particular situation.
- Use an economic principle to explain how to achieve a specific outcome.

For example, economists note that individuals and businesses are willing to borrow money in a period of inflation, as long as interest rates are not too high. The main driver of this fact is the desire to minimize costs. Since prices are going up, the value of money is going down. Thus, borrowers will be repaying their loans with cheaper dollars, making it less costly to borrow.

Apply the Skill

As you have read, the Federal Reserve has several tools, some of which have a contractionary effect on the economy and some of which have an expansionary effect. Suppose that a natural gas pipeline disaster depletes the flow of gas substantially. Electric utilities that rely on natural gas see huge increases in the cost of this fuel, causing electricity rates to sharply rise as well. Utilities that rely on other fuel sources raise their rates, too. As a result, businesses across the economy raise their prices. Within a few months, the inflation rate reaches double digits.

What Fed tool would be most effective in responding to this situation? What economic principle explains why it would be the most effective?

The Loanable Funds Market

One-fifth of Americans are adding nothing to their savings, according to a Bankrate survey. Why not?

Taylor Tepper, Bankrate.com, March 14, 2018

Essential Question: How do the interactions of borrowers and savers determine the equilibrium interest rate of loanable funds?

The loanable funds market, like so many other parts of the economy, is one of supply and demand. In this case, the supply is money, in the form of savings. U.S. families save a smaller portion of their incomes than their counterparts in many other countries, from Luxembourg and Switzerland to South Korea and Australia. Instead of encouraging people to save money, the consumer-driven U.S. economy entices them to spend. On average an adult in the United States spends $18,000 a year on nonessentials, but 60 percent of these same people do not have enough in savings to cover a $1,000 emergency. As you will see in this topic, the lack of savings has a direct impact on the supply of loanable funds, interest rates, investments, and economic growth.

How the Loanable Funds Market Works

The market for loanable funds, like other markets in an economy, is governed by the laws of supply and demand. The **loanable funds market** is a model of the way money from savers makes its way into the hands of borrowers.

Supply and Demand The supply of loanable funds comes from **national saving,** which consists of all of a nation's private saving and public saving. It includes the money people deposit in bank accounts to save for future use, business profits, and government budget surpluses. Interest is the reward paid to savers. Lenders—usually financial institutions—then supply funds to the loanable funds market. High interest rates on deposits provide an incentive to save, and thus a larger supply of loanable funds. There is less incentive to save when interest rates are low, with the result that there might be a shortage of loanable funds.

The demand for loanable funds usually comes from the desire to make a financed purchase of some sort. A family might want to purchase a new car or a new house, while a business may want to build a new office or purchase new equipment. Businesses and individuals are more likely to borrow when interest rates are low, because that keeps their costs down. As interest rates rise, the cost of borrowing goes up, people and businesses are less likely to borrow, and there is a drop in **investment spending**.

Interest Rates The interest rate is the price of a loan. It is also the amount that people receive for the use of the money they save or that they pay to borrow money. As you learned in Topic 4.2, there are two types of interest rates. The rate that is usually cited when banks advertise interest rates is the nominal interest rate. The real interest rate is the nominal interest rate minus the rate of inflation. For example, if the nominal interest rate is 7 percent and the rate of inflation is 2 percent, the real interest rate is 5 percent. Throughout this topic, the term *interest rate* will refer to the real interest rate.

Graphing the Market for Loanable Funds

The graph for loanable funds is similar to the other supply and demand graphs you have studied. The supply curve is directly proportional to the interest rate, so it slopes upward from left to right. There is an inverse relationship between real interest rates and the quantity demanded, so the demand curve slopes downward from left to right. The point at which the two curves intersect is the equilibrium level, where the supply of and demand for loanable funds are equal. The interest rate at this point is the **equilibrium interest rate.**

Whenever there is a change in either the supply or demand of loanable funds, the interest rate adjusts to the equilibrium level for the usual reasons. In reality, interest rates vary greatly depending on their amount, duration, and purpose. The interest rate on short-term credit card debt is often six times the rate on long-term home loans. For clarity, the loanable funds model simplifies this by assuming only one average interest rate.

If the interest rate fell lower than the equilibrium level, the supply of loanable funds would be lower than the demand for them, and lenders would raise their interest rates. This would encourage saving, which would increase the supply of loanable funds. But at the same time, higher interest rates would discourage borrowing, and thus decrease the demand for loanable funds.

If, on the other hand, the interest rate was higher than the equilibrium, the supply of loanable funds would exceed the demand for them. In order to attract borrowers, lenders would lower their interest rates, and thus restore equilibrium.

Determinants of Supply and Demand in the Loanable Funds Market

The national savings rate measures the part of the gross domestic product (GDP) that is saved in a nation. It includes savings from personal income, business earnings, and tax revenues. In the United States, the Commerce Department's Bureau of Economic Analysis (BEA) tracks this data as an economic indicator of the nation's financial health, since investments are funded through savings. Retirement plans such as 401(k)s and IRAs make up a large part of national savings. A general rise in incomes does not ensure a higher rate of savings, since it may be accompanied by a rise in consumption. The U.S. national savings rate has declined significantly since the mid-1960s. As of 2017, the United States ranked 113th out of 181 nations, with personal, business, and government savings accounting for only 17.5 percent of the GDP.

Economists often use a closed economy—that is, one that does not interact with other economies—in order to keep their models simple. In such a model, national saving is equal to investment. In fact, no such economy exists in the world today. In an open economy—one that interacts freely with other economies—investment equals national savings plus the net inflow of capital from abroad. Other factors can enter the picture as well and alter the outcomes. For example, government policies can affect the supply of or demand for loanable funds.

Incentives to Save and to Invest Americans save a much smaller portion of their income than people in many other countries. U.S. tax laws are at least partly responsible for this: Since interest income is taxable, it reduces the future payoff and thus reduces the incentive to save. If a country has high interest rates that discourage investments, it could change the tax laws to encourage people to save more. This could increase the supply of loanable funds, lowering the interest rate and stimulating investment. In periods of low interest rates, a sign that businesses can borrow money easily and at a low cost, changes to encourage savings would have little effect.

From time to time Congress passes investment tax credits to make investing more attractive. This gives a tax advantage to businesses that invest in capital improvements, such as buying new equipment or building new factories. Such an incentive would increase the demand for loanable funds at all interest levels, but it would not directly affect the supply of loanable funds. However, the increased demand would raise interest rates, which would encourage more saving, thus increasing the supply of loanable funds.

The Effects of Incentives to Save and to Invest

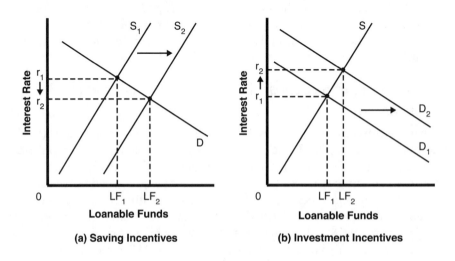

(a) Saving Incentives

(b) Investment Incentives

Graph (a) shows how saving incentives increase the supply of loanable funds, shifting it to the right, from S_1 to S_2. The equilibrium interest rate drops from r_1 to r_2, and the equilibrium quantity of loanable funds saved and invested rises. In graph (b), an investment tax credit raises the demand for loanable funds, shifting it to the right, from D_1 to D_2. The equilibrium interest rate rises from r_1 to r_2, and the equilibrium quantity of loanable funds saved and invested rises.

Government Budget Deficits or Surpluses A federal budget deficit exists when government spending exceeds tax revenue. In order to finance these deficits, the government borrows in the bond market. This reduces the supply of loanable funds that is available to finance investment by individuals and companies. Hence, it has the potential to push up interest rates, thereby discouraging both individuals and businesses from borrowing. If government borrowing causes a decrease in private borrowing, it is called "crowding out." Depending on what the government is borrowing to finance, it can reduce the economy's growth rate. (Crowding out is discussed in greater detail in Topic 5.5.)

A budget surplus (or a decrease in the deficit) can have the opposite effect. When the government spends less than it collects in taxes, the budget surplus increases the supply of loanable funds. This has the potential to reduce the interest rate and stimulate investment and economic growth. However, decreasing the federal deficit or running a surplus might also reduce aggregate demand, which could reduce economic growth.

The Effects of Government Budget Deficits and Surpluses

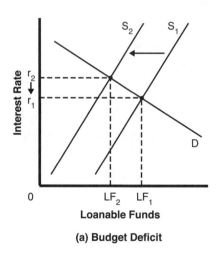

(a) Budget Deficit

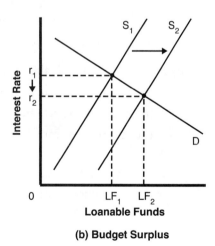

(b) Budget Surplus

In graph (a), a budget deficit lowers national saving, so the supply of loanable funds decreases, and the supply curve shifts to the left, from S_1 to S_2. The equilibrium interest rate rises from r_1 to r_2, and the equilibrium quantity of loanable funds saved and invested falls. Graph (b) illustrates a budget surplus. The supply of loanable funds increases, and the supply curve shifts to the right, from S_1 to S_2. The equilibrium interest rate drops from r_1 to r_2, and the equilibrium quantity of loanable funds saved and invested increases.

ANSWER THE TOPIC ESSENTIAL QUESTION

1. In one to three paragraphs, explain how the interactions of borrowers and savers determine the equilibrium interest rate of loanable funds.

KEY TERMS

loanable funds market	investment spending
national saving	equilibrium interest rate

MULTIPLE-CHOICE QUESTIONS

1. Which of the following will result in an increase in the real interest rate?
   (A) An increase in household saving
   (B) An increase in national saving
   (C) An increase in the supply of loanable funds
   (D) An increase in the government budget surplus
   (E) An increase in the demand for loanable funds

2. Why is the supply of loanable funds upward sloping?
   (A) As the real interest rate decreases, people are willing to save more.
   (B) As the real interest rate increases, people are willing to save more.
   (C) As the real interest rate decreases, people demand more loanable funds.
   (D) As the real interest rate decreases so does demand.
   (E) As the real interest rate increases, so does the government's demand for loanable funds.

3. What happens when a government spends more than it collects in tax revenues?

(A) There is a budget surplus amounting to an increase in the demand of loanable funds.

(B) There is a budget surplus amounting to a decrease in the supply of loanable funds.

(C) There is a budget deficit amounting to a decrease in the supply of loanable funds.

(D) There is a budget deficit amounting to an increase in the supply of loanable funds.

(E) There is a balanced budget amounting to an increase in the demand for loanable funds.

FREE-RESPONSE QUESTIONS

(a) Explain what happens to the demand for loanable funds if the government were to offer a tax credit on interest earned.

(b) Briefly explain what might cause the shift in the graph below.

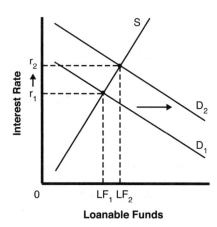

(c) Briefly explain what might cause the shift in the graph below.

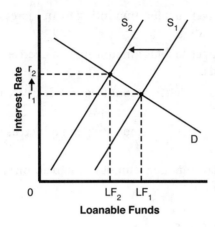

(d) Briefly explain what might cause the shift in the graph below.

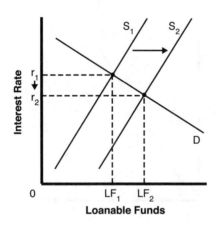

(e) What effect would a government budget surplus have on the supply of and demand for loanable funds?

Economists can demonstrate the effects of a change by using accurately labeled visuals. For example, look back at the graphs under "The Effects of Incentives to Save and to Invest" in the topic text. The two supply-demand curves show what happens in the loanable funds market if incentives are in place to encourage either savings or investments.

Apply the Skill

Suppose the economy is in the midst of a deflationary period. Falling prices encourage consumers to refrain from purchasing big-ticket goods and services. They reason that price reductions will continue and that, as a result, their money will be worth more and have more purchasing power in the future than it does now. Draw and accurately label a supply-demand curve that shows the original supply (S1) and demand (D1) in the loanable funds market and the interest rate (r1) in that market. Also show the effect of consumers' increased savings on supply and demand (S2 and D2, as appropriate) and the new equilibrium interest rate (r2). Graph and label the original and new quantity of loanable funds (use LF) on the horizontal axis. Use arrows to show any changes in supply, demand, and interest rates. Label all axes and curves correctly.

UNIT 4

Long Free-Response Question

1. Country X is currently in a recession, and the Central Bank decides to take action to bring the country back to full employment.

   (a) Identify an open-market operation that the central bank should engage in.

   (b) Draw a correctly labeled graph of the money market to show the change you indicated in part (a) and to show the effect on the nominal interest rate.

   (c) Using an aggregate demand and aggregate supply graph, show the original status of Country X, labeling full employment Y_f and equilibrium output and price level as Y_1 and PL_1, respectively. Then show the effect of the monetary policy action you indicated in (a) on the graph, and label the new equilibrium price level PL_2.

   (d) What is the effect of the open-market operation you indicated in part (a) on the price of bonds?

   Use the following table showing assets and liabilities for Investime Bank in Country X to answer questions (e) through (h).

Assets		Liabilities	
Required Reserves	$8,000	Demand Deposits	$80,000
Excess Reserves	$80,000	Owner's Equity	$20,000
Loans	$12,000		
TOTAL	$100,000	TOTAL	$100,000

   (e) What is the reserve requirement?

   (f) Suppose Amanda deposited $2,000 in to her checking account at this bank. Calculate each of the following:

   (i) The immediate change in the M1 measure of money

   (ii) The change in required reserves

   (g) What effect does the above transaction have on each of the following?

   (i) The supply of loanable funds

   (ii) The real interest rate

   (h) If the nominal interest rate is 5 percent and the real interest rate is 3 percent, calculate the inflation rate.

UNIT 5

Long-Run Consequences of Stabilization Policies

The 2020 COVID-19 pandemic was not just a major health crisis. It plunged the United States, and much of the world, into the most severe financial crisis since the Great Depression. When it shut down major parts of the U.S. economy in 2020, Congress responded by passing economic stimulus legislation to put money in the hands of consumers and to help struggling businesses and the tens of millions of people who lost their jobs. The Federal Reserve lowered the federal funds interest rate to 0 percent, bought trillions of dollars in securities, lent money directly to securities firms and major corporate employers, and created a program to support loans to small- and mid-sized businesses.

Extraordinary circumstances require extraordinary measures, and these were extraordinary uses of fiscal and monetary policy. Fiscal policy is the use of taxation and government spending to achieve financial goals for the nation, in this case the passage of economic stimulus legislation. Monetary policy refers to programs used by central banks, such as the U.S. Federal Reserve, to try to increase or decrease the level of business activity by regulating the nation's supply of money and credit.

In normal times, governments use a combination of fiscal and monetary policies to try to maintain a healthy economy by stimulating consumer spending, production, and employment and stabilizing prices and interest rates. When a financial crisis arises, such as the Great Recession or the COVID-19 pandemic, governments use these policies to try to return their economies to a healthy state as quickly as possible. In this unit, you will learn how governments use fiscal and monetary policy decisions to stabilize the economy.

"A bigger allowance would help me stimulate the economy!"

CartoonStock.com

Topic Titles and Essential Knowledge

Topic 5.1 Fiscal and Monetary Policy Actions in the Short Run

- A combination of expansionary or contractionary fiscal and monetary policies may be used to restore full employment when the economy is in a negative (i.e., recessionary) or positive (i.e., inflationary) output gap.
- A combination of fiscal and monetary policies can influence aggregate demand, real output, the price level, and interest rates.

Topic 5.2 The Phillips Curve

- The short-run trade-off between inflation and unemployment can be illustrated by the downward-sloping short-run Phillips curve (SRPC).
- An economy is always operating somewhere along the SRPC.
- The long-run relationship between inflation and unemployment can be illustrated by the long-run Phillips curve (LRPC), which is vertical at the natural rate of unemployment.
- Long-run equilibrium corresponds to the intersection of the SRPC and the LRPC.
- Points to the left of long-run equilibrium represent inflationary gaps, while points to the right of long-run equilibrium represent recessionary gaps.
- Demand shocks correspond to movement along the SRPC.
- Supply shocks correspond to shifts of the SRPC.
- Factors that cause the natural rate of unemployment to change will cause the LRPC to shift.

Topic 5.3 Money Growth and Inflation

- Inflation (deflation) results from increasing (decreasing) the money supply at too rapid of a rate for a sustained period of time.
- When the economy is at full employment, changes in the money supply have no effect on real output in the long run.
- In the long run, the growth rate of the money supply determines the growth rate of the price level (inflation rate) according to the quantity theory of money.

Topic 5.4 Government Deficits and the National Debt

- The government budget surplus (deficit) is the difference between tax revenues and government purchases plus transfer payments in a given year.
- A government adds to the national debt when it runs a budget deficit.
- A government must pay interest on its accumulated debt, thus increasing the national debt and increasingly forgoing using those funds for alternative uses.

Topic 5.5 Crowding Out

- When a government is in budget deficit, it typically borrows to finance its spending.
- A loanable funds market model can be used to show the effect of government borrowing on the equilibrium real interest rate and the resulting crowding out of private investment.

- Crowding out refers to the adverse effect of increased government borrowing, which leads to decreased levels of interest-sensitive private sector spending in the short run.
- A potential long-run impact of crowding out is a lower rate of physical capital accumulation and less economic growth as a result.

Topic 5.6 Economic Growth

- Economic growth can be measured as the growth rate in real GDP per capita over time.
- Aggregate employment and aggregate output are directly related because firms need to employ more workers in order to produce more output, holding other factors constant. This is captured by the aggregate production function.
- Output per employed worker is a measure of average labor productivity.
- Productivity is determined by the level of technology and physical and human capital per worker.
- The aggregate production function shows that output per capita is positively related to both physical and human capital per capita.
- An outward shift in the PPC is analogous to a rightward shift of the long-run aggregate supply curve.

Topic 5.7 Public Policy and Economic Growth

- Public policies that impact productivity and labor force participation affect real GDP per capita and economic growth.
- Government policies that invest in infrastructure and technology affect growth.
- Supply-side fiscal policies affect aggregate demand, aggregate supply, and potential output in the short run and long run by influencing incentives that affect household and business economic behavior.

Source: *AP® Macroeconomics Course and Exam Description.* Effective Fall 2019 (College Board).

Topic 5.1

Fiscal and Monetary Policy Actions in the Short Run

"[T]he Fed and its chair [leadership] must be permitted to act independently and in the best interests of the economy, free of short-term political pressures and, in particular, without the threat of removal or demotion of Fed leaders for political reasons."

Former Fed chairs Paul Volcker, Alan Greenspan, Ben Bernanke, and Janet Yellen, Open Letter, *The Wall Street Journal*, August 5, 2019

Essential Question: What are the short-run effects of fiscal and monetary policy on macroeconomic outcomes?

Four former chairs of the Federal Reserve System wrote an open letter to *The Wall Street Journal* warning of the dire consequences of turning the Fed into a political tool. President Donald Trump had publicly pressed Fed Chair Jerome Powell—a Trump appointee—to lower interest rates to boost employment and economic growth in the short run.

This tension between government and the Fed was not a new phenomenon. In the early 1970s, President Richard Nixon succeeded in forcing the Fed to take measures aimed at lowering interest rates to reduce unemployment in order to help him get re-elected. The result was an inflationary boom followed by a recession from which the nation did not recover until the early 1980s. In this topic and throughout this unit, you will learn about the many aspects of government (fiscal) and Federal Reserve (monetary) policy—their purposes, their interplay, and their outcomes.

The Goals of Fiscal and Monetary Policies

There are two powerful tools that can be used to regulate the economy: fiscal policy and monetary policy. As you have learned, the national government sets fiscal policy, while the nation's central bank sets monetary policy. Fiscal policy influences the economy through taxation and government spending, whereas monetary policy influences it by controlling the supply of money and managing interest rates. When they work together, they can promote sustainable growth.

The two policies work together to manage the business cycle and close output gaps. (An **output gap** is the difference between the actual output of an economy and its potential output.) Healthy economic growth is between 2 and 3 percent per year, unemployment around 3.5 to 4.5 percent, and inflation at about 2 percent. Interest rates should be high enough to encourage saving, but not so high that they discourage borrowing by individuals and businesses.

Monetary Policy As you will recall, a nation's central bank is the financial institution that is authorized to produce and distribute money and credit for a nation, as well as conduct its monetary policy. A country's central bank may or may not be an agency of the national government. In the United States, the central bank is the Federal Reserve System. The president appoints the Federal Reserve's chair, who must report to Congress on monetary policy. However, the Fed's decisions do not have to be approved by the president or Congress. The Federal Reserve is supposed to be independent and free from political pressure.

As you learned in Topic 4.6, the Fed has three important tools that it can use to implement monetary policy. It most commonly uses **open-market operations** to control the money supply. It can increase the money supply by buying U.S. government **securities** such as U.S. Treasury bills and decrease it by selling securities. It can also change the reserve requirements for banks, increasing or decreasing the amount of money banks must hold in reserve. The third tool is the discount rate, the interest rate charged to banks that need to increase their reserves by borrowing from the Fed, which indirectly affects the interest rates that consumers receive on their deposits or pay to borrow money.

Fiscal Policy Fiscal policy, on the other hand, is set by the president and Congress. Fiscal policy plays an important part in a nation's economy by increasing or decreasing tax rates and public spending. While it might seem elementary to assume that ideally, the nation's budget should balance tax revenues and public spending, this idea is a matter of vigorous debate among economists and other policy makers. When tax receipts are not adequate to pay for public spending, governments borrow money by issuing debt securities such as government bonds and thus, accumulate debt. Fiscal policy plays a key role, alongside monetary policy, to promote a healthy economy. But in some cases, lawmakers have been known to put the needs of their constituents before national economic priorities.

How Fiscal and Monetary Policies Work Together

As you learned in Unit 2, capitalist economies experience business cycles. These are periods of expansion and contraction of economic activity that occur over time. Economists use several indicators to determine the current stage of a cycle, including the interest rates, gross domestic product, consumer spending, and unemployment. The expansion phase is characterized by rapid economic growth, low interest rates, increased production, and inflation. The contraction phase is characterized by a slowdown in economic growth, higher unemployment, and stagnating prices.

When expansion gets out of control, it can result in a high rate of inflation and adversely affect the standard of living. Out-of-control contraction can result in a severe recession or even a depression, leading to high unemployment and a general decline in the standard of living. Both can be corrected by a combination of fiscal and monetary policies, which can be expansionary or contractionary in nature. The more common form is **expansionary policy**, which is used to reverse economic contraction by stimulating economic growth. The goal of **contractionary policy** is to reverse economic expansion by slowing economic growth to curb inflation.

Policy Goal	Fiscal Policy Tools	Monetary Policy Tools
Contraction	• Decrease spending • Decrease transfer payments • Raise taxes	• Sell bonds • Raise the discount rate • Raise the reserve requirement
Expansion	• Increase spending • Increase transfer payments • Lower taxes	• Buy bonds • Lower the discount rate • Lower the reserve requirement

Expansionary Policy As you have seen, fiscal and monetary policies can influence output, price level, interest rates, and unemployment. Expansionary fiscal policy consists of an increase in government spending (often referred to as stimulus spending) or a decrease in taxes, or both. Expansionary monetary policy consists of an increase in the money supply or a lowering of the discount rate, which lead to lower real interest rates. This makes borrowing more attractive and stimulates business investment. Both expansionary fiscal and monetary policies increase aggregate demand, resulting in increased output, lower unemployment, and increased real GDP.

As seen in the Closing a Recessionary Gap graphs on the next page, a recessionary gap can be closed either through self-correction or as a result of expansionary policy. Left alone, wages will fall as long as unemployment is below its natural level. This is because with so many people out of work and competition for jobs intense, people will accept a lower wage just so they have an income. Lower wages mean that aggregate supply can increase because wages and output costs decrease, making it less expensive to produce overall. This, in turn, will gradually shift the short-run aggregate supply curve, moving the economy toward equilibrium.

However, public officials can use expansionary fiscal or monetary policy to stimulate aggregate demand. If the government cuts taxes, consumption will increase as people have more after-tax income to spend, thus increasing aggregate demand. This can lead to higher inflation, which will raise the nominal interest rate. The central bank can use expansionary monetary policy to bring the nominal interest rate down to its original level.

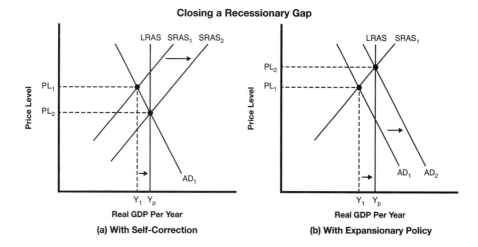

Closing a Recessionary Gap

(a) With Self-Correction

(b) With Expansionary Policy

Graph (a) illustrates the gradual closing of a recessionary output gap that takes place without implementing expansionary policies. The short-run aggregate supply shifts from $SRAS_1$ to $SRAS_2$ as a result of a fall in nominal wages in the long run. Graph (b) shows the effects of expansionary policy on aggregate demand, shifting it from AD_1 to AD_2 and closing the gap. (Y_1 represents actual output, and Y_p is potential output. The space between the two is the recessionary output gap.)

Contractionary Policy The goal of contractionary policy is to slow economic growth and bring inflation under control. It is the opposite of expansionary policy, consisting of cuts in government spending or an increase in taxes. Because neither of these options is popular, democratically elected politicians are reluctant to enact them. Central banks, which are more insulated from public opinion, can more easily adopt contractionary monetary policy that might cause higher unemployment and higher interest rates for borrowers. However, changes in monetary policy may take several months for their impact to become noticeable.

In the Closing an Inflationary Gap graphs on the following page, when no action is taken to correct an inflationary gap, nominal wages rise in response to a shortage of labor, and the short-run aggregate supply curve begins to shift to the left, eventually bringing the economy to its potential output. However, by using contractionary policy, such as reducing government spending on goods and services, public officials can stabilize the economy by reducing the level of real GDP. Such a policy would shift the aggregate demand curve to the left and restore real GDP to its potential.

Graph (a) illustrates the gradual closing of an inflationary output gap that occurs without implementing contractionary policies. The short-run aggregate supply shifts from $SRAS_1$ to $SRAS_2$ as a result of a rise in nominal wages in the long run.

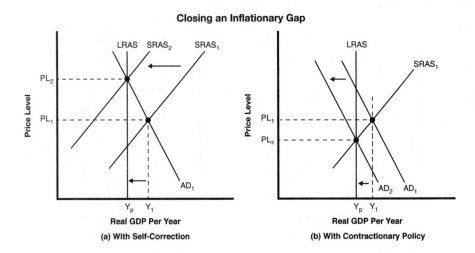

Closing an Inflationary Gap

(a) With Self-Correction

(b) With Contractionary Policy

Graph (b) shows the effects of contractionary policy to reduce aggregate demand, shifting it from AD_1 to AD_2 in order to close the gap. (Y_1 represents actual output, and Y_p is potential output. The space between the two is the inflationary output gap.)

Interactions of Fiscal and Monetary Policies The short-run impacts of different combinations of fiscal and monetary policy are summarized in the table Interactions of Fiscal and Monetary Policy. In each box, the first bulleted item refers to an expansionary or contractionary fiscal policy, the second to an expansionary or contractionary monetary policy, and the third bullet to the expected results. (Note that the results of conflicting fiscal policy and monetary policy cannot be determined without more specific information.)

EFFECTS OF THE INTERACTION OF FISCAL AND MONETARY POLICY			
		Monetary Policy	
		Expansionary	Contractionary
Fiscal Policy	Expansionary	• Aggregate demand increases, aggregate supply remains constant • Unemployment rate/output decreases • Price level increases	Uncertain/Indeterminate
	Contractionary	Uncertain/Indeterminate	• Aggregate demand decreases, aggregate supply remains constant • Unemployment rate/output increases • Price level decreases

1. In one to three paragraphs, explain the short-term effects of fiscal and monetary policy on macroeconomic outcomes.

KEY TERMS

output gap
open-market operations
securities
expansionary policy
contractionary policy

MULTIPLE-CHOICE QUESTIONS

1. Which of the following is an example of expansionary fiscal policy?
   (A) Raising taxes
   (B) Increasing government spending
   (C) Cutting government spending
   (D) Increasing the money supply
   (E) Lowering interest rates

2. The goal of expansionary fiscal and monetary policy is
   (A) an increase in output and a decrease in price level
   (B) an decrease in output and a decrease in price level
   (C) an increase in aggregate demand to reduce unemployment
   (D) a decrease in aggregate demand to decrease the price level
   (E) removing money from the system to slow the progression of a recession

3. Assume the economy is experiencing an inflationary period. Which of the following would happen if an expansionary monetary policy were to be applied?

	Employment	Price Level	Aggregate Demand
(A)	Increase	Increase	Decrease
(B)	Decrease	Decrease	Decrease
(C)	Increase	Increase	Increase
(D)	Decrease	Decrease	Increase
(E)	Increase	Decrease	Increase

(a) Assume that the United States economy is experiencing a period of inflation. Identify an open market operation and one fiscal policy that would slow down an overheated economy while bringing it back to full employment.

(b) What is the impact of expansionary fiscal and monetary policy on price level and unemployment?

(c) Assume the U.S. economy is in a recession. If no fiscal or monetary policy were to be implemented, what would be the eventual impact on nominal wages, price level, and unemployment?

(d) Now assume that the central bank and the government both take action to bring about full employment to the country during the recession. Identify one fiscal and one monetary policy action that can be combined to achieve this goal.

(e) Identify a scenario in which fiscal and monetary policy would work in tandem to increase output but keep nominal interest rates stable.

THINK AS AN ECONOMIST: *USE ECONOMIC PRINCIPLES TO EXPLAIN HOW A SPECIFIC OUTCOME OCCURS WITH MULTIPLE CONTRIBUTING VARIABLES*

Fiscal and monetary policy are the responsibility of different government entities. The president and Congress control fiscal policy, which they implement by raising or lowering either taxes or federal spending. The Federal Reserve Board controls monetary policy, which it enacts by using open-market operations, changing the reserve requirements for banks, or manipulating the discount rate. The Fed uses these tools to increase or decrease the money supply.

The president and Congress can work together on fiscal policy, responding to short-run problems, such as slowdowns in economic growth or increases in unemployment. If they disagree, they generally try to find a compromise they can both accept. In contrast, the Fed operates independently of these two branches of government. As a result, its actions could either reinforce or run counter to those of the president and Congress.

Apply the Skill

Suppose a sudden economic crisis strikes the nation. Rapidly rising inflation causes companies to cut back on output and lay workers off. The president is primarily concerned about high inflation while Congress focuses on the workers who have lost their jobs. The president and Congress agree to a set of strong measures that include cutbacks on federal spending and a tax surcharge of 10 percent on all earners. Fed officials are equally alarmed by inflation but believe that the government's fiscal policy will take too long to slow inflation. It sells Treasury bills and raises the discount rate in an effort to reduce the money supply. What will be the effect of these policy actions?

The Phillips Curve

"By most accounts, Federal Reserve policy makers have been very successful in recent years. The evidence? Low inflation and extremely low unemployment. But the Fed's success has also undermined one of the basic theories it has relied on to understand the economy and how inflation and unemployment are related. It's called the Phillips curve."

Ari Shapiro, "Is It Time for the Fed to Say Goodbye to the Phillips Curve Theory?" on *All Things Considered*, National Public Radio, October 29, 2018

Essential Question: How does the Phillips curve model represent the relationship between inflation and unemployment and the effects of macroeconomic shocks on both?

Policy makers use a variety of tools to help them predict economic trends so they can use fiscal and monetary policy to maintain a healthy economy. In many instances, trade-offs are involved. This is the case with the Phillips curve, which suggests that there is an inverse relationship between inflation and unemployment: when inflation is low, unemployment is high, and vice versa. This poses a dilemma to policy makers who are forced to decide between the lesser of two problems.

What Is the Phillips Curve?

In 1958, the economist A. W. Phillips published an article in which he compared the rates of unemployment and wages in the United Kingdom between 1861 and 1957. He had found that there appeared to be an inverse relationship: during years when there was high unemployment, wages tended to be steady or fall, and when unemployment was low, wages tended to rise. Because other prices tend to rise and fall in the same pattern as wages, his findings can be extended to the relationship between inflation and unemployment.

Researchers found that the same patterns that Phillips found in the United Kingdom also existed in the United States. They believed that increasing aggregate demand could increase the demand for labor. As unemployment shrinks, companies increase wages to compete for workers and raise prices to pay for increased wages. They called the inverse relationship of wages or prices and unemployment the **Phillips curve**. The following graph shows a theoretical Phillips curve.

Short-Run Phillips Curve

Inflation Rate (y-axis, 0 to 10)

Unemployment Rate (x-axis, 0 to 10)

Many economists believed that the Phillips curve illustrated a stable relationship, and that they could maintain a low rate of unemployment if they were willing to accept a higher inflation rate. The rates of inflation and unemployment during the decade following Phillips's publication of his findings appeared to support the idea of the Phillips curve, and many governments began to use the Phillips curve to set fiscal and monetary policy.

Critics of the Phillips Curve The economist Milton Friedman published a paper in 1968 in which he argued that monetary policy could only lower unemployment by raising inflation in the short run. His view was supported by other **monetarists**, economists who believe that the money supply is the primary factor affecting demand in the short run. According to classical theory, growth in the money supply is the primary determinant of inflation, but it only alters prices and nominal incomes. It does not affect output or factors that affect the rate of unemployment. Friedman concluded that there was no reason to expect a relationship between the rate of inflation and the rate of unemployment in the long run.

Using the Phillips Curve to Make Predictions

Phillips did not say that when unemployment went down, prices would go up. He just pointed out that when unemployment went down, wages tended to rise. Other economists developed the Philips curve and used it as a predictor of what might happen in the economy. During the 1960s economists believed that increasing aggregate demand would result in an increase in the demand for labor, decreasing unemployment and causing a rise in wages, which would be passed on to consumers in the form of higher prices for goods and services. Many governments set a target inflation rate and used fiscal and monetary policy to expand or contract their economies in order to achieve that rate.

Policy makers viewed the Phillips curve as a new tool that could help guide fiscal and monetary policy. An economy might experience either a recessionary or an inflationary gap. These are differences between real output and potential output with full employment. An economy with a recessionary gap would have high unemployment and little or no inflation. Expansionary policies such as tax cuts, increased government spending, or increases in the money supply would increase aggregate demand and move the economy to a point on the Phillips curve with lower unemployment and higher inflation. An economy with an inflationary gap would have very little unemployment and a higher rate of inflation. Contractionary policies such as higher taxes, cuts in government spending, or reductions in the money supply would move the economy to a point on the Phillips curve with higher unemployment but lower inflation. (For graphs illustrating the closing of recessionary and inflationary gaps, see Topic 5.1.)

Failure of the Phillips Curve During the 1960s, the Phillips curve seemed to provide an accurate depiction of the trade-offs between inflation and unemployment: low inflation was accompanied by high unemployment, while low unemployment was accompanied by a high inflation rate. (See graph (a), 1960–1969, on the following page.) Then around 1970 the inverse relationship between inflation and unemployment started to break down in the United States, partly as a result of fiscal policy and partly as a result of monetary policy. Government spending rose as the Vietnam War escalated, and the Fed tried to counteract the resulting expansionary fiscal policy by holding down interest rates. Inflation had risen significantly during the 1960s, from 1–2 percent early in the decade to 5–6 percent at the end of the decade, but unemployment actually rose as well.

In 1971, President Richard Nixon announced three new fiscal policies he hoped would help him get re-elected: a 90-day wage and price freeze, a 10-percent tariff on imports, and the removal of the United States from the gold standard. Abandoning the gold standard caused the value of the dollar to plummet, which raised the price of imports even more. Nixon's Federal Reserve chair, a former presidential adviser, agreed with Nixon's policies, including trying to reduce interest rates to stimulate the economy until after the election.

As a result, the United States experienced a period of rising unemployment and rising inflation, along with stagnant economic growth—a combination of economic factors known as stagflation. Under those circumstances, any changes in monetary policy to lower unemployment by increasing inflation could only have a temporary effect. The economic downturn worsened in 1974, when the Organization of Petroleum Exporting Countries (OPEC) began an oil embargo. The reduced supply of oil caused the world price of oil to double—a supply shock that rippled through the economy, affecting everything from the costs of production and transportation to the cost of oil to heat homes. This caused a shift in the aggregate supply curve, and along with it, a shift in the Phillips curve. The Fed decided to accommodate the supply shock by increasing the money supply. By 1980, the inflation rate was 14 percent.

Rethinking the Phillips Curve Between 1971 and 1991, there did not appear to be a smooth relationship in the long run between inflation and unemployment. (See graph (b), 1971–1991, on the following page.) Economists were forced to rethink the Phillips curve. They realized that workers and consumers were able to adapt their expectations about future rates of inflation based on current conditions. As a result, the inverse relationship between inflation and unemployment existed only in the short run. In the long run, the Phillips curve could shift outward. This led to a distinction between the Phillips curve in the long run and in the short run. An economy is always operating somewhere along the **short-run Phillips curve** (**SRPC**). Any change in the model for aggregate demand and aggregate supply has a corresponding change in the Phillips curve model.

U.S. Inflation and Unemployment Rates

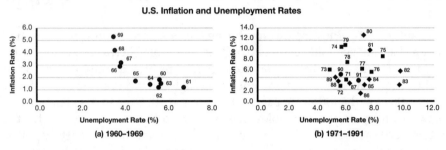

(a) 1960–1969

(b) 1971–1991

The relationship between inflation and unemployment fit the Phillips curve pattern.

The long-term relationship between inflation and unemployment had broken down.

Source: Federal Reserve Bank of San Francisco & U.S. Bureau of Labor Statistics

Economists determined that there is a natural rate of unemployment that is normal even in a healthy economy. In 2020, the Federal Reserve considered the natural rate of unemployment to be 3.5–4.5 percent and the target inflation rate to be around 2 percent. Because expectations can adapt to changes in inflation rates, the **long-run Phillips curve** (**LRPC**) is a vertical line at the natural rate of unemployment. When employment is below the natural rate, inflation speeds up; when employment is above the natural rate, inflation slows down. When the unemployment rate equals the natural rate, inflation is stable. A change in the natural rate of unemployment also changes the LRPC.

When the government pursues expansionary economic policies, inflation increases as aggregate demand shifts to the right, and the SRPC is thrown out of equilibrium. As aggregate demand increases, firms hire more workers to increase output, and unemployment decreases. However, because of higher inflation, workers' expectations of future inflation change, shifting the SRPC to the right to a new stable equilibrium point, at which the rate of unemployment has returned to its natural rate. The economy is in equilibrium at the point where the SRPC and LRPC intersect.

Expansionary and Contractionary Policies and the Phillips Curve

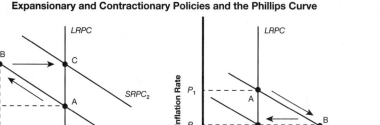
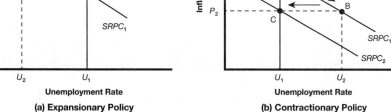

(a) Expansionary Policy (b) Contractionary Policy

Graph (a), Expansionary Policy, illustrates the effect of expansionary monetary policy in both the short and long run. Expansionary policy moves the economy up along SRPC₁ from point A to point B. As expected, inflation rises, the SRPC shifts to the right, and the economy moves to point C. At that point, both expected and actual inflation are higher, and unemployment has returned to its natural rate.

Graph (b), Contractionary Policy, illustrates the effect of contractionary monetary policy in both the short and long run. When the Fed takes action to reduce inflation, the economy moves along SRPC₁ from point A to point B. In time, expected inflation falls, and the SRPC shifts to the left. When the economy reaches point C, there is a return to equilibrium and unemployment returns to its natural rate.

The Phillips curve has gradually flattened over time, and since 2000 the correlation between unemployment and changes in inflation has been nearly zero. Inflation has barely moved as unemployment rose and fell. Between 2009 and 2020, unemployment fell from 9.9 percent to 3.6 percent, while inflation hovered between 1 and 2 percent. The weakened relationship between inflation and unemployment in recent years has led many to question the relevance of the Phillips curve. One reason for this is globalization. It has become more difficult for workers to negotiate for higher wages when large multinational companies can move jobs overseas, so employers no longer raise wages in response to a tight labor market.

Macroeconomic Shocks and the Phillips Curve

An already sick economy in the early 1970s was worsened by the oil embargo and subsequent doubling of the cost of crude oil. This was an example of a supply shock. There are also demand shocks. Such shocks are unexpected events that affect businesses' costs of production and thus the prices they charge, causing dramatic changes in future output. Supply and demand shocks may be either positive or negative, and will result in corresponding shifts in the SRPC.

SUPPLY AND DEMAND SHOCKS		
	Supply Shock	**Demand Shock**
Positive	• New manufacturing techniques • Lower labor costs • Increase in the supply of money	• Interest rate cuts • Tax rate cuts • Higher wage rates
Negative	• Higher labor costs • Environmental disasters • Wars	• Environmental disasters • Terrorist attacks • Stock market crashes

Shocks to aggregate supply or aggregate demand cause the SRPC to change. An adverse shock gives policy makers a less favorable trade-off between inflation and unemployment. Major adverse changes in aggregate supply or demand can worsen the short-run trade-off between unemployment and inflation. Supply shocks cause the SRPC to shift.

- A negative supply shock causes the aggregate supply curve to shift to the left, resulting in reduced output, and the SRPC to shift to the right, as reduced output leads to higher inflation and higher unemployment.

- A positive supply shock has the opposite effect, resulting in a shift of the SRPC to the left. (For graphical examples of these shifts in the SRPC, see the graphs under Expansionary and Contractionary Policies and the Phillips Curve.)

See below how demand shocks correspond to movement along the SRPC.

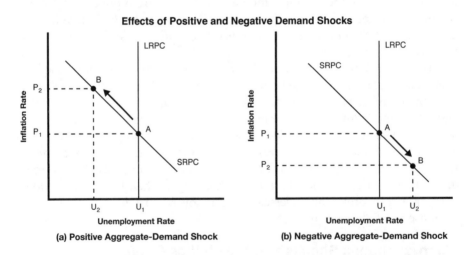

Effects of Positive and Negative Demand Shocks

(a) Positive Aggregate-Demand Shock

(b) Negative Aggregate-Demand Shock

Graph (a), Positive Aggregate-Demand Shock, shows the effect of a positive demand shock on the Phillips curve. An increase in aggregate demand is accompanied by movement from point A to point B. As the inflation rate rises it is accompanied by a corresponding drop in the rate of unemployment. Graph (b), Negative Aggregate-Demand Shock, shows the effect of a negative demand shock on the Phillips curve. A decrease in aggregate demand is accompanied by movement from A to B. The fall in inflation rate is accompanied by a corresponding rise in the rate of unemployment.

ANSWER THE TOPIC ESSENTIAL QUESTION

1. In one to three paragraphs, explain how the Phillips curve model represents the relationship between inflation and unemployment and the effects of macroeconomic shocks on both.

KEY TERMS

Phillips curve   short-run Phillips curve (SRPC)
monetarist   long-run Phillips curve (LRPC)

MULTIPLE-CHOICE QUESTIONS

1. According to the Phillips curve model, an increase in the expected rate of inflation will cause
   (A) a corresponding rise in employment
   (B) the short-run Phillips curve to shift to the right
   (C) the short-run Phillips curve to shift to the left
   (D) the long-run Phillips curve to move to the left
   (E) the long-run Phillips curve to move to the right

2. Where does expansionary monetary policy eventually move the economy in relation to the long-run Phillips curve?
   (A) It shifts it to the right of the LRPC.
   (B) It shifts it to the left of the LRPC.
   (C) It moves it higher on the LRPC.
   (D) It moves it lower on the LRPC.
   (E) It moves it above the LRPC.

3. What impact would a negative supply shock have on the Phillips curve?
   (A) It would cause the SRPC to shift to the left as both inflation and unemployment fall.
   (B) It would cause the SRPC to shift to the right as both inflation and unemployment rise.
   (C) It would cause movement upward along the SRPC as inflation rises and unemployment falls.
   (D) It would cause movement downward along the SRPC as inflation falls and unemployment rises.
   (E) It would have no measurable impact on the SRPC.

1. Assume the United States economy is experiencing an inflationary period caused by an increase in government spending.

   (a) On the short run Phillips curve, would the economy, in its current state, be characterized by a point to the right of, left of, or on the long run Phillips curve?

   (b) Draw a Phillips curve to illustrate your answer in part (a) and place point A on the graph to indicate the current state of the economy.

   (c) Identify a fiscal policy that would aid in closing the inflationary gap.

   (d) On the graph you drew in part (b), illustrate the implementation of fiscal policy that you indicated in part (c) on the Phillips curve by placing point B on the curve.

   (e) Assume the price of oil increased significantly. Describe what change would take place on the Phillips curve due to this supply shock.

THINK AS AN ECONOMIST: *DEMONSTRATE YOUR UNDERSTANDING OF AN ECONOMIC SITUATION ON AN ACCURATELY LABELED GRAPH OR VISUAL*

The short-run Phillips curve shows the relationship between the unemployment rate and the inflation rate as a function of aggregate demand and aggregate supply. The clear relationship between unemployment and inflation that economists posited in the 1970s has proven less clear in recent decades. The reason is, in part, because producers and consumers respond to changes in economic conditions as they take place. Those responses change outcomes. These responses are particularly evident on the short-run Phillips curve.

Apply the Skill

Suppose that engineers make a technological breakthrough with rechargeable batteries needed in automobiles. The new batteries last five times longer than existing batteries and recharge in half the time. Manufacturers find that smaller versions can be used on a host of other products, from laptop computers to washing machines. The result of this discovery is a sudden boom in short-run aggregate supply, and manufacturers increase output to get their new products to market.

Draw a graph showing the effect of this boom on the short-run Phillips curve. Label the graph correctly to show the original and new short-run Phillips curves. Include the long-run Phillips curve as well.

Money Growth and Inflation

"A steady rate of monetary growth at a moderate level can provide a framework under which a country can have little inflation and much growth. It will not produce perfect stability; . . . but it can make an important contribution to a stable economic society."

Milton Friedman, *The Counter-Revolution in Monetary Theory* (1970)

Essential Question: How does monetary policy affect inflation?

As you have read, the Federal Reserve tries to keep the annual inflation rate at 2 percent in the long run in order to maintain price stability and maximum employment. At that rate, people can hold money without concern that it will lose purchasing power. A higher inflation rate would reduce people's confidence in long-term financial decisions, and a lower rate might lead the economy into deflation, with falling wages and prices. The Federal Open Market Committee uses monetary policy to help keep the inflation rate at 2 percent.

Inflation and the Value of Money

Inflation, a general rise in prices of consumer goods and services has been the norm in the United States since 1950. At times, inflation has been very high—in 1974 it was over 10 percent. The only full year of deflation was during the financial crisis of 2009, when prices fell slightly for the year. Overall, the average inflation per year between 1950 and 1970 was 3.4 percent.

The steady increase in prices had a large impact on the value of money. Prices in 2020 were 970 percent higher than in 1950. This means that it would cost about $10.70 in 2020 dollars to buy what a dollar would have bought in 1950. In other words, a dollar in 2020 is worth less than a dime was worth in 1950.

Measuring Inflation Several economic indicators can be used to measure inflation. You have already read about the best-known of these, the Consumer price index (CPI), which the Bureau of Labor Statistics uses to tracks the prices on a basket of goods and services. Another is the personal consumption expenditures price index (PCEPI or, simply, PCE) from the Bureau of Economic Analysis. Like the CPI, the PCE is a monthly report that measures price changes in consumer goods and services in the U.S. economy.

The Federal Reserve prefers to use the PCE to measure inflation because it measures a broader set of goods and services than the CPI. In a recent year (2018), the CPI measured the rate of inflation as 1.9 percent, while the PCE measured it as 1.5 percent. However, not all prices increase at the same rate, and some prices actually go down. For example, while the cost of new vehicles rose 0.7 percent in 2018, the cost of televisions dropped 19 percent.

The Value of Money Inflation means that a particular amount of money will purchase less over time. Even though price indexes are used to determine the rate of inflation, the value of the basket of goods and services remains the same. As the overall price level rises, the value of money falls, so people have to pay more than they did a year before for the same thing. To put it another way, a cup of coffee that cost 25 cents in 1950 would cost $2.68 in 2020. The value of the cup of coffee did not change, but the value of money did.

Money Supply and Money Demand

Like so many other things in economics, the value of money is determined by supply and demand. As you learned in Unit 4, the Fed controls the supply of money. It can expand the quantity of money in the money supply by buying government bonds. When people deposit the dollars they receive for those bonds in banks, the money supply expands even more as a result of the money multiplier effect.

The demand for money, on the other hand, is determined by many factors. One is the amount of money people want to hold as currency, which depends on the interest rate they could receive if they bought interest-bearing bonds instead of keeping currency in their wallets or checking accounts. But the main reason people choose to hold money is that it is a medium of exchange: They use it to buy the goods and services they need and want. As prices rise, people tend to hold more money in currency rather than in bonds. In other words, a higher price level increases the quantity of money demanded.

As with other types of supply and demand, there is an equilibrium point at which supply and demand balance. In this case, the quantity of money demanded balances the quantity of money supplied. It is this equilibrium of money supply and money demand that determines the price level and hence the value of money.

In the graph Price Level and Money Supply and Demand atop the following page, the horizontal axis shows the quantity of money, the left vertical axis shows the value of money, and the right axis shows the price level. As you will recall, the supply curve is vertical because the money supply is set by the Fed, while the demand curve slopes downward. This indicates that, as its value decreases so that it buys less, people tend to hold a larger quantity of money to pay for goods and services. At point A, the quantity of money demanded and the quantity of money supplied have balanced. This equilibrium determines the price level and the value of money. (As you can see, there is an inverse relationship between the price level and the value of money.)

Price Level and Money Supply and Demand

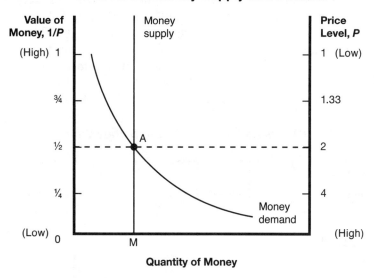

Quantity of Money

The Quantity Theory of Money A change in the money supply results in a change in the price level, which in turn affects the value of money. According to the **quantity theory of money** (QTM, also called the Fisher equation), there is a direct relationship between the quantity of money in an economy and the price level of goods and services. The QTM is based on the **equation of exchange**, first developed by 19th-century classical economists and revised by 20th-century economists Irving Fisher and Milton Friedman. The Fisher equation is:

$$M \times V = P \times T$$

In this equation, M = money supply, V = velocity of money, P = average price level, and T = volume of transactions of goods and services (real output). (The letters Q or Y sometimes take the place of T in this equation. All three are acceptable)

The impact of changes in the money supply depends on several factors:

- The velocity of money is stable. (Velocity of money is explained below.)
- Real output is limited to full-employment output.
- Any increase in the money supply causes an increase in price level.

If the quantity of money doubles, price levels also double, which causes inflation. As a result, consumers have to pay twice as much for the same amount of goods and services. By the same token, if the quantity of money drops, price levels drop, causing deflation, and consumers will pay less for goods and services. In the long run, the growth rate of the money supply determines the growth rate of the price level, and as a result, the rate of inflation.

In the graph Price Level and Increase in the Money Supply below, the immediate effect of increasing the money supply is to create an excess supply of money. Before, the economy was in equilibrium at point A. When the Fed increases the money supply, the supply curve shifts to the right. The price level and the value of money adjust to bring supply and demand back to equilibrium at point B. A rapid increase in the money supply can lead to a rapid increase in inflation as the production of goods and services lags. As you learned in the last topic, unemployment falls as a result of a rise in the rate of inflation.

Price Level and Increase in the Money Supply

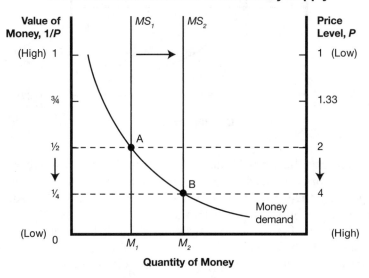

If the Fed decided to slow down an overheated economy by decreasing the money supply, the supply curve would have shifted to the left, and the point where it intersected the money demand curve would have become the new equilibrium. As a result of the decrease in the money supply the price level would have fallen, and the value of money would have risen. Any reduction in the money supply should be gradual to bring the economy to full employment. (Economists consider full employment to be the point at which the rate of unemployment is at or below the natural rate of unemployment.)

The Velocity of Money Another way of looking at the quantity theory of money is by considering something called the **velocity** of money. This is a ratio of nominal gross domestic product (GDP) to a measure of the money supply (either M1 or M2). It can be thought of as the rate of turnover in the money supply—that is, the number of times a unit of currency is used to purchase final goods and services included in the GDP, which is the total output of goods and services produced by an economy. It can be used alongside GDP, unemployment, and inflation as an indicator of an economy's health.

To calculate the velocity of money, divide the GDP by the money supply:

$$V = Y \div M$$

In this equation, V = velocity of money, Y = quantity of output (or GDP), and M = money supply (either M1 or M2). The Federal Reserve uses the M2 money supply to calculate the velocity of money, as in the following graph.

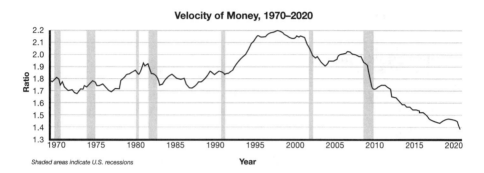

Velocity of Money, 1970–2020

Shaded areas indicate U.S. recessions

This graph shows the velocity of money calculated quarterly between the beginning of 1970 and the end of 2019. While it looks as though there were wild fluctuations over that period, in actuality they are really quite small, ranging from just over 1.4 to 2.2. Notice that the velocity of money dropped to its lowest levels in recent history in the second decade of the 21st century. This is partly because the Great Recession destroyed wealth, and those who didn't lose their homes, jobs, or retirement savings were afraid to spend money to buy anything they didn't need.

The Taylor Rule In 1993, Stanford University economist John Taylor published a study in which he proposed guidelines for central banks to use to alter interest rates in response to changes in economic conditions. The Taylor rule or principle was meant to help central banks set rates for short-term stabilization while maintaining long-term growth. It is based on three factors:

1. Targeted inflation levels versus actual inflation levels

2. Full-employment levels versus actual employment levels

3. A short-term interest rate consistent with full employment

In other words, the Taylor rule is used to determine what interest rates will be when there are shifts in the economy. It recommends that the Fed raise interest rates when inflation is high or when employment exceeds full employment levels, and lower interest rates when levels of inflation and employment are low. While the Taylor rule is unable to account for certain economic shocks such as a stock market or housing market crash, many central banks find it helpful in setting monetary policy.

1. In one to three paragraphs, explain how monetary policy affects inflation.

KEY TERMS

---

quantity theory of money   equation of exchange   velocity

MULTIPLE-CHOICE QUESTIONS

---

1. What economic indicator does the Fed prefer to use to measure inflation?

   (A) The discount rate

   (B) The consumer price index

   (C) The producers price index

   (D) The gross domestic product

   (E) The personal consumption expenditures price index

2. On the money market graph, what happens to the supply curve when the Fed increases the money supply?

   (A) It shifts to the right.

   (B) It shifts to the left.

   (C) It shifts upward.

   (D) It shifts downward.

   (E) It does not move because it is always a vertical line.

3. What happens to the demand for money when an economy enters an inflationary period?

   (A) The demand for money decreases.

   (B) The demand for money increases.

   (C) The demand for money stays the same.

   (D) The demand for money becomes stable.

   (E) The demand for money begins to determine the supply of money.

(a) Assume the United States is in an inflationary period. Indicate what would happen to the demand for money, aggregate demand, and, thereby, the price level and the level of unemployment.

(b) According to the quantity theory of money, calculate the velocity of money if the real output is $200 billion, the money supply is $50 billion, and the price level is 1.5.

(c) Explain the quantity theory of money.

(d) Calculate the nominal gross domestic product if the velocity of money is 3 and the money supply is $500.

(e) In your own words, explain what is meant by the velocity of money.

THINK AS AN ECONOMIST: *DETERMINE THE OUTCOME OF AN ECONOMIC SITUATION USING ECONOMIC CONCEPTS*

The velocity of money is the ratio of nominal gross domestic product (GDP) to a measure of the money supply (either M1 or M2). It can be thought of as the rate of turnover in the money supply—that is, the number of times a unit of currency is used to purchase final goods and services included in the GDP.

Apply the Skill

Look at the graph "Velocity of Money, 1970–2020" in the topic. The velocity of money from 1995 to 2000 ranged from 2.1 to 2.2. The velocity of money from 2015 to 2019 ranged from 1.5 to 1.4.

In which of those periods of time was the economy healthier, based on the velocity of money? Explain the reasoning for your answer.

Government Deficits
and the National Debt

Contrary to the prevailing wisdom in Washington these past few years, we cannot simply spend as we please, and defer the consequences to the next budget, the next administration, or the next generation. . . . This will not be easy. It will require us to make difficult decisions and face challenges we have long neglected.

Barack Obama, Remarks at Opening of Fiscal Responsibility Summit,
February 23, 2009

Essential Question: What are the long-run implications of monetary and fiscal policy as they pertain to the national debt?

Barack Obama began his presidency in the wake of the 2008 financial crisis. The month after he took office, Congress approved his economic stimulus package, which helped end the recession and start the nation on the road to economic recovery. But during Obama's eight years in office, the national debt, the amount of money the country owes its creditors, effectively doubled—from $10 trillion to $20 trillion. And, as if to show that increasing the national debt is a bipartisan exercise, the national debt increased another 21 percent in the first two years of the Trump administration. Does a large growing national debt spell doom for a country? How do the budgetary decisions made by politicians and their appointees affect people and countries in the long run?

Government Budgets

Government budgets typically include funding for education, public safety and defense, transportation, and social welfare (including unemployment compensation, retirement benefits, and health care), as well as subsidies for industries. Most government budgets are divided into two main categories:

- Purchase of goods and services for education, health care, transportation, defense, and so on.
- Transfer payments to individuals (through Social Security) or industries (through subsidies).

Much of a national budget may be mandatory expenditures such as retirement benefits and health care that cannot be cut without legislative action.

Governments get the majority of their money either directly or indirectly through taxes—taxes on income, profits, property, and goods (often as sales or value-added taxes) as well as Social Security payroll taxes. They may also rely for part of their funding on fines or taxes on polluters or others who inflict societal damage, profits from state-owned businesses such as petroleum companies, or the sale of goods and services.

A **balanced budget** is achieved when tax revenues are adequate to cover government expenditures. However, modern government budgets rarely balance, so most governments have to resort to borrowing, either by issuing financial securities or, in some cases, by taking out loans from private financial institutions or international organizations such as the World Bank.

Budget Surpluses A government's budget surplus is the difference between revenues and public spending for a given year. Budget surpluses are usually a result of fiscal policy that either increases taxes or reduces spending or both. When there is a surplus, the extra funds can be used to reduce the public debt, which in turn reduces interest payments and helps the economy in the future. A budget surplus can also be used to fund infrastructure, public works, new programs, or existing programs, such as retirement benefits or health care.

Budget Deficits If spending exceeds revenues, the difference is negative, and there is a budget deficit. A budget deficit can be caused by fiscal policy designed to stimulate the economy, such as tax cuts or increased government spending, or by unexpected events, such as wars, natural disasters, or unexpected shocks such as the oil embargoes of the 1970s. During recessions, a temporary deficit can be a good thing. When there is high unemployment, increased spending on unemployment insurance and economic stimulus packages, along with tax cuts, can help restore confidence and shore up the economy.

Budget deficits can have negative consequences in the long run, however. Year on year, budget deficits are added onto the national debt. The government must pay interest on this debt, which can be substantial. Any funds used to pay interest on the debt are funds denied for arguably more useful things—education, national parks, highways and bridges, national defense, or tax cuts.

Deficits can also slow economic growth since private saving can either be used to fund private investments or government deficits, but not both at the same time. When the government is forced to borrow, it can make it more difficult for individuals and businesses to finance new investments. This means that some businesses may find it harder to upgrade equipment or expand as quickly as they might like. Higher deficits over an extended period of time can have an adverse impact on productivity.

In order to reduce budget deficits, governments may need to change fiscal policy by raising taxes or cutting public spending, or by using a combination of the two. During the Clinton administration (1993–2001), the United States actually had a budget surplus for a few years, which resulted from a combination of tax increases, budget cuts, and a booming economy. But this period stands out as an anomaly in the recent past, with every other administration accruing national debt only over the past 50 years. Continuing budget deficits can lead to inflationary monetary policies. For example, the central bank may increase the money supply, which in turn leads to an increase in the price level. Continuing to increase the money supply will eventually result in a recession and a decline in economic activity.

There are only a few ways that governments can cover deficits other than through fiscal or monetary policies. They can print more fiat currency, but this poses the risk of devaluing the nation's currency and leading to hyperinflation, a situation in which prices rise rapidly and uncontrollably. Another option is to sell assets such as government real estate, gold, or petroleum reserves, or even government-owned and operated enterprises, such as railroads or utilities (power, water, and so on), thus raising revenues for the government.

Such privatization can have mixed results for investors, customers, and workers, however. This was the case in the United Kingdom, which sold its publicly-run rail, energy, water, telecommunications, airline, steel, and automotive enterprises in the 1980s when Margaret Thatcher was prime minister. Investors with access to enough capital were able to buy some of these enterprises at bargain prices, but these individuals were very few. Some industries became more efficient in private hands. But the power of unions in the UK was vastly diminished, which led to rising inequality and a pervasive sense of disaffection among the British working classes.

The Federal Budget The U.S. federal budget is a product of the government's fiscal policy and represents public spending. The president presents a budget proposal to Congress, which uses it as a guide in creating its own budget resolution and creating the appropriations bills that provide funding for the various categories of government expenditures. However, only a small part of the federal budget is discretionary, and that is the only part for which spending can be increased or decreased as part of the government's fiscal policy.

In the United States, individual and corporate income taxes and Social Security payroll taxes account for over 90 percent of revenues each year. Federal revenues have averaged 17.3 percent of the gross domestic product (GDP) over the past 50 years. In FY 2019, revenues were expected to be $3.451 trillion and expenditures $4.411 trillion, resulting in a deficit of $960 billion—nearly a trillion dollars. The pie charts on the following page break down revenues by source and outlays (expenditures) by category.

Federal Revenues and Expenditures for Fiscal Year 2019

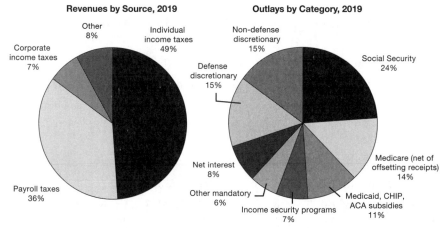

Revenues by Source, 2019

Other 8%

Corporate income taxes 7%

Individual income taxes 49%

Payroll taxes 36%

Outlays by Category, 2019

Non-defense discretionary 15%

Defense discretionary 15%

Social Security 24%

Medicare (net of offsetting receipts) 14%

Net interest 8%

Other mandatory 6%

Income security programs 7%

Medicaid, CHIP, ACA subsidies 11%

Source: Congressional Budget Office

Approximately 62 percent of the federal budget was allocated for mandatory expenditures: Social Security, Medicare, Medicaid and other health care expenses, income security programs, and miscellaneous mandatory expenses. Another 8 percent went to pay interest on national debt, money the government has had to borrow to make up for budget deficits. Two discretionary categories received 15 percent apiece. Defense discretionary funding includes allocations for the Pentagon and military programs. Non-defense discretionary funding pays for the government, education, infrastructure (such as federal highways), international affairs, and research, among other things.

Before the Great Depression, which began in 1929, policy makers aimed to make sure the federal budget was balanced except during major wars. As you can see in the following graph, the United States maintained a fairly balanced budget until the late 1960s, when there were occasional slight deficits. During the period of stagflation in the mid-1970s, those deficits were becoming larger, and they became larger still as a result of the Reagan-era tax cuts. President Clinton achieved a balanced budget in 1997 and budget surpluses for fiscal years 1998 to 2001.

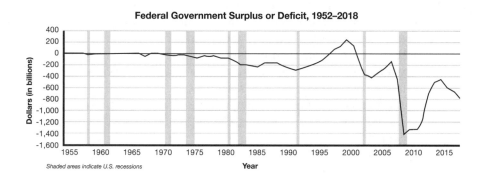

Federal Government Surplus or Deficit, 1952–2018

Dollars (in billions)

Shaded areas indicate U.S. recessions

Year

A number of factors contributed to the increasing budget deficit of the early 2000s:

- Rising mandatory spending on Social Security, Medicare, and similar programs
- Increased military spending as a result of the war on terror
- Recessions in 2001 and 2008–09 that slowed economic growth and reduced tax revenues
- The Economic Stimulus Act of 2009 that helped end the Great Recession
- The fact that U.S. salaries have not kept up with inflation
- Tax cuts under Presidents Bush, Obama, and Trump

As a result of the Trump tax cuts of 2017, deficits were projected to be $1 trillion a year between 2020 and 2029. Then, in 2020, massive federal borrowing in response to the coronavirus caused these projected deficits to increase sharply. As you will recall, tax cuts and increases are also a part of a government's fiscal policy.

National Debt

National debt is the amount of money a government owes its creditors. It is cumulative, which means that every year that a government operates at a deficit adds to its debt. Most modern governments spend more money than they take in, so they need to borrow money in order to fund essential programs. Total debt for most European countries is growing, but usually below the rate of growth of national income. Most national governments base the amount they borrow on what is required to maintain economic stability and growth. When handled responsibly, national debt can be used to promote long-term economic growth and prosperity.

However, at some point a national debt can get so large it creates a drag on the economy. Identifying this point is complicated because it reflects a country's overall economic strength. For example, in 2020, the United States had the eighth-highest national debt in the world, and it was one of the 16 (out of 184) nations with a debt-to-GDP ratio above 100 percent. This meant that the federal government owed more money than the entire output of the country for one year. Some economists were concerned that the debt was so large it would slow growth. Some economists responded that other wealthy countries, such as Singapore, had debts that were more than 100 percent of their GDP, while many poor countries, such as Bangladesh and Guatemala, had debts less than 50 percent of their GDPs.

One important factor in determining how much money a government can borrow is whether investors are willing to lend it money. The U.S. government can borrow extensively because investors trust it will not default (be unable or unwilling to pay its debts). The United States has come close to defaulting only when Congress has threatened to cut off funds to repay money that has already been borrowed.

Ownership of the U.S. National Debt The federal debt falls into two categories:

- Public debt accounts for about two-thirds of the money borrowed by the government. This includes U.S. Treasury bills, notes, and bonds sold to individuals, financial institutions, corporations, and foreign governments. The governments of China and Japan each own between 5 percent and 10 percent of the national debt.

- Intragovernmental debt accounts for the other one-third of federal borrowing. Federal agencies such as the Social Security Trust Fund, military and federal employee retirement funds, and the Federal Reserve each purchases debt with surplus funds that it wants to save with very little risk for future use.

As of January 1, 2020, the U.S. national debt was $23.2 trillion dollars and growing rapidly, while the GDP was $21.727 trillion. The Federal Reserve estimated that by 2029, the interest alone on the national debt will amount to approximately 17 percent of the GDP—about the same percentage as the entire federal budget currently accounts for. This is money that will not be available for other uses. The following graph shows how the federal debt has grown since 1966.

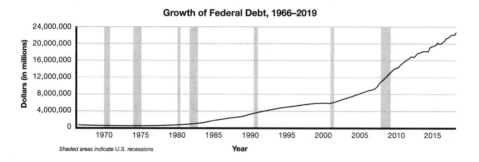

Growth of Federal Debt, 1966–2019

The high debt-to-GDP ratio theoretically increases the risk of holding government securities, and thus makes them less attractive to investors. As demand for Treasury securities decreases, interest rates must be increased. The value of the dollar is tied to the value of Treasury securities, so lower demand for them also decreases the value of the dollar. This in turn means that foreign holders of Treasury securities get paid in currency that is worth less, which will encourage foreign investors to look elsewhere. If these things come to pass, the portion of its annual budget the government is forced to pay as interest on the debt will explode.

Reducing the Debt Over the years, political candidates and legislators have proposed and debated a number of ideas for federal debt reduction. There have been several attempts to pass a constitutional amendment requiring a balanced budget. The movement began in the late 1970s, when Republicans tried to cut spending under the Carter administration. There were other attempts to pass a balanced budget amendment in the 1980s when the deficit shot up following the Reagan administration's tax cuts, and in 1995. Congress again failed to pass a balanced budget amendment in 2011.

Congress has the ability to limit the national debt by means of a debt ceiling. This is the maximum amount of money that the U.S. government can borrow by issuing bonds. Between 2001 and 2019, however, Congress increased the debt ceiling 14 times, and the 2019 Bipartisan Budget Act suspended the debt ceiling until July 31, 2021.

These and other struggles in regard to the national debt show how contentious and difficult the issue is. Debating how large a deficit the United States can carry and still remain prosperous is an ongoing political issue.

ANSWER THE TOPIC ESSENTIAL QUESTION

1. In one to three paragraphs, describe the long-run implications of monetary and fiscal policy.

KEY TERMS

balanced budget	budget deficit
budget surplus	national debt

MULTIPLE-CHOICE QUESTIONS

1. What effect does fiscal policy have on a government's budget?

   (A) Fiscal policy alone determines the amount of revenue a government will have to work with.

   (B) Fiscal policy determines both the revenues and outlays in a government's budget.

   (C) Fiscal policy can increase or decrease the money supply.

   (D) Fiscal policy determines the rate of interest that the government will pay on its debt.

   (E) Fiscal policy has no effect on a government's budget.

2. A balanced budget is achieved when

(A) tax revenues exceed government spending

(B) government spending exceeds tax revenues

(C) the government stops excess spending and lowers income tax

(D) tax revenues can cover all government expenditures

(E) the government increases its outlays regardless of tax revenues

3. The national debt is created when a government

(A) operates at a deficit more than it operates at a surplus

(B) spends more money than it takes in

(C) borrows money from other entities and receives equal amount of tax revenue

(D) decreases its spending and increases its tax revenues

(E) engages in expansionary fiscal policy

FREE-RESPONSE QUESTIONS

(a) What other sources of income do governments have in addition to taxes?

(b) Identify and describe the two major categories of government expenditures.

(c) How is a government's budget surplus calculated?

(d) What is the difference between government deficit and government debt?

(e) What steps can governments take to reduce or eliminate debt?

THINK AS AN ECONOMIST: *DETERMINE THE OUTCOME OF AN ECONOMIC SITUATION USING ECONOMIC CONCEPTS*

Each year Congress passes a budget that the president signs. That budget shows either a surplus (if receipts are greater than spending) or a deficit (if the reverse is true). The last budget surplus in the United States came in 2001. To fund the deficits, the government must borrow money. The total amount borrowed is the total federal debt.

Because debt numbers are so large, economists use comparative measures to make them more understandable. One of those comparatives is debt per capita, or per person. Like GDP per capita, this simply divides the gross number (dollars of debt) by the number of people. Some economists argue this is the most revealing measure since it puts the debt in personal terms.

Another comparative is debt as a percentage of GDP, which measures total debt against the country's total economic output. Some economists prefer this way of viewing the debt. They point out that the national debt reached a high of 119 percent in 1946—reflecting spending for World War II—but fell in subsequent years, reaching a low of 31 percent in 1971.

Apply the Skill

Study the figures on the national debt in five years over the first two decades of the 21st century. Look at the rate of change for each of the three measures. Based on these numbers, what do you think is the likely economic outcome if the federal debt continues to grow at similar rates? Explain why you think so.

FEDERAL DEBT						
	Total Debt (billion)	Change	Debt Per Capita	Change	Debt as Percentage of GDP	Change
2000	$5,674.2	n/a	$19,947.77	n/a	55.0%	n/a
2005	$7,932.7	+39.8%	$26,729.39	+25.4%	60.4%	+9.8%
2010	$13,561.6	+71.0%	$43,737.02	+63.6%	89.9%	+48.8%
2015	$18,150.6	+33.8%	$56,513.16	+29.2%	98.9%	+10.0%
2019	$22,719.4	+25.2%	$69,063.79	+22.2%	105.5%	+6.7%

Sources: Federal Reserve Bank of St Louis

Under Keynesian economics, a government will help an economy in recession if it spends money. When the U.S. federal government was implementing policies to bring the country out of the Great Depression, it used government programs to put people back to work, invested in infrastructure, and shored up the financial system. More recently, the federal government spent large amounts of money to help mitigate the effects of the Great Recession of 2008–2009.

However, Keynesian economics does not provide a reason for deficit spending in times of expansion. "The boom, not the slump," Keynes once remarked, "is the right time for austerity at the Treasury."

Towards a Balanced Budget Conservative politicians and economists believe that the best policy to reduce national debt is to not incur it in the first place. This would require a balanced budget or a budget where spending amounts equal revenue. Chris Edwards, director of tax policy at the Cato Institute, believes that long term U.S. deficit spending risks putting the economy in a "death spiral" in which the amount of money needed to service the debt—pay interest on the debt to creditors—will consume large amounts of the federal budget. If there is too much debt, the country will scare away investors and the economy will struggle.

Maya MacGuineas, director of the Committee for a Responsible Federal Budget, believes that working toward a balanced budget and reducing the national debt would have the following benefits to the U.S. economy: (1) greater investment and economic growth, (2) higher income and wages, (3) lower interest rates, (4) declining government interest payments, (5) increased ability to respond to problems, and (6) reduced risk of financial problems.

Incurring Debt As stated, Keynesian economic theories dictate that during an economic downturn, government spending should increase, even if it means the federal government must incur debt to do so. The reasoning behind this is shared by many economists, even those who believe in a balanced budget.

In a paper titled, "Rising Government Debt: Causes and Solutions for a Decades-Old Trend," economist Pierre Yared explained how incurring debt can be useful at times. First, he explained that if trying to raise revenue with tax increases would inhibit economic growth or recovery in the short term, issuing longer term bonds that can be paid back when the economy has recovered is a useful expansionary fiscal tool. Second, in times of recession, credit markets become more inflexible as financial institutions are less likely to extend credit. The federal government becomes the "borrower of first resort" and, using money it borrows, can then free up the movement of financial capital by enacting business and consumer tax cuts or issuing loans to businesses.

The handling of issues related to national debt is politically treacherous, though, as implementing policies to reduce the debt comes with many hard decisions The debate between those who believe in a balanced budget and those who view government debt to be a useful fiscal policy is ongoing.

Topic 5.5

Crowding Out

"If government spends an amount equal to 50 percent of the national income, only 50 percent is left to be available for private purposes, and that is true however the 50 percent that government spends is financed."

Milton Friedman, Letter to Chris Edwards (1993)

Essential Question: What is crowding out, and how does fiscal policy affect it?

The national income is measurable year by year. As Milton Friedman points out, if the government spends half of that amount, only half of it is left for the private sector. As you learned in Topic 4.7, the same is true of the loanable funds market: the supply of loanable funds has a limit, so when there is a budget deficit and the government is forced to borrow, a reduction in the quantity of funds available for private investment occurs.

What Is Crowding Out?

The phenomenon is known as **crowding out**—the adverse effects of public sector borrowing on the private sector. Crowding out occurs when a government's expansionary fiscal policy increases the budget deficit—in other words, the government is spending more than it takes in. This can happen because of tax cuts or increases in public spending or a combination of the two fiscal policies.

The idea of crowding out gained popularity in the 1970s and 1980s as monetarists—economists such as Milton Friedman who focused on using monetary policy rather than fiscal policy to improve an economy's performance—reacted to the growing share of the gross domestic product for which the public sector accounted because of increasing public spending.

How Does Crowding Out Work? As you learned in the last topic, a budget deficit exists when government spending exceeds its tax revenues. In order to finance such deficits, the government needs to borrow money. It does this by selling Treasury bills, notes, and bonds to the public. In order to sell more bonds, the government may have to raise interest rates on its bonds to make them more attractive to buyers. Higher interest rates on Treasury securities drives up interest rates elsewhere in the economy, which discourages private investment and spending.

The larger the budget deficit is, the more demand there is for loanable funds. As you will recall from Topic 4.7, the supply of loanable funds is national saving—the sum of private saving and government saving. When there is a budget deficit, government saving is negative, reducing national saving and therefore the quantity of loanable funds available. Not only is national saving reduced, but government borrowing on this scale takes an ever-greater percentage of all the savings available for investment, crowding out businesses that want to invest in physical capital.

As the demand for loanable funds rises, so does the real interest rate. This higher interest rate is one way in which government borrowing crowds out private investment, since higher interest rates tend to reduce private borrowing. Even a slight rise in the interest rate can be enough to discourage private borrowing for expansion. If the interest rate gets high enough, the number of entities able to afford the cost of borrowing (other than the government) would shrink drastically. The following graphs show the effects of a budget deficit on the supply of, and demand for, loanable funds.

Effect of Government Budget Deficits on Loanable Funds

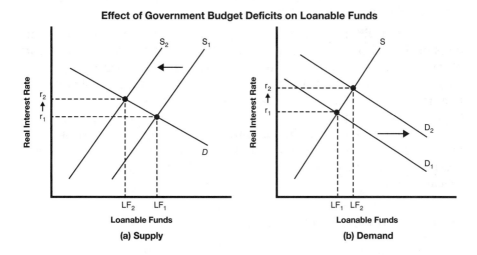

(a) Supply

(b) Demand

In the graph (a), a budget deficit lowers national saving, so the supply of loanable funds decreases, and the supply curve shifts to the left, from S_1 to S_2. The equilibrium interest rate rises from r_1 to r_2, and the equilibrium quantity of loanable funds drops. In graph (b), as the budget deficit grows, the demand for loanable funds shifts to the right, from D_1 to D_2. The equilibrium interest rate rises as well, from r_1 to r_2.

The Effects of Crowding Out

The purpose of expansionary fiscal policy is usually to stimulate GDP and create jobs. Crowding out has a tendency to limit the stimulus because higher government spending causes private sector spending and investment to drop. Since the government and the private sector invest in different goods and services, this shift can have a large impact on how the economy develops.

When Crowding Out Does Not Occur Not all deficit spending causes crowding out. Sometimes it results in crowding in. This occurs when government investments stimulate additional private investment. For example, when the government invests in infrastructure, such as roads, bridges, seaports, and airports, private industry can deliver goods to market more easily. Power generators and telecommunications facilities can help create new industries or bring economic prosperity to areas that were formerly depressed.

Public spending on education and research also has a positive effect on the economy. Programs for early childhood education, like Head Start, aim to raise children out of poverty. Most college students today benefit from federal student grant or loan programs. Government-funded medical research has improved health and extended life expectancy.

In addition, many common consumer products are at least partially the result of research for defense and the space program. The Internet, lasers, microwaves, LEDs, solar cells, penicillin, CAT scans, LASIK, prosthetic limbs, EpiPens, GPS, drones, camera phones, wireless headsets, duct tape, super glue, and memory foam are just a few products that were originally developed for use by the defense or space programs.

Long-Run Effects If crowding out results in a reduction in private investment, it also reduces economic growth over the long run. A large part of investment spending consists of businesses expanding their operations or buying new equipment, for which they usually borrow money. Higher interest rates reduce borrowing, which means less investment in capital. This reduces the economy's ability to produce goods and services in the long run. It also discourages the use of credit by consumers to make large purchases or obtain mortgages, which slows economic growth. This in turn reduces government tax revenues, leading to even more government borrowing, which can become a vicious cycle.

ANSWER THE TOPIC ESSENTIAL QUESTION

1. In one to three paragraphs, explain what crowding out is and how fiscal policy affects it.

KEY TERMS

crowding out

---

1. What is the main cause of crowding out?

    (A) A reduction in the money supply

    (B) An increase in the money supply

    (C) Contractionary fiscal policy

    (D) Expansionary fiscal policy

    (E) Deflation

2. Why does the supply of loanable funds decrease when there is a budget deficit?

    (A) There is a greater demand for loanable funds by the public.

    (B) There is a reduced demand for loanable funds by the government.

    (C) There is a decrease in national saving.

    (D) The public sector gets crowded out of the loanable funds market.

    (E) The private sector demands more loanable funds because of the low interest rate.

3. Which of the following is one of the effects of crowding out?

    (A) Reduced private investment

    (B) Increased private investment

    (C) Lower unemployment

    (D) Larger budget deficits

    (E) Lower interest rates

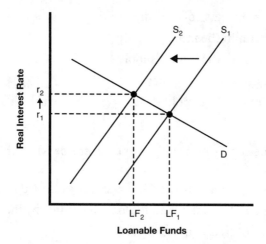

(a) How does the graph above illustrate crowding out?

(b) What effect do government budget deficits have on private investment?

(c) How does crowding out limit the economic stimulus intended by expansionary fiscal policy?

(d) What are some ways that government spending can stimulate the economy by increasing the demand for goods?

(e) What are the effects of crowding out in the long run?

THINK AS AN ECONOMIST: *DETERMINE THE EFFECTS OF CHANGES ON OTHER ECONOMIC MARKETS*

In trying to determine what economic policies to implement, government decision-makers must consider the impact of policy changes on multiple markets. For example, they may consider an increase in tariffs with a trading partner in order to protect a particular industry. However, those higher tariffs can have an impact on consumer spending. If the tariffs cover a wide range of products and are high enough, consumer spending could drop. That can have an impact on employment. Policy makers need to consider all possible ramifications of the policies they implement before moving forward.

Apply the Skill

Suppose the federal government is running a trillion-dollar deficit with a GDP of $21.2 trillion. A spike in unemployment leads Congress and the president to sign a $500 billion stimulus package. That package has to be funded by increased borrowing. What would the likely short-term effects of this borrowing be on the bond market and the market for loanable funds? What are the likely long-term effects on private research and development and employment? Explain the reason for each development.

Economic Growth

Productivity is the most important determinant of the standard of living of a group of people, a nation or a planet.

Bill Conerly, "Productivity and Economic Growth," *Forbes*, May 19, 2015

Essential Question: How does the economy expand and contract but grow in the long run?

Worker productivity drives long-term economic growth. Essentially, it refers to how well a business or an economy does things, how efficiently it uses its time and workers. Increasing productivity means being able to accomplish more in the same amount of time. Economists use different methods to measure economic growth and the factors that drive it.

What Is Economic Growth?

Economic growth refers to an increase in the aggregate production of goods and services in an economy from one period of time to another. It often correlates with increased **productivity**, or output per unit of input, which is usually calculated as a ratio of gross domestic product (GDP) to hours worked.

Determinants of Economic Growth Several factors affect economic growth:

- **Physical capital.** An increase in the amount or quality of capital goods, such as buildings, machinery, vehicles, and tools, tends to improve productivity.

- **Human capital.** As workers become more skilled through education, training, or experience, they become more productive. The higher the average level of education is in an economy, the higher the human capital and labor productivity are.

- **Labor force.** Increasing the labor force tends to increase an economy's overall production.

- **Technology.** Innovations and inventions such as the assembly line and robotics make existing businesses more productive and also can spawn new industries.

Economic growth is heavily dependent on rates of saving and investment. As you have learned, major capital investments often are funded by loans, and the loanable funds market is dependent on national saving—the total of private and public saving.

As economic growth increases profits for businesses, stock prices rise. This gives companies capital to invest in expansion. Unemployment decreases, and people have more money to spend on goods and services, and those purchases add to the GDP. More people in the workforce also means increased income tax revenues, which generate funds that governments can invest in more human capital, infrastructure, and research, adding to productivity. These factors make economic growth essential for improving people's standard of living.

Measuring Economic Growth There are several ways of measuring economic growth. Rather than focusing on the total *amount* of goods produced, economists look at the *value* of those goods. As you will recall, one of the functions of money is as a unit of account. The World Bank uses gross national income to measure growth.

In the United States, economic growth is most commonly measured in changes in the dollar value of the real gross domestic product, or **real GDP**, which is the nominal GDP adjusted for inflation. When all other factors are equal, there has been economic growth if the real GDP increases from one year to the next. (Note that GDP measures final production—for example, the finished automobile, not all the individual parts that went into it. It also includes exports, but not imports.)

Because the size of the workforce can fluctuate, the **real GDP per capita** is a better indicator of economic growth. To determine this, divide the real GDP by the total population:

$$Real\ GDP\ per\ capita = \frac{Real\ GDP}{Population}$$

The Bureau of Economic Analysis (BEA) keeps records on real GDP, and the Federal Reserve Bank of St. Louis maintains a database of real GDP per capita since 1947 on its website. The real GDP per capita is used to compare the standard of living between countries or over time. As shown in the following graph, real GDP per capita has generally been rising but has fallen during recessions.

Real GDP Per Capita, 1948–2019

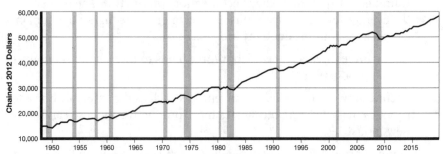

The production possibilities curve can be used to determine possible outcomes of additional resources, such as the expansion of the labor force, better management techniques, or improved technology. Any or all of these resources could potentially allow goods to be produced more efficiently. In these cases, the resulting differences can be represented graphically, as shown in Topic 1.2.

Phases of Economic Growth

As you have learned, economies go through business cycles. In the United States, the National Bureau of Economic Research (NBER) tracks business cycle stages using quarterly GDP growth rates. Analysts track the business cycle to determine whether an economy is expanding or contracting. If an economy is growing too fast, it overheats, and inflation kicks in. As people lose confidence in the economy, it contracts. If it contracts too much, it becomes a recession. The graph below shows how an economy can expand and contract. Expansion is the ascending or rising line, the peak is where it changes direction and begins to descend or fall as the economy contracts until it reaches the trough, or lowest point, before beginning to ascend again as the economy begins to expand. Periods of recession have a shaded background.

Expansions and Contractions of the U.S. Economy, 1948–2019

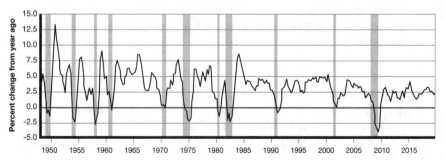

Long-Run Economic Growth

Viewed in terms of cycles of expansion and contraction, the economy between 1948 and 2019 appears to be very volatile. In the long run, however, real economic growth during the same period was relatively steady, with a few minor exceptions, as seen in the following graph. Notice that this graph follows a trajectory very similar to that of the real GDP per capita graph on the following page, although the vertical axis in this graph is in billions of dollars and the vertical axis in that graph is in dollars.

Real Economic Growth, 1948–2019

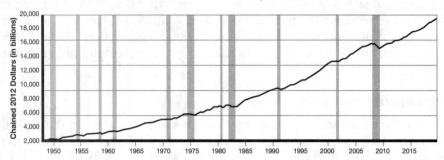

Of the major factors that drive economic growth—increased human and physical capital, increased labor, and improved technology—technology is the most influential. Additional output as a result of adding an extra unit of capital or labor declines over time, in accordance with the law of diminishing returns. This means that a country cannot sustain long-run growth just by adding capital or labor. However, the law of diminishing returns does not apply to human capital and technology, partly because there is no way of measuring them.

Aggregate Production Function The **aggregate production function** is a measure that shows how an economy's aggregate output, or real GDP, depends on the determinants of economic growth: physical and human capital, labor force, and technology. Thus, aggregate employment and aggregate output are directly related because, when other factors are constant, firms need to employ more workers in order to produce more output. This is captured by the aggregate production function.

Sustained economic growth occurs only when labor productivity—the amount of output per worker—increases steadily over time. Two primary factors determine labor productivity: the quantity of capital per hour worked and the level of technology. Technological change can be accomplished by means of better machinery and equipment, increased worker knowledge and skills, and better management and organization of production.

Productivity is determined by the level of technology and physical and human capital per worker. The aggregate production function shows that there is a positive relationship of per capita output to both physical and human capital per worker. Output per employed worker is a measure of average labor productivity. The graph on the following page shows how productivity depends on the quantities of capital per worker.

Aggregate Production Function

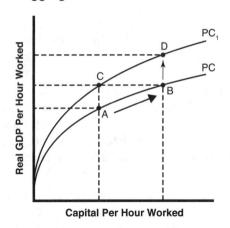

In the graph, if the amount of capital per worker changes, this is shown by a movement along the production function (from A to B, or from C to D). On the other hand, if the level of technology changes, it is a shift of the production function (from A to C, or from B to D). Notice that the production functions are concave: their slopes decrease as the variable on the horizontal axis increases. This is a result of the law of diminishing returns, which states that when one input increases (here, capital per hour worked), while the other input is fixed (here, level of technology), those increases yield smaller gains in terms of real GDP.

A study of nine major advanced economies between 1990 and 2013 found negative correlations between the contributions of either labor or capital alone and economic growth, but a positive correlation for all three factors, suggesting that the real driver of long-run economic growth is technological progress.

Economic Growth in Historical Perspective

The British economist Thomas Malthus made a dire prediction in an essay he published in 1798: the human race, he believed, was destined to starve to death due to overpopulation. He used arithmetic and geometric series to prove that food increases more slowly than population. According to Malthus, food production could only increase at an arithmetic rate, which means adding the same quantity each year. For example, the series 1, 3, 5, 7, 9 is arithmetic because each number is 2 more than the previous one.

However, population could increase at a geometric rate, multiplying by the same ratio each year. For example, the series 1, 2, 4, 8, 16 is geometric because each number is twice the previous one. He concluded that the reason humans were not dying off in the face of these odds must be a result of economic choices, such as limiting family size. Technological advances in agriculture also played a large part in increasing food production.

Diverging Economies In 1750, the empires of China and India accounted for about two-thirds of global output. Europe and North America were small, both in population and in economic production. Then the Industrial Revolution took hold, first in Great Britain and then in the rest of Europe and North America. By 1970, the world diverged into two groups: the West and "the Rest," the developing world. In the West, industrialization, technology, government support, and a market economy eventually led to great wealth, improved health care, and lower birth rates. It included 1 billion people, a life expectancy of 70 years, two-child families, and an average income of $10,000 or more per person. The "Rest" consisted of 3 billion people with shorter life expectancies, three times as many children per woman, and one-tenth the income of the West.

Convergence Between 1970 and 2000, those diverging trends were beginning to be replaced by convergence. Developing nations rapidly began to catch up with the West, starting with Japan and then Korea, China, India, and elsewhere. Most countries employed some mixture of elements used in the West: industrialization, technology, government support, and a market economy. Economic changes led to dramatic social changes. As countries provided basic education and better health care, child mortality declined and people had smaller families. If convergence continues, the gap between the West and other countries will be difficult to notice.

ANSWER THE TOPIC ESSENTIAL QUESTION

1. In one to three paragraphs, explain how the economy expands and contracts but grows in the long run.

KEY TERMS

| economic growth | real GDP | aggregate production function |
| productivity | real GDP per capita | |

MULTIPLE-CHOICE QUESTIONS

1. The term *human capital* refers to
   (A) the number of workers in an economy
   (B) equipment furnished to workers by their employers for use on the job
   (C) cash recruitment incentives offered to new employees
   (D) skills acquired through education, training, or experience
   (E) capital per hour worked

2. Which of the following is most likely to promote long-term economic growth?

(A) Private savings

(B) Technological progress and increased human capital

(C) Production of consumer goods

(D) Private consumption of consumer goods

(E) Public consumption of consumer goods

3. An increase in capital stock will have which of the following effects on income per capita and aggregate production?

	Income Per Capita	Aggregate Production
(A)	Decrease	Increase
(B)	Decrease	Decrease
(C)	Decrease	Indeterminate
(D)	Increase	Decrease
(E)	Increase	Increase

FREE-RESPONSE QUESTIONS

(a) Briefly explain what real GDP is and how it is used to calculate real GDP per capita.

(b) Assume the country of Vinland has a population of 100 and real gross domestic product in 2020 was $550,000 and the country of Taraq has a population of 180 and real gross domestic product in 2020 was $630,000. Which country's real gross domestic product per capita is greater?

(c) List and explain the four factors that contribute to long-term economic growth.

(d) In what way does savings factor into economic growth?

(e) Explain how aggregate output and aggregate employment are related.

THINK AS AN ECONOMIST: *USE ECONOMIC PRINCIPLES TO EXPLAIN HOW A SPECIFIC OUTCOME OCCURS WHEN THERE ARE MULTIPLE CONTRIBUTING VARIABLES*

Economists identify four factors that can play a role in economic growth: increased physical capital, increased human capital, increased size of the labor force, and improved technology. They have determined that of these factors, technology produces the highest levels of growth.

Apply the Skill

As stated in the text, economic growth correlates with productivity. The Bureau of Labor Statistics measures productivity as unit labor cost, which is found with this formula:

$$Unit\ labor\ cost = \frac{Total\ labor\ compensation/hours\ worked}{Output/hours}$$

Given this formula, rank the four factors that play a role in economic growth from greatest to least contribution to productivity. Explain the reasons for the order of your ranking.

Public Policy and Economic Growth

"Long-term economic growth depends mainly on nonmonetary factors such as population growth and workforce participation, the skills and aptitudes of our workforce, the tools at their disposal, and the pace of technological advance."

Jerome Powell, "The Economic Outlook and Monetary Policy," February 22, 2017

Essential Question: How do public policies affect economic growth?

As you will recall, economic growth is usually measured as the percentage of increase in real gross domestic product from one period to the next. Between 1950 and 2014, real GDP grew at an average rate of 3.3 percent a year. The Congressional Budget Office projected a GDP growth rate of only 2.1 percent a year through 2025. The CBO reasoned that the economy would have a reduction in the number of hours worked as baby boomers retired and fewer people entered the workforce to replace them. This problem would be compounded by the fact that businesses would be reluctant to invest in capital stock when the labor force was growing slowly. What could federal, state, and local governments do to increase the growth rate?

What Is Public Policy?

Public policy is a collective term for the plans and actions at any level of government that affect that government's constituents:

- It is policy made by the government, although it may be the result of ideas from members of the public outside the government.

- It is what the government chooses to do or not to do about a particular issue on behalf of the public.

- It may take the form of laws or regulations with the intention of solving a problem or bringing about a desired state.

- It is an ongoing process that evolves over time.

Anyone in the government may initiate public policy—members of the executive, legislative, and judicial branches of government at any level; agency bureaucrats, political parties, interest groups, the media; even an individual who sees a problem or issue that needs to be addressed by the government.

How Does Public Policy Affect Economic Growth?

Many public policies affect a country's (or state's, or city's) economy, either directly or indirectly, and sometimes both directly *and* indirectly. You have already learned how fiscal and monetary policies can be used to directly encourage economic growth. Besides tax cuts, increasing the money supply, or reducing interest rates, other public policies can be used to promote economic growth, some of which involve public spending.

Human Capital A country can improve its long-term economic growth by investing in education and health care. As you will recall, human capital is knowledge, skills, and experience necessary to do a job. Investment in education is at least as important to a country's long-run economic success as investment in physical capital. Studies have shown a direct relationship between education and a country's GDP per capita: As the average number of years of education increases, so does the GDP per capita. In the United States, each year of schooling a person has raises that person's wage by an average of 10 percent.

Investing in education ensures that a country will have the necessary human capital to ensure long-term economic growth. Thus, one way governments can raise living standards is by providing good schools and encouraging people to take advantage of them. Another benefit of education is the greater probability that recipients of that education will generate new ideas that will further improve productivity and thus lead to greater economic growth.

Health policy also shapes human capital, and hence productivity and economic growth. Healthier workers are more productive workers. In the United States, the government has implemented several policies to promote nutrition (including SNAP, the federal government's Supplemental Nutrition Assistance Program) and immunization, control tobacco, and combat obesity and substance abuse. It has also provided health care or health insurance through the Veterans Health Administration, the Medicaid program (for low-income individuals), and the Affordable Care Act.

Property Rights The issue of **property rights,** the ownership and control of a specific good or resource, goes to the very heart of how a market economy works. Governments, groups, and individuals own and use property. Rights include a legitimate claim to use a good, to earn income from it, and to transfer it to another person or entity. Property rights protect not just land or other property, but also the goods, services, and finances associated with it. Property ownership falls into three primary categories:

- **Private property** is property owned and managed by an individual or a legal group of owners, such as a corporation or partnership.

- **Public property** is property owned by the public at large and controlled by the government or community. Schools, highways, and parks are examples of public property.

- **Collective property** is controlled or owned by a group or combination of individuals or entities that jointly control access to and use of the property. Grazing land in the U.S. West is an example.

Protecting property rights is a responsibility of the federal, state, and local governments. By enforcing the rights of property owners, governments play an important role in a market economy. For example, laws discourage theft and courts make sure that buyers and sellers live up to the terms of their contracts.

Free Trade Free trade allows countries to concentrate on producing the goods in which they have a comparative advantage and makes trade mutually beneficial. Since World War II, the United States and Europe have generally supported freer trade. Governments can promote free trade by reducing tariffs, quotas, and other barriers. Tariffs are duties that governments impose on imported or exported goods, and quotas are limits on the amounts of goods that can be imported. Both are government policies designed to protect domestic producers.

Throughout modern history, governments across the world passed or raised tariffs in order to raise money or to protect industries from foreign competition. This has often been successful in building domestic industry, but it includes a trade-off. The burden of tariffs has traditionally fallen on consumers. For example, after President Donald Trump imposed tariffs on trade with China in 2018, the effect was a reduction in U.S. real income of $1.4 billion per month by the end of the year.

In addition, in an integrated global economy, tariffs that help one industry can harm another within the same country. Products assembled in one country often include parts manufactured around the world. For example, cars made in U.S. auto plants typically include between 25 percent and 60 percent parts made in other countries. If producers cannot get the parts they need at the price they expect, they either cannot assemble a product or they have to raise the cost of production. Either of these conditions can cause companies to reduce production and lay off workers. One study found that the steel tariffs alone could cause 40,000 workers in the U.S. automobile industry to lose their jobs. And when China retaliated with tariffs on U.S. soybeans, Chinese importers turned to Brazil, leaving U.S. farmers in the lurch. Once a market has been lost, it is difficult to get it back.

Research and Development One way in which the government encourages research and development is by protecting intellectual property through copyrights, patents, trademarks, and trade secrets. Most technological advances come from private research by firms and individual inventors. By allowing them to profit from their inventions, the patent system provides an incentive for individuals and firms to engage in research, thereby driving innovation. Technological advances by U.S. inventors have given rise to new industries, raised living standards, and made the United States the innovative, wealthy, and powerful country it is today.

The government also conducts research directly by hiring scientists, engineers, and others to work on specific projects. NASA, the National Science Foundation, and the National Institutes of Health are just a few of the many government agencies that engage in research. The government also finances research and development indirectly, through grants and tax breaks. These grants are usually awarded to fund research that is valuable to the government or to society as a whole. Much of government-funded research is for high-risk, basic research that underlies future innovation.

Environment Environmental policies include laws and regulations aimed at protecting the environment, conserving natural resources, and slowing climate change. Many of these regulations attempt to protect public health by improving air and water quality, regulating waste disposal, and dealing with oil and chemical spills. Opponents of government regulations argue that the costs of implementing environmental policies harms business and results in a loss of jobs.

Government can also use tax policies, research funding, and direct investments to encourage use of certain types of energy. For example, it has provided various subsidies for fossil fuel industries such as coal and oil as a way to promote inexpensive energy. In more recent years, it began to support non-fossil fuels. In 2007, the U.S. journalist and author Thomas Friedman coined the term *Green New Deal* to describe efforts to combat climate change by transitioning from fossil fuels to renewable sources of energy, such as solar panels and wind turbines.

Supply-Side Economics

Classical economic theory holds that supply, or the production of goods or services, is the main driver of economic growth. **Supply-side fiscal policies** are government attempts to create a better climate for business through tax cuts and deregulation with the goal of increasing productivity and shifting the long-run aggregate supply curve to the right. Proponents argue that if companies temporarily overproduce, the excess inventory will cause prices to fall and consumer demand will increase to offset the excess supply.

Supply-Side Economics

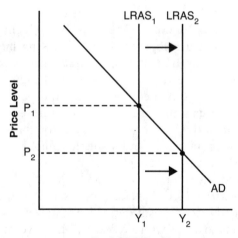

Real GDP Per Year

Proponents of supply-side economics believe that lower tax rates will boost employment and spur investment in capital. They argue that any reductions in the tax rates will be offset by increased revenues as a result of increased employment and productivity. They tend to favor reducing government spending to free up more resources for the private sector. "Supply-siders" also tend to favor free markets and fewer government regulations on businesses.

The Laffer Curve In 1974, the economist Arthur Laffer developed what has come to be known as the Laffer Curve. The idea behind it is that lower tax rates, along with less government regulation, boost economic growth. The Laffer Curve formed the basis for the supply-side economic policies of President Ronald Reagan, popularly known as Reaganomics or "trickle-down" economics.

Figure 20.2 **Laffer Curve**

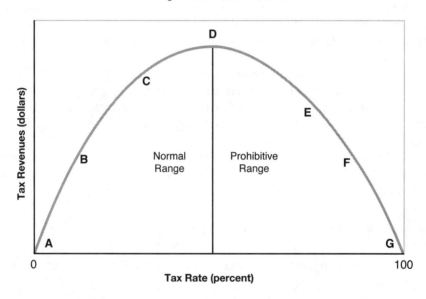

At the left side of the curve, a tax rate of zero results in no government revenue and, as a result, no government. At the right side of the curve, with a tax rate of 100 percent, there would also be no tax revenue because no one would work if the government took all personal income and business profits. At point B, there is some tax revenue, and at point C there is even more, but as the government keeps raising taxes, there are diminishing additional revenues. Eventually, after reaching the maximum level at point D, higher tax rates actually result in lower revenue, which is why Laffer referred to this as the prohibitive range.

You will notice that Laffer did not include any actual percentages in his diagram. Tax cuts increase government revenue in the prohibitive range. Then they increase consumer spending and demand, which encourages business growth and hiring, resulting in increased government revenues in the long run.

This in turn helps reduce government spending on social welfare programs such as unemployment benefits.

Limitations of Supply-Side Economics If taxes are lowered outside the prohibitive range, the economy will not be stimulated enough to offset the reduced revenues. Demand drops and business suffers from lack of customers. During a recession or period of slow growth, tax cuts harm the economy. Government spending on social welfare programs and jobs boost the economy and keep it from sliding into a depression.

In order to work as Laffer predicted, companies would need to use increased revenue from tax cuts to create jobs. If they perceive potential demand for their goods and services, they are likely to do this. However, if they predict that a lack of demand means that increasing production will not increase profits, they have no incentive to create more jobs. Instead of using money from tax cuts to create jobs, businesses are likely to save it, send it to stockholders as dividends, buy back stock, or expand operations overseas. As the U.S. economy has become more technology intensive and less labor intensive, businesses are more likely to use tax cuts to invest in computers and automation than to hire new workers.

The National Bureau of Economic Research found that for every dollar of income tax cut, only 17 cents are generated from greater spending, and every dollar of corporate tax cut returns 50 cents in revenue. Unless there is a corresponding cut in government spending, the result is an increase in the budget deficit, which adds to the national debt.

The Treasury Department has found that tax cuts boost a weak economy in the short run. In the long run, however, they can increase inflation, leading the Federal Reserve to raise interest rates, which slows economic growth.

ANSWER THE TOPIC ESSENTIAL QUESTION

1. In one to three paragraphs, explain how public policies affect economic growth.

KEY TERMS

property right
supply-side fiscal policies

---

1. Which of the following public policies is most likely to promote long-run economic growth?

   (A) A decrease in unemployment benefits

   (B) A decrease in income taxes

   (C) An increase in transfer payments

   (D) An increase in funding for public education

   (E) An increase in public infrastructure

2. What is the most common reason modern governments impose tariffs?

   (A) To raise money

   (B) To reduce the budget deficit

   (C) To protect domestic producers

   (D) To help domestic producers reduce their prices

   (E) To boost real income

3. How does the patent system encourage inventors?

   (A) By allowing them to profit from their inventions

   (B) By easing government regulations

   (C) By helping finance production

   (D) By providing government grants

   (E) By providing tax breaks

FREE-RESPONSE QUESTIONS

   (a) Briefly define public policy.

   (b) Which of the five types of public policy discussed in this topic has the greatest immediate impact on the general public? Explain your answer.

   (c) Supply-side economics is an example of what kind of public policy?

   (d) Assume the United States economy is in long-run equilibrium. Identify one supply-side economic policy that could be implemented to spur long-run growth.

   (e) Briefly explain how supply-side economics works.

THINK AS AN ECONOMIST: *USE ECONOMIC CONCEPTS TO EXPLAIN HOW A SPECIFIC OUTCOME OCCURS WHEN THERE ARE MULTIPLE CONTRIBUTING VARIABLES*

Government policy makers hope to implement policies that promote economic growth. Growth means rising incomes and a rising standard of living, which contribute to people's sense of well-being.

Policy makers have a range of policy options for promoting growth. With as complex a system as a national economy, it can be difficult to determine which policy option will have the desired result.

Apply the Skill

You are the economic advisor to the president of Dragonia. The country has a middle-income economy with a slowly growing industrial sector, but a substantial part of the workforce practices agriculture. The president wants to apply to the World Bank for a low-interest loan as part of an economic development program. The loan is contingent on showing that the public policies to be enacted will promote high economic growth. What public policies would you place at the center of the economic development program? Identify at least three policies and explain why they would have the desired effect.

UNIT 5

Long Free-Response Question

1. Assume the country of Strongland is operating at full employment with a balanced budget.

   (a) Draw a correctly labeled Phillips curve that illustrates the country's current economic situation and label it *A*.

   (b) The government engages in a war that it decides to finance by borrowing. What effect will this have on each of the following?

      (i) The government's budget balance

      (ii) The real interest rate

   (c) Given your answer in part (b) (ii), what will be the impact on each of the following?

      (i) Private interest-sensitive spending. Explain.

      (ii) Long-run economic growth. Explain.

   (d) On your graph in part (a), show the effect of military spending and label it point B.

   (e) Identify the open market operation that the central bank should use to bring the country back to full employment.

   (f) What is the effect of the monetary policy identified in (e) on the price level?

   (g) Now assume that the price of oil increases. What is the effect of each of the following?

      (i) Price level

      (ii) Short-run Phillips curve

UNIT 6

Open Economy—International Trade and Finance

United States citizens traveling abroad soon discover that they need to exchange their U.S. dollars for the currency of the country or region they are visiting—pounds or pesos, euros or yen, or any of the many other currencies in use around the world. This is complicated by the fact that each currency's exchange rate, the price of one currency in terms of another, changes almost constantly.

In an open economy, countries interact with the rest of the world through trade and financial markets. All of these transactions need to take the exchange rate into consideration. Changes in the value of a country's currency are tied to the demand for that country's goods, services, and financial assets. The value of a country's currency can affect economic activity within a country as well as between countries. Fiscal and monetary policy can influence aggregate demand, output, price levels, and interest rates, all of which affect exchange rates.

As the value of one country's currency rises in relation to that of another, it imports more and exports less. Conversely, if the value of a country's currency falls in relation to another country's, it imports less and exports more. This is an example of the law of supply and demand. Tariffs and quotas are attempts to lower the demand for a country's goods. Tariffs raise prices by imposing a monetary penalty on imports, but often result in retaliatory tariffs. Quotas, on the other hand, merely restrict the quantity of a particular good that can be imported. In this unit, you will learn about macroeconomic policies that influence trade and finance between countries.

"I haven't heard from Stanley since the strong U.S. dollar lured him overseas."

CartoonStock.com

Topic Titles and Essential Knowledge

Topic 6.1 Balance of Payments Accounts

- The current account (CA) records net exports, net income from abroad, and net unilateral transfers.

- The CA is not always balanced; it may show a surplus or a deficit. A nation's balance of trade (i.e., net exports) is part of the current account and may also show a surplus or a deficit.

- The capital and financial account (CFA) records financial capital transfers and purchases and sales of assets between countries.

- The CFA is not always balanced; it may show a surplus (financial capital inflow) or a deficit (financial capital outflow).

- The balance of payments (BOP) is an accounting system that records a country's international transactions for a particular time period. It consists of the CA and the CFA.

- Any transaction that causes money to flow into a country is a credit to its BOP account, and any transaction that causes money to flow out is a debit. The sum of all credit entries should match the sum of all debit entries (CA+CFA=0).

Topic 6.2 Exchange Rates

- In the foreign exchange market, one currency is exchanged for another; the price of one currency in terms of the other is the exchange rate.

- If one currency becomes more valuable in terms of the other, it is said to appreciate. If one currency becomes less valuable in terms of the other, it is said to depreciate.

Topic 6.3 The Foreign Exchange Market

- The demand for a currency in a foreign exchange market arises from the demand for the country's goods, services, and financial assets and shows the inverse relationship between the exchange rate and the quantity demanded of a currency.

- The supply of a currency in a foreign exchange market arises from making payments in other currencies and shows the positive relationship between the exchange rate and the quantity supplied of a currency.

- In the foreign exchange market, equilibrium is achieved when the exchange rate is such that the quantities demanded and supplied of the currency are equal.

- Disequilibrium exchange rates create surpluses and shortages in the foreign exchange market. Market forces drive exchange rates toward equilibrium.

Topic 6.4 Effect of Changes in Policies and Economic Conditions on the Foreign Exchange Market

- Factors that shift the demand for a currency (such as the demand for that country's goods, services, or assets) and the supply of a currency (such as tariffs or quotas on the other country's goods and services) change the equilibrium exchange rate.

- Fiscal policy can influence aggregate demand, real output, the price level, and exchange rates.

- Monetary policy can influence aggregate demand, real output, the price level, and interest rates, and thereby affect exchange rates.

Topic 6.5 Changes in the Foreign Exchange Market and Net Exports

- Factors that cause a currency to appreciate cause that country's exports to decrease and its imports to increase. As a result, net exports will decrease.

- Factors that cause a currency to depreciate cause that country's exports to increase and its imports to decrease. As a result, net exports will increase.

Topic 6.6 Real Interest Rates and International Capital Flows

- Interest rates across countries change the relative values of domestic and foreign assets. Financial capital will flow toward the country with the relatively higher interest rate.

- Central banks can influence the domestic interest rate in the short run, which in turn will affect net capital inflows.

Source: *AP® Macroeconomics Course and Exam Description.* Effective Fall 2019 (College Board).

Topic 6.1

Balance of Payments Accounts

In Globalization 1.0, which began around 1492, the world went from size large to size medium. In Globalization 2.0, the era that introduced us to multinational companies, it went from size medium to size small. And then around 2000 came Globalization 3.0, in which the world went from being small to tiny.

Thomas Friedman, U.S. journalist, author, and Pulitzer Prize winner (b. 1953)

Essential Question: How do balance of payments accounts measure the goods, services, and financial trade between countries?

A person living in Montreal can purchase a German car that was assembled in South Carolina and contains parts manufactured in China and Mexico. Sixty years ago, this kind of international production was virtually impossible, not to mention the impractical supply chain nightmare involved. But as globalization exploded in the latter 20th century, along with high-speed financial technologies, the world and its economies have grown increasingly smaller. International transactions can now be executed instantly with a few clicks on a smartphone. And millions of those transactions occur hourly every day. Keeping track of all this global import and export business on a macroeconomic level requires a unique set of criteria and indicators to understand what has happened—and is happening—between trading economies.

Balance of Payments Accounts (BOP)

Countries keep track of all their transactions with other countries by using **balance of payments accounts**. These are usually calculated quarterly or annually. They encompass all transactions that countries' individuals, governments, and businesses complete with the same entities in other countries. BOP accounts include:

- exports of goods, services, and capital to other countries
- imports of goods, services, and capital into the country
- capital flow out of and into the country
- transfer payments (i.e. remittances and foreign aid out of an into the country)

BOP accounts are truly macroeconomic, as they summarize all business between a country and the rest of the world. To get a sense of how BOP accounts work, consider this very simplified version of an annual BOP from the fictional country of Freelandia.

	Payments *from* other countries	Payments *to* other countries	Net
1. Sales/purchases of goods and services	2,220	2,980	−760
2. Factor income	929	712	217
3. Transfers	—	—	−83
Current account (1 + 2 + 3)			−626
4. Official asset sales and purchases	488	91	397
5. Private sales and purchases of assets	1,733	1,445	288
Financial account (4 + 5)			685
Total			59

Amounts in billions of dollars

For the year 2018, Freelandia's BOP accounts ended up in the black, or in positive territory, despite some large deficits in certain areas. (Accounts with figures in negative territory are said to be "in the red.") Here is what each row and column of the table means:

1. **Sales/purchases of goods and services:** This is closest to pure export/import numbers. Column 2 shows how much money Freelandia brought in for all sales to other countries (exports). Column 3 shows how much Freelandia paid to other countries for goods and services (imports).

2. **Factor income:** This is what countries pay for using factors of production owned by people in other countries. For example: profits from Hong Kong Disneyland go to the U.S.-based Disney company, so those profits would go in column 2. Profits earned by U.S. car dealers selling Japanese cars go in column 3 because the ownership is overseas.

3. **Transfers:** These are funds that people living in one country send to people in another country. (The U.S. government only estimates the net on transfers.)

4. **Official asset sales and purchases:** These are transactions between governments—primarily governments' central banks.

5. **Private sales and purchases of assets:** These are transactions between private entities in different countries. If a German auto company purchases an American auto company, that would show up in column 2. U.S. investors buying stock in a Spanish company would show up in column 3.

Activity like sales of goods and services, factor income, and transfers (rows 1–3) are treated differently than official (or government) asset sales and private asset purchases (rows 4 and 5). This is primarily because these transactions impact the future in different ways. If a U.S. farmer sells corn to an Asian client, the transaction is finished when the goods and money are exchanged. This is called a current account transaction, as there is no question of future liability. But if a U.S. trader sells bonds to a Swiss client, there is a liability involved because eventually, the U.S. trader will have to pay interest and repay the principal in the future. This is known as a capital and financial account transaction.

Current Account The **current account (CA)** is a country's export net income over a period of time. It is concerned with short-term transactions: the receipt and payment in cash for goods and services, factor income, and transfers. In Freelandia's current account, you can see there is a $760 billion deficit between the goods Freelandia sold to other countries as exports and what Freelandia paid to other countries for their imported goods. Even though the factor income and transfers are net gains for Freelandia, the net sum of current accounts remains high. This deficit is often referred to as a country's **trade balance** (or imbalance in Freelandia's case). Remember, the transactions that comprise the CA do not create any liabilities for the future—these are completed deals.

SURPLUSES AND DEFICITS IN THE CURRENT ACCOUNT (CA)		
	Surplus	Deficit
Credits > Debits	√	
Credits < Debits		√
Exports > Imports	√	
Exports < Imports		√

Trade between the United States and China has shown BOP account deficits for decades. In 2017, the U.S. deficit was $53 billion. This means there is more **outflow of funds** to China than there is **inflow of funds** to the United States. Americans buy lots of computers, cell phones, and items of clothing that are made in China. The Chinese buy lots of commercial aircraft, soybeans, and semiconductors from U.S. producers. The United States runs the largest BOP deficit of any nation. But it also posts some of the largest capital and financial account numbers in the world (though not in China's league). You will see later why that helps balance these deficits.

Capital and Financial Account The inflow and outflow of funds that impact a country's foreign assets and liabilities is measured by the **capital and financial account (CFA)**. These are transactions that have future liabilities. Some of the components of the CFA include:

- foreign investment, loans, and reserves
- banking and other capital exchanges
- debt forgiveness between countries
- real estate transactions
- stocks and bonds

Money that leaves a country is recorded as a debit. But CFA money is investment money, so the expectation is that, in the future, there will be a return on that money. The return, whether it is on a direct investment or a capital gain from an investment, is recorded as a credit in the BOP. When a country has to pay out a capital gain, that would be recorded as a debit in the BOP.

SURPLUSES AND DEFICITS IN THE CAPITAL FINANCIAL ACCOUNT (CFA)		
	Surplus	Deficit
Inflow > Outflow	√	
Inflow < Outflow		√
Investments in > Investments out	√	
Investments in < Investments out		√

How the BOP Works

As the totals in the Freelandia table show, the country ran a deficit in its current account, which means it paid more money to other trading countries than it took in. But Freelandia had a surplus in its capital financial account—it sold more assets to foreign countries than it bought from other countries. The net of the CA and CFA accounts shows as a surplus of $59 billion. But economists will tell you that the surplus is a statistical error that reveals the imperfect nature of BOP accounts. That is because the rule of balance of payments accounting is that current accounts and capital financial accounts should balance each other out and sum to zero. According to the International Monetary Fund's Balance of Payments Manual, the BOP formula is:

Current account (CA) + Capital financial account (CFA) = 0

So why is this formula true? After all, Freelandia's BOP account table clearly shows CA + CFA *does not* add up to zero.

The BOP diagram on the following page may help you understand how this unique math works out. The diagram shows the money that flows *between* countries—not the money that flows *within* a country. You can see that there is money flowing into the United States from other countries for goods and services (consider these exports). There is also money flowing out of the United States to other countries for goods and services (consider these imports). At the same time, capital and financial assets are flowing both ways as well—inflow and outflow to and from the United States and all other countries. These two different tracks (CA and CFA) are represented by the same size arrows in the diagram, suggesting that they equal out. The negative outflow of funds for Freelandia is ultimately matched by the inflow of funds from other countries.

Another way to think about this macroeconomic concept is this: if a woman in Taiwan buys a dress from Brazil, Taiwan gains a dress and Brazil gains the equivalent in money. For the BOP account to reach a zero sum, the value exchange is added to the BOP ledger—which makes it balanced (or zero). Remember: economists contend that BOP account surpluses and deficits are really just statistical errors.

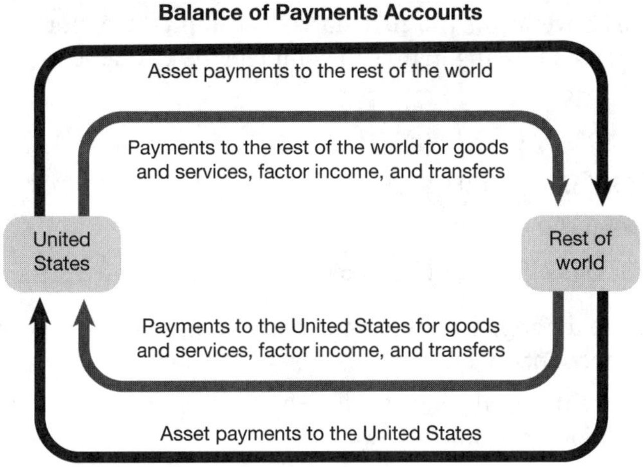

Balance of Payments Accounts

The inner, gray arrows represent the current account (CA) inflow and outflow of funds. The outer, black arrows represent the capital financial account (CFA) inflow and outflow of funds.

ANSWER THE TOPIC ESSENTIAL QUESTION

1. In one to three paragraphs, explain how balance of payments (BOP) accounts measure the goods, services, and financial trade between countries.

KEY TERMS

balance of payments (BOP) account   outflow of funds
current account (CA)   inflow of funds
trade balance   capital and financial account (CFA)

	Payments *from* other countries	Payments *to* other countries	Net
Sales/purchases of goods and services	1,751	_____(1)	-812
Factor income	534	412	122
Transfers	131	202	-71
Current Account			$_____(2)

Amounts in billions of dollars

1. The table above shows the 2020 current accounts (CA) for Zambonia. Determine the missing figures to complete the CA table total.

   (A) (1) $939   (2) $863
   (B) (1) $939   (2) -$619
   (C) (1) $2,563   (2) -$761
   (D) (1) $2,563   (2) -$619
   (E) (1) $2,563   (2) $863

2. What is the difference between current accounts (CA) and capital financial accounts (CFA)?

   (A) CAs are the total goods trade deficit; CFAs are the total assets deficit for a nation.

   (B) CAs show long-term trade trends; CFAs show short-term asset sales.

   (C) CAs are the most recent BOP account figures; CFAs are the most recent liability figures.

   (D) CAs are a nation's net income; CFAs are the net change in assets and liabilities.

   (E) CAs measure only net goods and services trades; CFAs measure all asset and liability trades.

3. The balance of payments is

   (A) when the sum of the current account (CA) and capital financial account (CFA) are zero

   (B) when the current account (CA) is greater than the capital financial account (CFA)

   (C) when the capital financial account (CFA) is greater than the current account (CA)

   (D) when the capital financial account (CFA) and the current account (CA) are equal to one

   (E) when foreign investment exceeds domestic investment

1. Which component of the balance of payments accounts is affected by the following economic developments? Explain your answers for each.

   (a) A U.S. company sells a brand-new airplane to an Australian airline.

   (b) German investors buy stocks in an American parcel shipping service.

   (c) South Vietnam purchases from the United States a fleet of used machines for chewing up old asphalt when resurfacing roads. The United States ships the entire fleet to South Vietnam.

   (d) A Russian oligarch who owns homes in the United States buys a luxury corporate yacht, which he keeps in the United States.

   (e) The Amazon Basin floods for nearly a week, causing massive loss of property, record-breaking damages, and several hundred deaths. The U.S. government approves sending a foreign aid package to help the worst-hit countries: Peru, Bolivia, and Brazil.

THINK AS AN ECONOMIST: *DESCRIBE ECONOMIC CONCEPTS*

Countries exist in a world economic system and constantly engage in trade with other countries. That trade consists of the exchange of goods and services and of financial assets. Economists use two different accounts to measure the flow of those two sets of exchanges, the current account (CA) and the capital financial account (CFA).

Apply the Skill

The two accounts are separate entities, but economists say that they must balance. That is, CA + CFA = 0. In your own words, explain what each account measures and why they must net to zero. Use the example of a country with a trade imbalance.

A country is said to have a trade deficit when it imports more than it exports. The United States has carried a trade deficit with its trading partners since the late 20th century. In response, government officials in charge of U.S. trade policy have often tried to reduce this trade deficit. So, what are people who are worried about the trade deficit worried about?

Trade Deficits Are a Symptom of Something Else The existence of a trade deficit is seen by many as a sign of weakness in U.S. trade policy or competitiveness. Further, the U.S. trade deficit is viewed as an outgrowth of unfair trade practices exercised by some U.S. trading partners. People see that exports are lower than imports, and they jump to the conclusion that the United States is "losing the trade war." Further, economist and advisor to President Trump, Peter Navarro, has stated that the U.S. trade deficit inhibits economic growth in the United States.

However, a number of economists say that none of these reasons are the fundamental cause of the trade deficit. Instead, economist Joseph Stiglitz believes that the cause of the trade deficit is rooted in the domestic U.S. economy. He says, "The United States has a problem, but it's not with China. It's at home: America has been saving too little." In other words, because U.S. consumers save too little, the United States must attract foreign investment to finance U.S. government debt, buy U.S. real estate, and invest in U.S. stocks. Alternatively, Michael Pettis, a senior fellow at the Carnegie-Tsinghua Center for Global Policy, believes the trade deficit is a sign of too much foreign savings and too little foreign consumption.

Trade Deficits Are Unimportant—or Even Healthy The strongly negative view of trade deficits as a critical problem holding back the U.S. economy, or as a sign of some sort of fatal flaw, is not universally held. In fact, some economists believe that a trade deficit might even be a sign of a growing or strong U.S. economy. As the economy grows, people earn more income with which they buy more goods and services, both foreign and domestic.

In addition, capital inflows demonstrate that foreign investors believe the United States offers low-risk and high-return assets. In other words, a trade or current account deficit is unrelated to a capital account surplus. As *The New York Times* economics reporter Neil Irwin observes, "In effect, the flow of capital is the reverse of the flow of goods. And the trade deficit will be shaped not just by the mechanics of what products people in the two countries buy, but also by unrelated investment and savings decisions. The cause and effect goes both directions."

So, are trade deficits something to be worried about? Maybe . . . or maybe not.

Topic 6.2

Exchange Rates

A nation's exchange rate is the single most important price in its economy.

Paul Volcker, U.S. economist, former chairman of the Federal Reserve (1927–2019)

Essential Question: How are currency exchange rates determined and impacted by changes in import and export activity?

If you order something online from a site based in Shanghai, there is a currency exchange rate issue that comes into play that you probably never even think about. You go to your cart, pay for the item, and that is it, right? You are most likely to be aware of exchange rates when you travel to another country. Before you can even take a taxi from the airport or buy a meal, you need to exchange your U.S. dollars for the country's currency. The higher the exchange rate, the more your dollar will buy. The price of goods made in one country has to be translated into the currency of other countries where the goods are being shipped to and sold. The exchange rate is central to all import and export business and investment between nations. Determining those rates is crucial for all countries that trade in today's wide-open market.

Foreign Exchange Markets and Rates

Stated simply, the **exchange rate** is the price at which currencies from different countries are traded. If you are going on vacation to Mexico, you will want to know what kind of purchasing power your dollar will have in pesos, Mexico's currency. If your trip was on February 22, 2020, the exchange rate would be 18.89 pesos for every 1 U.S. dollar. So, 100 U.S. dollars would get you 1,889 pesos. The exchange rate formula is this:

$$U.S.\ dollars \times Exchange\ rate = Pesos$$
$$100\ U.S.\ dollars \times 18.89 = 1,889.00\ pesos$$

If lunch in a town in Mexico costs 28 pesos, that is 1.49 in U.S. dollars. Before you make that purchase, the exchange rate is determined. The rate is tracked and changes constantly, all day, every day, though usually in small increments.

More often than not, goods and services are paid for in the currency where they are produced—European products are purchased in euros, Japanese products in yen, U.S. goods in dollars, etc. International transactions need a way to exchange one currency for another, and that is what the **foreign exchange market** does. (This is also sometimes called "forex" or "FX.") It is not a physical place—it is an electronic marketplace accessible to countries around the world. But every weekday around the clock, there are trillions of dollars traded in currency between countries, which is why the forex is the world's biggest financial market. Keep in mind that in open economies, the laws of supply and demand determine how valued a currency is.

SAMPLE FOREIGN EXCHANGE MARKET RATES			
	U.S. Dollars	**Yen**	**Euros**
One U.S. dollar exchanged for	1	107.94	0.7034
One yen exchanged for	0.009264	1	0.006516
One euro exchanged for	1.4217	153.46	1

The table shows the price for each type of currency if purchased with the currency in the left column. For example, US$1 can be exchanged for €0.7034—this means it takes €0.7034 to buy US$1. If you wanted to buy euros with U.S. dollars, it would cost US$1.4217 to purchase €1. Both these numbers show the exchange rate between the euro and the U.S. dollar: 1/1.4217 = 0.7034. To write out these exchange rates, you can use one of two ways—and both are correct as there is no set rule on how to do it:

- €0.7034 to US$1
- US$1.4217 to €1

Changes in how much of one country's currency it takes to purchase another country's currency are often expressed as strengthening or weakening. If, for example, it took more U.S. dollars to purchase the same number of Mexican pesos, the U.S. dollar would be described as weak and the peso strong. If the opposite were true, analysts would call the peso weak and the dollar strong.

Fixed Exchange Rates Most countries have a central bank that deals with exchange rate policies and concerns. One key policy this authority handles is the **exchange rate regime**, which is the system a country uses to establish the exchange rate of its own currency against other currencies. There are a variety of regimes a country can choose to set its exchange policy, but the two primary regimes are fixed rates and floating rates.

A **fixed exchange rate** (also called a "pegged currency") is a regime where a country ties its official exchange rate to another country's currency. Fixed exchange rates give exporters and importers more certainty and reduces the risk of fluctuations in currencies. For example, Hong Kong's regime is to set its exchange rate at HK$7.80 to US$1 (or US$0.13 to HK$1). If the value of Hong Kong's currency falls below the pegged rate, the central bank buys HK dollars with U.S. dollars that it has in reserve to maintain the pegged rate. If the HK currency rises beyond the pegged rate, they sell more HK dollars until the value gets back to the pegged rate. (Many countries with fixed exchange rates tie their regime to the U.S. dollar because of its stability.)

There are disadvantages to the fixed exchange rate regime:

- It limits a country's ability to change interest rates to spur economic growth.
- It limits the market's ability to make adjustments if a currency is overvalued or undervalued.
- It requires very large currency reserves to make the limited changes to remain at the pegged level.
- It can lead to unofficial (or dual) exchange rates (more on this later).

Because exchange rates are determined by supply and demand for a country's goods, pegged/fixed regimes have limited abilities (noted above) to respond when their currency fluctuates due to increased demand. This is why many countries do not choose a fixed regime.

Floating Exchange Rates A **floating exchange rate** regime is where a country's currency price is determined by the forex market, which is based on supply and demand. The United States and the European Union employ a floating regime. India, the world's largest democracy, and China, the biggest economy in the world, use a managed floating regime that allows the central bank more control to make adjustments than a free-floating regime. (Some have called China's approach a "fudge" regime because it plays a little loose with the competitive nature of forex and lets the central government "fudge" the yuan currency to China's benefit.)

In a floating exchange rate system, long-term currency prices change based on the economic strength of a country and its interest rates in relation to the same in another country. Supply and demand, exports and imports—basics of economic competition—are at the heart of determining floating exchange rates. If demand is low and a country's supply grows, the currency will fall in relation to other currencies. And the opposite is true as well: great demand causes a currency exchange rate to rise.

Another aspect of a floating exchange rate system is that central banks can buy or sell their own currencies to try to adjust the exchange rate with other countries. This is usually done to calm down a market that is volatile. Because a currency that rises too high or falls too low can make a negative impact on a nation's economy and ability to trade internationally, central banks can step in to try to even things out. For example, a central bank could raise interest rates to control the flow of investment money into its country.

Dual Exchange Rates Countries will sometimes use a **dual**—or unofficial—**exchange rate** regime. This is where a country uses an official fixed exchange rate for imports and exports and current account transactions, and an unofficial floating rate for specific goods or capital account transactions. Dual exchange rates are usually employed as a short-term solution to a specific crisis, such as soaring inflation or a severe unemployment shock. They also can occur as a result of currency devaluation, the planned reduction of the value of a country's currency versus that of another. (Currency revaluation is the reverse of this process.)

These dual rates have the benefit of helping a government maintain production and export of goods as well as keeping international investment in the country alive. But there are drawbacks as well. The exchange rates can be manipulated by importers and exporters to increase their currency profits. A black market can also develop to try to avoid the high exchange rates set by the central bank.

Venezuela provides a good example of how central bank and government intervention can go awry. When problems with the country's economy arose in the 1990s, Venezuela began altering its currency controls in an attempt to respond to exploding inflation and lack of food and medicine. Starting in the early 2000s, Venezuela tried many different exchange and currency regimes—none of which worked and many that made the problem worse. Political changes and national control of the oil industry did not help things, either. Venezuela tried dual exchange regimes, they devalued their currency more than once, and they tried using different exchange rates for different types of goods. In the end, this amount of exchange-rate management hurt, rather than helped, Venezuela's trading economy.

Currency Appreciation and Depreciation Currency exchange rates change daily—usually incrementally—based on a number of things: export/import activity between countries, fiscal policy and government actions within countries, and interest rate changes. **Currency appreciation** is when the value of one country's currency increases in relation to another country's currency. Remember that exchange rates are always calculated between two countries, so in a floating exchange regime, it is possible for a country's currency to appreciate in relation to one country and depreciate in relation to another country.

Several factors influence relative currency exchange rates:

- **Consumer tastes:** One country's consumers prefer certain goods and services that are produced in another country. For several decades, for example, U.S. consumers have preferred foreign car brands, such as Honda and Toyota (Japan), over domestic cars. This causes a depreciation in U.S. currency relative to the currency of Japan.

- **Relative inflation:** One country's price level is higher than that of another. In recent years, for example, the inflation rate in Venezuela has been higher than that of the United States, prompting Venezuelans to come to the United States to purchase goods and services. This caused the U.S. dollar to appreciate relative to Venezuela's currency, the bolivar.

- **Relative incomes:** One country's income level is higher than that of another. For example, when the United States was able to climb out of the Great Recession and its income levels increased, this allowed U.S. consumers to look abroad to purchase foreign goods and services. This caused a depreciation in the U.S. dollar relative to the currencies in countries from which U.S. consumers made purchases.

- **Relative interest rates:** One country's interest rates are higher than those of another. The country with the higher interest rate becomes a more desirable country in which to invest, as the investor would gain a larger return on investment. This causes a depreciation of currency in the country that is investing in the other country.

Appreciation of currencies is primarily determined by aggregate demand. If demand for U.S. goods increases, the exchange rate will appreciate as well. For example, the forex notation for the exchange rate between the United States and the European Union is written like this: USD/EUR = 0.92. The first currency (USD) is called the base currency and represents one unit ($1). The second currency listed (EUR) is the amount of that currency needed to equal one unit of the base currency. This can be written as a fraction as well: USD/EUR = 1/0.92. If the U.S. dollar appreciates by 0.11 cents, the exchange rate will change to USD/EUR = 1/1.03. That means it will now take €1.03 to purchase $1 USD. The same notation applies when a currency depreciates, only the amount to purchase the base currency goes down.

What effect does currency appreciation have on an economy? You might think the answer would be clearly positive because the value of a currency goes up, but that is not the case. It is a more complicated cause and effect response.

- If foreigners have to spend more because the USD appreciates and goods become more expensive, export costs will rise.
- If foreigners buy fewer U.S. exports, then GDP will begin to fall because of the drop in demand. A drop in GDP is commonly interpreted as a weakening of the economy.
- However, because exchange rates are linked to demand, if the USD appreciates and demand for U.S. goods drops, foreign goods (imports) become cheaper and American consumers have more purchasing power with the stronger dollar.

Lower import prices and a stronger dollar can help keep inflation in check.

Currency depreciation is when the value of a currency in a floating exchange rate regime falls. This can happen as a result of negative economic developments in a country, interest rate volatility, or political instability that would keep investors away. Currency depreciation can serve a positive purpose: to improve a country's competitiveness in exports or close the gap in a country's trade deficit. When implemented gradually and with no extreme economic shocks, depreciation is a useful tool.

Currency depreciation is most often seen in countries with persistent inflation issues, large current account deficits, and very low interest rates. When a country's interest rates are kept low, investor dollars—always looking for the highest yields—tend to stay away from investing in that country. In high inflation countries, even if central banks increase interest rates to try to stem inflation, too much inflation can cause instability and make it hard to compete in global export markets. When countries enact severe currency depreciations—as Venezuela did in the example above—foreign investors can get spooked and pull their investments from the country, which only makes the trade and currency problem worse. All of these situations can work as a vicious cycle to cause currency depreciation.

The effects of currency depreciation on a country are varied and depend on the current economic situation. Some possible effects include:

- weakening of currency in foreign exchange markets (resulting in less import purchase power)
- uncertainty for producers within the country and investors in the country
- faster-growing trade deficits
- greater reliance on import goods and, ultimately, higher inflation

Currency depreciation and appreciation both play a role in balancing a country's exchange rate. As with most economic issues where striking an equilibrium is the goal, avoiding severe swings in either direction makes it much easier for governments and central banks to manage the impact of exchange rates.

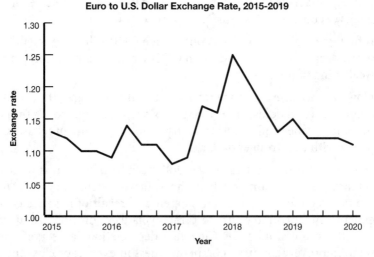

Between January 2014 and January 2020, the exchange rate between euros and U.S. dollars has fluctuated within a range of $0.10 cents. Only in the 14-month period between June 2017 and September 2018 did the euro appreciate much beyond the $0.10 USD range. Both the United States and the European Union use floating exchange rate regimes.

ANSWER THE TOPIC ESSENTIAL QUESTION

1. In one to three paragraphs, explain how currency exchange rates are determined and impacted by changes in import and export activity.

KEY TERMS	
exchange rate	floating exchange rate
foreign exchange market	dual exchange rate
exchange rate regime	currency appreciation
fixed exchange rate	currency depreciation

MULTIPLE-CHOICE QUESTIONS

1. When the U.S. dollar decreases in value relative to the euro, it has
   - (A) depreciated
   - (B) appreciated
   - (C) equalized
   - (D) changed to a fixed exchange rate
   - (E) changed to a floating exchange rate

2. Under a floating exchange rate regime, a currency's value is directly determined by
   - (A) the loanable funds market
   - (B) the money market
   - (C) the foreign exchange market
   - (D) a country's fiscal policy
   - (E) a country's monetary policy

3. Relative income and relative inflation are factors that determine
   - (A) the value of a country's currency in the money market
   - (B) the value of a country's currency in the inflation market
   - (C) the value of a country's currency in the foreign exchange market
   - (D) supply and demand of a country's currency and import
   - (E) a country's current account

1. Use the following scenario to answer the questions below:

China and the United States are trading partners. The currency in China is the yuan. The United States has relatively higher inflation than China.

(a) In what way does the higher inflation rate affect the United States dollar?

(b) Given your answer in part (a), what is one effect on trade for the United States?

(c) Given your answer in (a), do the U.S. goods sold in China become more expensive, less expensive, or remain the same?

(d) What can the Federal Reserve do to help the U.S. dollar appreciate relative to China's currency, the yuan?

(e) Assuming that the value of the U.S. dollar appreciates relative to China's currency, will the new exchange rate encourage or discourage U.S. exports? Why?

THINK AS AN ECONOMIST: *IDENTIFY AN ECONOMIC CONCEPT USING QUANTITATIVE DATA*

Economists use quantitative data to identify and explain economic concepts. In doing so, they present the data, discuss it, and explain how it demonstrates the concept.

Economists use exchange rates to measure the value of one currency against others on the world market. The exchange rate measures demand for a country's currency.

Apply the Skill

Look at the data in the table, which shows the exchange rate among several different currencies, including the U.S. dollar. Calculate the value, in each other currency, of the $23.50 an American consumer spends on an imported good from that country. Identify the currencies against which the U.S. dollar is weaker and those against which it is stronger and explain why.

U.S. Dollar	Canadian Dollar	Mexican Peso	Chinese Yuan	EU Euro	Australian Dollar
$1	1.42	24.6	7.06	0.902	1.56

Topic 6.3

The Foreign Exchange Market

[Trade's] ultimate object, however, it pretends, is always the same, to enrich the country by the advantageous balance of trade.

Adam Smith, Scottish Economist, *Wealth of Nations*, (1776)

Essential Question: What role do supply and demand play in the foreign exchange market and the equilibrium exchange rate?

When they travel to a foreign country, people want to know the currency exchange rate so they know how far their money will go during their visit. Those exchange rates may vary incrementally throughout each day of a trip, and that is because currency exchange rates are determined on a macroeconomic level via the foreign exchange market. Around the world, people making purchases, manufacturers filling supply orders, political developments, and the daily financial activities of investors, corporations, and banks all contribute in various ways to determining how much one country's currency is valued against another country's currency. And at the heart of these rates and transactions is the most fundamental of economic factors: supply and demand.

The Foreign Exchange Market

The **foreign exchange market**—which is also called forex, FX, or the currency market—is a virtual marketplace where exchange rates for currencies around the globe are set. These markets are comprised of countries' central banks, investors, commercial businesses, companies dealing specifically in forex sales and purchases, and a variety of investment firms. Currencies are bought and sold and exchanged in the foreign exchange market, which is "open" 24 hours a day, five days a week (it is "closed" on weekends). This is where companies, banks, and governments convert their home currencies into the currencies from other countries. To get an idea of how busy the forex is and how much money passes through it every day, in 2019, the daily average turnover of currencies was 6.6 trillion U.S. dollars. Yes, that was *trillion*.

Because the world's ability to freely trade goods and services between countries has increased rapidly and over the past 30 years, what happens in the marketplace in certain large economies, like those of the United States, China, and the European Union, will have a more immediate impact on economies large and small worldwide. This is in large part due to the foreign exchange market and how it affects international trade. Currencies on the forex are always traded in pairs, meaning the value of one currency is always relative to the currency it is being exchanged for: U.S. dollar to yen, yen to euro, euro to peso, peso to U.S. dollar—you get the idea.

Exchange rates between currencies are just as important to vacationers visiting other countries as they are to central banks, investors, and businesses selling their goods and services around the world. Rates are ultimately based on supply and demand—the volume of goods supplied in a country to import overseas and the demand for foreign goods in that same country. The foreign exchange market serves as a processing system for this supply and demand.

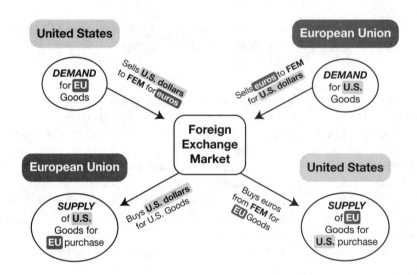

As euros go into the forex to buy U.S. dollars, U.S. interests can buy those euros to purchase EU goods. As more U.S. dollars go into the forex to buy euros, EU interests can buy those dollars to purchase U.S. goods. The equal exchange of currencies is a balanced exchange that countries strive for. However, supply and demand and a variety of other possible developments can create an imbalance that countries try to avoid as much as possible.

The Equilibrium Exchange Rate

In general terms, equilibrium is achieved when supply and demand are balanced. This was examined with the AD-AS curve analysis in Unit 3. The **equilibrium exchange rate** works similarly: it is the exchange rate where the demand for U.S. dollars is equal to the quantity of U.S. dollars being supplied.

Supply of currency works hand in hand with demand for currency. Supply of currency is based on a country's demand for imported goods from other countries. For example, if Mexico imports cars from Germany, it must pay in euros, and to buy euros it must sell (supply) pesos. The more cars Mexico imports, the bigger supply of pesos that make it into the foreign exchange market.

The following graph depicts the foreign exchange market and an equilibrium point between euros and U.S. dollars.

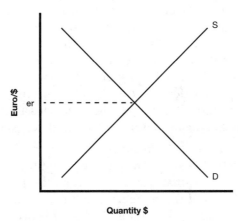

Forex Market Equilibrium (U.S. dollar)

The exchange rate affects both exports and imports. The **demand curve** for U.S. dollars slopes downward because as the dollar appreciates (becomes more valuable), prices for U.S. goods cost Europeans more euros, so they tend to buy fewer imported goods from the United States. If the euro appreciates and the U.S. dollar weakens (depreciates) against it, products from the United States become cheaper to Europeans and they will buy more goods (and U.S. dollars). The **supply curve** slopes upward for similar reasons: the more euros it costs to buy a U.S. dollar, the more dollars Americans will supply the foreign exchange market.

This equilibrium rate (er) also comes into play with countries' balance of payments accounts. (See Topic 6.1.) Recall that two of the major types of international transactions are:

- purchases and sales of goods and services (current account)
- purchases and sales of assets (capital and financial account)

With the equilibrium exchange rate reflected in the graph, the balance of payments on the current account and the balance of payments on the capital and financial account would essentially be zero. This means U.S. imports and exports are about even for the period being assessed.

Disequilibrium occurs when there is a deficit or surplus in a country's balance of payments (BOP). This can result in shortages or surpluses in the foreign exchange market. Disequilibrium can be caused by a variety of factors:

- changes in consumer tastes that affect imports or exports
- inflation or deflation
- a country's currency is revalued or devalued
- political instability

Countries try to prevent this imbalance, and a persistent state of disequilibrium can cause serious crises for most countries. But the foreign market is predisposed to push exchange rates toward equilibrium. For example, if the demand for U.S. dollars is low in comparison to the euro, the cheaper cost to buy American goods will incentivize Europeans to buy more American goods with their stronger euros. And as more U.S. exports are sold to Europeans, price levels will rise and cause the dollar to strengthen and the euro to lose some of its purchasing power. Because currencies are exchanged on a one-to-one basis, it is not possible for two currencies to appreciate against each other at the same time—one currency has to depreciate as the other currency appreciates. So the bias of the exchange market towards equilibrium helps a depreciated currency to appreciate because of the most basic of market forces—supply and demand.

Currency Supply and Demand As previously discussed, a nation's currency value is determined by how much demand there is for the currency and how much supply of that currency is available. Exchange rates reflect that relationship. **Demand for currency** is a direct result of the demand for a country's export goods and investors looking to invest in the country. If U.S. companies develop a new, affordable, and easy-to-install solar panel that European consumers want to buy, there will be an increased demand for U.S. dollars on the foreign exchange market because so many people need U.S. dollars to buy the new solar panels. This development looks just like a demand curve you have seen before:

Forex Market for Dollars and Euros

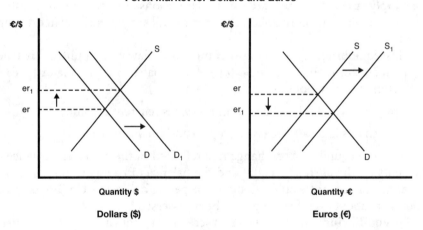

Because of an increase in export sales of solar panels, the demand curve for U.S. dollars against euros shifts to the right, which means the dollar has appreciated. Remember that as a currency appreciates (costs more to buy), fewer people from other countries will be able to afford exported products from the United States. In purchasing solar panels from the United States, Europeans must supply euros to the foreign exchange market. Thus, the euro depreciates relative to the U.S. dollar, as shown in the right-hand graph.

1. In one to three paragraphs, explain what role supply and demand play in the foreign exchange market and the equilibrium exchange rate.

KEY TERMS

foreign exchange market	supply of currency	disequilibrium
exchange rate	demand curve	demand for currency
equilibrium exchange rate	supply curve	

MULTIPLE-CHOICE QUESTIONS

1. If there is a spike in export goods and services from Mexico to Germany, what will happen to the peso-euro exchange rate?
   (A) The euro will appreciate because more will be spent to purchase pesos.
   (B) Because the demand for pesos will be high, it will depreciate against the euro.
   (C) The peso will appreciate relative to the euro.
   (D) The euro will depreciate at the same rate that the peso appreciates.
   (E) Both currencies will appreciate because of increased demand for both.

2. If the demand curve for U.S. dollars shifts to the left, what happens to the equilibrium exchange rate of euros to dollars?
   (A) The equilibrium rate will result in more expensive dollars.
   (B) The U.S. dollar will depreciate and cost more euros.
   (C) The equilibrium rate will result in a rise in euros.
   (D) It will remain the same; the rate is based on the supply of dollars.
   (E) It will cost fewer euros to purchase a U.S. dollar.

3. Why does the supply curve for a currency slope upward?
   (A) When demand for a country's goods rises, the country needs to supply more currency.
   (B) There is always a demand for currencies in a global economy.
   (C) The more goods a country imports, the more currency supply is needed.
   (D) Even in low export years, a country's currency must always remain in high supply.
   (E) It shows how equilibrium in the currency's exchange rate is maintained.

1. Answer each of the following questions using the idea that the United States and Argentina are trading partners.

   (a) Argentinian tourists increase visits to the United States during winter. What effect will this have on the supply of Argentine pesos in the foreign exchange market?

   (b) The U.S. government significantly increases personal income taxes. What effect will this have on the demand for the Argentine peso in the foreign exchange market? Explain your answer.

   (c) Argentinian interest rates increase. What effect will this have on the supply of U.S. dollars in the foreign exchange market? Why?

   (d) The United States experiences a severe recession. How does this affect the value of the U.S. dollar in relation to the Argentine peso?

   (e) Argentina experiences higher than normal inflation. How does this affect the value of the Argentine peso in relation to the U.S. dollar? Explain your answer.

THINK AS AN ECONOMIST: *DRAW AN ACCURATELY LABELED VISUAL TO REPRESENT AN ECONOMIC MARKET*

Forex, or the foreign exchange market, is an aggregate of all the currency trading that takes place around the globe. Companies, banks, and governments rely on this market to convert their home currencies into the other countries' currencies in order to complete transactions in international trade and business.

Apply the Skill

Forex is shaped by the laws of supply and demand. In this case, the determinant is the relative supply and demand of different world currencies. Complete the graphic below to indicate the effect of different exchange rates on a country's imports and exports.

	Effect on demand for Country A currency in Country B	Effect on supply of Country A currency in Country B
Currency of Country A appreciates		
Currency of Country A depreciates		
Currency of Country A is stable		

Topic 6.4

Change Affects the Foreign Exchange Market

In matters of industry, human enterprise ought doubtless to be left free in the main, not fettered by too much regulation, but practical politicians know [industry] may be beneficially stimulated by prudent aims and encouragements on the part of the government.

Alexander Hamilton, United States' First Secretary of the Treasury (1755–1804)

Essential Question: How do changes in policy and economic conditions impact the foreign exchange market?

In an open-trading global economy like the one that more or less exists today, every action has a reaction. If Saudi Arabia cuts its oil production, consumer companies large and small across the globe will feel the impact—not to mention the investors and petroleum suppliers worldwide. If a pandemic virus shuts down electronics production industries in China for five months, every related business will feel the ripple effects in supply and demand for their products. The foreign exchange market reacts to these substantive economic and policy changes as well. But the changes do not have to be as wide-reaching as these global scale events—monetary and fiscal policy adjustments by central banks or political legislation in individual countries can alter the forex rates as well.

Influencing the Equilibrium Exchange Rate

Recall that the equilibrium exchange rate is the rate where the demand for one country's currency is equal to the quantity of that country's currency being supplied (see Topic 6.3 for more details). Exchange rates are based on the supply and demand for a country's goods, which is why a graph of the forex supply and demand for any currency will look similar to the aggregate demand-aggregate supply (AD-AS) curve.

Economists distinguish between two versions of the exchange rate: the nominal exchange rate and the real exchange rate.

- The **nominal exchange rate** is the rate of exchange that does not account for the difference in aggregate price levels (inflation) for the same products in two different countries.

- The **real exchange rate** does account for differences in inflation (aggregate price levels) between countries. This is the rate economists use when analyzing imports and exports of goods and services. Even though a currency may depreciate in relation to another currency, the real exchange rate might not change.

Consider, for example, a hotel room in Mexico that costs 1,000 pesos. If the exchange rate is 10 pesos per U.S. dollar, that is equivalent to $100. Inflation spikes the cost of that same room by 50 percent as well as the exchange rate. Now it is 1,500 pesos per night. With the new exchange rate of 15 pesos per dollar—1,500 divided by 15—the room rate is still $100 U.S. dollars. The real exchange rate is applied to all traded goods and services, and a country's current accounts only use the real exchange rate. So in a forex currency supply and demand graph, the demand and supply curves will only shift and affect the equilibrium rate when there is depreciation or appreciation in the currency—causing higher and lower prices—in real terms.

Non-Fiscal Policy Impacts on the Forex Rate Some events that can impact the foreign exchange market are not specifically tied to fiscal or monetary policies. These tend to be unexpected occurrences, or, if anticipated, they are outside the traditional control of central banks and governments. Because of the global inter-connectedness of the forex market, there are literally millions of people interacting with it and trillions of dollars passing through it every day. Events all across the globe can affect exchange rates quickly—sometimes severely though usually less so.

Hurricanes, tornados, floods, earthquakes, and other similar calamities happen every year around the world. They can have devastating effects on an economy and its ability to maintain trade. They have an immediate negative effect on a nation's currency, as well as on the morale of the country's citizens. Infrastructure is essential for maintaining a productive economy. When infrastructure is severely damaged, it will slow or sometimes even stop production output for the country. Destruction of factories can set back major manufacturers for months or years.

In order to rebuild damaged areas after such an event, it is often necessary for a large amount of resources to be funneled into repairs—from both the private sector and the government. As a result, economic growth can be curtailed, which directly affects consumer spending. Nations recovering from environmental disasters usually have greatly depreciated currency, which affects what they can do on the foreign exchange market.

A country's trade position and its abilities on the forex can also sustain impacts due to political developments. These changes are usually far less severe than the environmental events described above. They are often smaller adjustments that do not threaten the security of an economy and its currency. Elections can change the priorities of a country and its economy, which may result in new monetary policies. Forex participants will try to predict what the consequences of the new leaders in a country will be. For example, if a presidential candidate who supports free trade and is courting foreign investment looks like she will be the new leader of a less-developed country, it can increase the value of that country's currency. Conversely, if this same person is in office but looks set to lose an election, the inherent uncertainty of the situation can result in a drop in currency value.

Unexpected political developments, like rampant citizen protests, national strikes, a scandal that leads to a change in leadership, or something as abrupt as a coup can cause chaos for a country's currency. Forex traders prefer stability in economies and currencies.

The most devastating development for a country and its currency is war. Much like an environmental disaster, a war can cause overwhelming damage to infrastructure, industries, and the leadership of a country—not to mention the horrible cost in human lives. It can take years, and even decades, for a country and its economy to recover from war. Because rebuilding a nation after a war is expensive, it must be financed by low interest rates. Those low interest rates as well as a lack of exports from the war-torn country depreciate the value of a country's currency because other countries demand less of the the war-torn country's currency from the forex market, leading to currency depreciation.

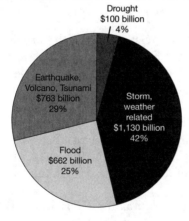

Environmental Disaster Damage, 1995-2015

Environmental disasters are among the most unpredictable events that can impact world economies and the foreign exchange market. As the diagram shows, between 1995 and 2015, there was over $2,655 billion in total damages to countries around the world. That is an average of more than $132 billion per year.

Trade Tariffs

Simply put, a **tariff** is a tax on imported goods from other countries. If a ton of iron ore from Australia costs $100, a tariff of $50 per ton changes the price to $150 per ton for U.S. companies wanting to buy this iron ore. The positive domestic result is that home countries do not have to raise their prices to compete with the imported goods. You can understand why free trade advocates so dislike tariffs. They directly affect the supply of and demand for goods.

Tariffs on imports have a double effect on trade: they make the cost of imported goods and raw materials more expensive for both U.S. manufacturers and U.S. consumers. It is ultimately the American consumer who pays for the tariff because producers pass along their increased costs in the form of higher prices for what they produce.

Another view of tariffs is that they involve trade-offs. Tariffs make imported goods more expensive for consumers and imported raw materials and parts more expensive for suppliers. But they can also have benefits:

- **Domestic Employment Protection:** Countries that use low-wage labor can make it hard for U.S. companies to compete on price, so tariffs can help maintain employment competition.

- **Consumer Protection:** If a country believes imported goods from another country could be dangerous or tainted, prohibitive tariffs can keep those goods out of the country.

- **Protecting Infant Industries or Economies:** A nascent economy or industry in a country can benefit from limited imports to promote domestic production and consumption.

- **National Defense:** Goods that deal with state secrets or national defense can be maintained domestically by keeping foreign imports out of the market. Similarly, countries often try to avoid becoming dependent on imports for vital products such as food.

- **Retaliatory Policy:** Governments can use tariffs to retaliate against other countries for real (or perceived) trade violations.

The Smoot-Hawley Act America's relationship with tariffs has been something of a rollercoaster. One of the first acts signed into law by the new Congress was a tariff act. In the late 1700s, the founders—Alexander Hamilton especially—believed tariffs were necessary to protect young industries against foreign competition, to promote a trade surplus, and to raise revenues for the government. Over its first 140 years, the United States raised and lowered tariffs regularly, but they were always high by modern standards. Between the end of the Civil War in 1865 and the start of World War I in 1914, they usually added 40 percent to 50 percent to the cost of imported goods, although some goods were exempt.

When the economic devastation known as the Great Depression began in 1929, Congress tried to protect domestic jobs by raising tariffs again. The **Smoot-Hawley Act** of 1930 increased tariffs to about 60 percent on covered goods, though it also increased the number of goods not covered. Other countries responded by increasing their tariffs on U.S.-made goods. The result of the higher tariffs was to further decrease trade, which was already in decline because aggregate demand around the world was decreasing. Smoot-Hawley pushed a deep depression even deeper.

When Franklin Roosevelt took office in 1933, his administration began to undo the impact of the high tariffs. However, not until the end of World War II in 1945 did the United States fully embrace a low-tariff policy for the first time. In 1947, the **General Agreement on Tariffs and Trade (GATT)** was signed by 23 nations, which minimized barriers to free trade like tariffs, quotas, and subsidies. Today, most tariffs are targeted to affect specific goods. Overall, tariffs raise the price of imported goods overall only by about 3 percent.

Import Quotas and Non-Tariff Barriers

An **import quota** is a non-tariff barrier that affects price levels, supply and demand, and the forex. Quotas are restrictions on how much of a particular good can be imported into a country. Unlike tariffs, which impose a monetary penalty on imports, quotas place limits on the total amount of goods an exporter can put into a country's market as a way to protect domestic producers. Quotas are administered by licenses that countries give to export entities that specify their limits. In the United States, the biggest import licenses (i.e. clothing, sugar) are issued to foreign governments rather than individual companies. Though import quotas do not impose taxes, their effect on export nations can actually be more costly as there can be no additional goods beyond the quota allowed to flood into the import country's marketplace.

The list of import quotas for goods entering the United States is long and extremely specific. Olives, various types of brooms, cotton, seasonings, animal feed, automobiles, beef, cheeses, and even ice cream are all imported goods on which the United States has restricted limits for importation. Most countries have some form of import quota system. These can vary greatly based on a nation's natural resources, its production and manufacturing systems, how its economy has developed and grown, and its history.

World Trade Organization (WTO) In 1995, the **World Trade Organization (WTO)** was created to oversee trade and mediate trade disputes between countries. The WTO essentially absorbed the GATT agreement created in 1947. As of 2020, there were 164 member countries in the WTO. It helps maintain communication between trading countries and since its inception has helped lower trade barriers globally.

The WTO has had positive and negative effects on international trade. **Multinational corporations**—companies based in more than one country—and consumers have benefitted greatly from the WTO's advocacy for expanding world trade. But the growth in international trade has had some negative effects. For example, higher-wage countries have lost jobs to lower-wage countries. Companies can get away with abusing their workers and damaging the environment because if a government tries to regulate it, the company can move easily to another country. Every year when the WTO conference convenes, it is met with great protests from human and economic rights activists.

United States-China Trade War When Donald Trump ran for president in 2016, he made what he called America's unfair trade deals with other countries a focal point of his campaign. Candidate Trump focused specifically on the North American Free Trade Agreement (NAFTA)—between Canada, Mexico, and the United States—and U.S.-China trade relations. In 2018, the Trump administration took action and started a full-blown trade war with China. The United States implemented a 25 percent tariff increase on certain Chinese imports, affecting an estimated $34 billion worth of Chinese goods. China retaliated by announcing tariffs on $34 billion worth of U.S. goods.

In addition to the United States, many other countries have complained of China's unfair trade practices, which include manipulating its currency, stealing intellectual property (especially technologies), and instituting restrictive trade barriers to limit the amount of foreign goods that are allowed on the Chinese market. The fact that the world's two biggest economies entered into a trade war was unsettling for investors, other economies dependent on China and the United States, as well as manufacturers and consumers in both countries. The war escalated throughout 2018 and into 2019—the United States hiked tariffs on Chinese goods a total of three times—and China responded in kind.

The scope of the trade war was beyond the purview of the WTO; the Trump administration felt the organization had treated the United States unfairly over the years. By the end of 2019, the world economy was feeling the effects of the trade war. Some economists estimated a loss of $700 billion in business. On the forex market, the U.S. dollar remained stable, even rising a little against the Chinese yuan. This is in part due to the reliability of U.S. dollars on the forex: other countries still demanded the currency. The yuan suffered more on the forex, dropping to its lowest point since the early 2000s. Chinese GDP was damaged to the point that some investors began pulling out of the market.

The Chinese consumer appeared to be better able to withstand the reduced U.S. imports, whereas U.S. consumers, businesses, and agriculture were impacted more seriously. Another influencing factor was that for more than two decades, the United States ran a large trade deficit with China. The trade war didn't reduce the situation. In fact, it made it worse. U.S. consumers, farmers, and manufacturers paid for the brunt of the trade war's consequences. In early 2020, China and the United States came to an understanding about new trade rules between them, although no specific plan had been enacted between the countries.

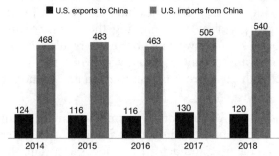

U.S.-China Trade Deficit, 2014–2018 (in billions of dollars)

■ U.S. exports to China   ■ U.S. imports from China

	2014	2015	2016	2017	2018
U.S. imports from China	468	483	463	505	540
U.S. exports to China	124	116	116	130	120

The United States has run a trade deficit with China for two decades. Between 2014 and 2017, the deficit remained fairly static, as had China's trade barriers to U.S. goods. In 2018, the U.S. deficit jumped as a result of the Trump administration's hike in tariffs on Chinese goods.

ANSWER THE TOPIC ESSENTIAL QUESTION

1. In one to three paragraphs, explain how changes in policy and economic conditions impact the foreign exchange market.

nominal exchange rate

real exchange rate

tariffs

Smoot-Hawley Act

General Agreement on Tariffs and Trade (GATT)

import quota

World Trade Organization (WTO)

multinational corporations

MULTIPLE-CHOICE QUESTIONS

1. What was the primary purpose of the Smoot-Hawley Act?

   (A) To restore U.S. trade after the crash of 1929

   (B) To encourage other countries to reduce tariffs on goods from the United States

   (C) To protect domestic producers from foreign imports

   (D) To establish quotas for all imported foreign goods

   (E) To restore the U.S. exchange rate equilibrium with Europe

2. What is the important difference between the nominal exchange rate and the real exchange rate?

   (A) The nominal exchange rate accounts for a nation's trade deficit.

   (B) The nominal exchange rate accounts for the difference in inflation.

   (C) The real exchange rate is used on the foreign exchange market.

   (D) The real exchange rate accounts for the difference in aggregate price levels.

   (E) There is no substantive difference between the two rates on the forex.

3. How does a tariff on imports benefit domestic producers of the same imported good?

   (A) It provides revenue that is given to the domestic producers.

   (B) It limits imports to a specified quantity for each license period.

   (C) It raises the price level domestic producers can sell their products.

   (D) It makes the domestic producers more efficient.

   (E) It allows producers more leeway in controlling nominal costs.

1. Use the following scenario to answer the questions below.

The United States and Brazil, where the currency is the real (pronounced *rey-al*), are trading partners. The United States is currently in a recession with high unemployment.

(a) Due to the recession, the United States is not investing in Brazil. How would a decline in U.S. investment affect the supply of the U.S. dollar in the foreign exchange market?

(b) How would the lack of investment affect the value of the U.S. dollar relative to Brazil's real?

(c) Assume the United States government engages in expansionary fiscal policy to decrease unemployment. Based on the eventual change in real gross domestic product, will the supply of U.S. dollars increase, decrease, or remain the same?

(d) Based on your answer in part (c), will the U.S. dollar appreciate, depreciate, or remain the same in relation to Brazil's real?

(e) Assume that to counteract the effect of the expansionary policy on Brazil's industry, the Brazilian government places a high tariff on imported goods. How will this tariff affect the value of the real?

THINK AS AN ECONOMIST: *DRAW AN ACCURATELY LABELED GRAPH TO REPRESENT CHANGING CONDITIONS IN AN ECONOMIC MARKET*

The supply and demand of money in the foreign exchange market reacts to market forces in similar ways to the supply and demand for goods or services. Economists use supply-demand curves to display the interaction of these two forces to set the equilibrium exchange rate. They can also use these curves to show changes in supply and demand that occur.

Apply the Skill

Consider the following situation. Priceyvania, a trading partner of the United States, is currently experiencing high inflation rates of about 20 percent a year. The government of Priceyvania prints more of the country's currency—the Pricey tag—to try to cover their citizens' increased demand for money. Draw a correctly labeled graph of the foreign exchange market showing the effect of Priceyvania's decision on the exchange rate of the Pricey tag versus the U.S. dollar. Use arrows to show the direction of changes. Label the axes and the demand curves appropriately.

Changes in the Foreign Exchange Market and Net Exports

Trade is the natural enemy of all violent passions. Trade loves moderation, delights in compromise, and is most careful to avoid anger. . . . [I]t makes them [people] inclined to liberty but disinclined to revolution.

Alexis de Tocqueville, French diplomat and political scientist (1805–1859)

Essential Question: How do changes in currency value affect net exports and aggregate demand?

Even in the foreign exchange market, supply and demand are the biggest determining factors of value. They influence export and import goods as well as currency appreciation and depreciation. A country's balance of payments reflects the demand for its goods and its demand for foreign goods. That balance impacts the value of the country's currency on the forex. A decline in the value of a country's currency makes a country's exports less expensive, which tends to increase net exports (and vice versa). These variations in the flexible exchange market influence the flow of goods and services between countries.

Net Exports and GDP

As you will recall, exports and imports are part of the formula for calculating a nation's GDP (gross domestic product). The most common way to calculate GDP is the expenditures method, which considers all investments, consumption of and spending on finished goods in a country (by both the private sector and government), and net exports. The formula for calculating GDP is:

$$GDP = C + I + G + (X - M)$$

- C = consumer spending on goods
- I = investment (or business) spending on goods like factories and equipment
- G = government spending on goods and service (i.e. Medicare, public works projects)
- X = exported goods to other countries
- M = imported goods from other countries

In this formula, (X – M) means total exports minus total imports—which is called **net exports**. A country's net export figure is used to calculate GDP. If a country exports more than it imports, that indicates the country has a **trade surplus**. A surplus creates economic growth because it means foreign demand is high, which means factories have to produce more goods and employment numbers are high to keep up with the demand. If a country buys more imported goods than it exports, that is called a **trade deficit**. A trade deficit means that demand for foreign goods is high, which indicates that the domestic economy is strong and consumers and businesses are buying more foreign goods.

Ideally, a country tries to strike a relative balance between exports and imports. This kind of balance suggests an economy is healthy and growing. If the net export number gets too high, it can indicate a weak domestic market or a surging foreign market. An exception to this is the United States: the U.S. trade deficit tends to get worse when the economy is strongest. The United States has had persistent trade deficits with countries like China, but because of its size and resources, it remains one of the most productive countries in the world. But in most countries, if the imports far outpace exports—creating a severe trade deficit—it will have a direct and downward effect on the country's foreign exchange rate. When a currency appreciates or depreciates, a country's imports and exports will react accordingly.

Net Exports and the Foreign Exchange Market

On the foreign exchange market, demand for a currency is inversely related to its value. This means that when a country's currency becomes cheaper to buy on the forex, the goods and services from that country are also cheaper to buy. And when goods and currency are cheaper, it will encourage foreign consumers and investors to buy more from that country. This increases exports from the country and increases imports to the foreign consumers' country. Necessarily, an increase in exports means an increase in supply, so the country's producers have to make more goods to keep up with the increased demand.

Supply on the foreign exchange market, however, works differently. Currency supply is directly related to the value of a currency. This means as a currency **appreciates** (rises in value), it becomes cheaper to buy foreign goods (imports), so the people who hold that currency will supply more of it to the forex so they can buy more foreign goods with their increased purchasing power. Because the foreign exchange market is binary—meaning two currencies are traded in relation to one another—if one currency appreciates, the other currency depreciates in relation to it. Think of it as a closed feedback loop where every action necessarily has a reaction.

Currency Appreciation The following example shows how this works. Assume the exchange rate between the United States and Mexico is 50 pesos to $1 dollar. A U.S. company makes a smartphone component that costs $10 domestically. Mexican manufacturers could import that component for 500 pesos (not including any shipping or tariffs costs). If the dollar appreciates against the peso—to 55 pesos per $1—the Mexican manufacturer could import that smartphone component for 550 pesos ($10 × 55). That is a 10 percent increase in cost to the Mexican manufacturer. They may look elsewhere for a cheaper price on that same component because, unlike fixed costs (such as wages), producers have flexibility on supply costs to save money and increase or preserve profits. So this appreciation of the U.S. dollar could ultimately reduce how competitive the U.S. export company can be in the Mexican market.

Currency Depreciation So what about when a currency **depreciates?** Assuming the same initial exchange rate—50 pesos to $1 dollar—imagine a different Mexican company that makes shorts and sells most of its product to the United States. A pair of shorts the exporter sends to the United States sells for $10, which means the Mexican company would make 500 pesos (again, not including shipping costs). If the peso depreciates to 55 per U.S. dollar, the exporter can sell the same shorts for about $9 and still receive the same amount of pesos (500). The 10 percent depreciation of the peso against the dollar makes the Mexican exporter more competitive in the U.S. market. The Mexican company can produce more shorts, which increases production to meet the increased demand.

You can see how this closed feedback loop works and impacts the forex currency rates and net exports. The dollar appreciating makes U.S. exports less competitive in Mexico, but it makes Mexican exports cheaper in the United States. The depreciation of the peso improves the competitive ability of short exports from Mexico but it makes the imports of U.S. smartphone components more expensive in Mexico.

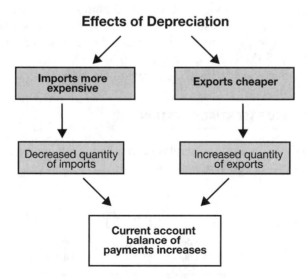

The closed feedback loop of imports and exports determines, and is determined by, the exchange rate between the two countries. If one currency appreciates, the other necessarily depreciates.

Net Exports and the Balance of Trade

As you have learned previously, demand plays a big role in a country's **balance of trade**, or net exports. If Spain has products that are in high demand around the world, Spain will export more goods and produce more of those goods to keep up with the demand. Net exports play a role in a country's balance of payments as well. The figure is calculated as part of the current accounts portion of the balance of payments. Depending on the economic situation of a country, the balance of trade—either a surplus or a deficit—can have a minimal effect or a damaging effect on the country's economy.

Trade deficits affect a smaller country, such as Haiti, more severely. Haiti is one of the poorest countries in the world. In 2018, it had a GDP of about 8 billion dollars, which is about 1/4 of the state of Vermont's GDP for that year. (Vermont has the smallest GDP of any U.S. state.) Haiti relies heavily on imports, and it has averaged a trade deficit of about $200 million a year. You can imagine how running a constant 2–3 percent trade deficit for years can take a toll on a small country's economy.

For a country like the United States, running a trade deficit in net exports is mitigated by the sheer mass and complexity of the total U.S. economy. Another factor is the fact that money consistently flows back into the country on account of the reliability of the U.S. dollar. In fact, the United States has run a trade deficit every year since 1976, meaning it imported more goods than it exported. During this period, the United States was the largest economy in the world with an active and reliable domestic consumer culture.

A main reason it ran a deficit during that period was because of the country's desire for oil imports, although the United States became a net exporter of oil after 2015. Another reason has to do with a combination of the movement of manufacturing jobs away from the United States to countries with lower prevailing wages and U.S. consumers' high demand for the low-cost consumer products made in these countries. But the trade deficit is mixed into a huge and robust economy, so the continual negative trade imbalance does not make a major impact when considering the entirety of U.S. economic activity.

ANSWER THE TOPIC ESSENTIAL QUESTION

1. In one to three paragraphs, explain how changes in currency value affect net exports and aggregate demand.

KEY TERMS

net exports	trade deficit	depreciates
trade surplus	appreciates	balance of trade

1. What is most likely to happen if the demand for U.S. exports rises and American consumers buy fewer imported goods?

   (A) The value of the dollar will appreciate.

   (B) The balance of payments will show a deficit.

   (C) The exchange rate for dollars will depreciate markedly.

   (D) The supply of goods will lag behind demand.

   (E) The value of foreign currencies against the dollar will depreciate.

2. When a nation's currency depreciates, which is the most likely result?

   (A) Imports will increase.

   (B) Nominal wages will increase.

   (C) Fewer people will buy dollars.

   (D) Import tariffs will be lifted.

   (E) Exports will increase.

3. Which best describes why a depreciating currency results in decreased imports?

   (A) Foreign countries take advantage of the depreciated currency to raise prices.

   (B) The weakened currency has less buying power in the foreign market.

   (C) It is too risky to buy the depreciated currency on the forex.

   (D) Tariffs make the price for foreign goods too expensive to import.

   (E) A country with a depreciated currency will try to reduce imports to avoid large trade deficits.

FREE-RESPONSE QUESTIONS

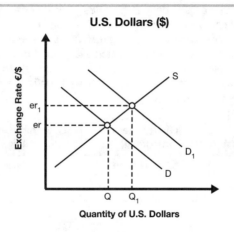

U.S. Dollars ($)

Quantity of U.S. Dollars

The graph shows the supply and demand curves for European exports and the forex rate for euros to U.S. dollars. Use the graph to answer the following:

(a) What does the D_1 line tell you about the demand for euros? What is the effect on the exchange rate for euros?

(b) What might have caused the change in demand for euros?

(c) With the change in the cost of euros, what do you expect will happen to net European exports to the United States? Why?

(d) Imagine aggregate demand increased once again even further to the right than D_1. How will that rightward shift ultimately affect European imports?

(e) Assuming aggregate demand increases once again from the D_1 line, explain how the European economy could react to adjust the value of its currency on the forex.

THINK AS AN ECONOMIST: *DETERMINE THE OUTCOME OF AN ECONOMIC SITUATION USING ECONOMIC MODELS*

Economists use models to analyze markets and explain the outcomes of economic situations. For example, economists note that market forces push a market toward equilibrium. When disequilibrium occurs, producers and consumers change their behavior until supply and demand meet at the market price again. This is true both on the microeconomic level, regarding individual firms and industries, and on the macroeconomic level, in terms of aggregate supply and demand.

Apply the Skill

As you have learned, one model economists use is the formula for calculating GDP. That formula is:

$$GDP = C + I + G + (X - M)$$

Net exports (exports minus imports, or X – M in the formula) thus form a part of GDP. A country that runs a trade deficit, then, has a negative value as part of its GDP calculation, which, of course, drags GDP down. Generally, economists say that a country that runs trade deficits over the long run will have a weakened economy. Yet the United States, which has had a trade deficit every year since 1976, is not seen the same way. The chart below shows the figures used to calculate the U.S. GDP in 2018. Use that data and the formula to explain why U.S. trade deficits are less problematic than trade deficits for other countries.

C (Consumer spending on goods)	I (Investment spending)	G (Government spending)	X – IM (Net exports)
$14,188 billion	$3,766 billion	$3,569 billion	−$659 billion

Source: Federal Reserve Bank of St. Louis

Real Interest Rates and International Capital Flows

It is not by augmenting the capital of the country, but by rendering a greater part of that capital active and productive than would otherwise be so, that the most judicious operations of banking can increase the industry of the country.

Scottish political economist Adam Smith, *The Wealth of Nations* (1776)

Essential Question: How do differences in the real interest rate affect capital flows, foreign exchange markets, and loanable funds markets?

No matter where you live on this planet, seemingly arcane macroeconomic concepts like real interest rates and capital flows probably affect your life whether you are aware of it or not. Technology has made the world small, metaphorically. Hence, investors anywhere, from Peru to Malaysia, can invest anywhere, from Sweden to Kenya. The easy flow of investment capital across the globe has created remarkable opportunities for consumers, businesses, and governments on all continents. And as with most things in a global economy, there are some resultant trade-offs in such an open market world economy.

Real Interest Rates

As you will recall from Topic 4.2, interest rates take two forms: nominal and real interest rates. The **nominal interest rate** is what most people think of when they think of or hear about an interest rate on a loan. Nominal rates are in dollar terms. A car dealership might offer a 3 percent interest rate on financing a new car. A bank loan may offer a 4.5 percent interest rate. This means that if you finance something like a new car, you will pay 3 percent for the loan—$3 of interest on every $100 dollars—over the course of the loan. The **real interest rate** differs from the nominal rate in that it accounts for inflation (which the nominal rate does not). This gives the borrower or investor a more precise gauge of their money's buying power. The formula for calculating the real interest rate is:

Nominal interest rate – Inflation rate = Real interest rate

For example, if the nominal rate on a car loan is 3 percent and the rate of inflation is 5 percent, the real interest rate the consumer/investor is paying is −2 percent, which means she is paying back the loan with money that has a lower "real" value. In other words, her money has more payment power when inflation is higher. The opposite is true as well: if the loan rate is 3 percent and the inflation rate is 2 percent, then the real interest rate is 1 percent—which is an advantage to the lender because the borrower is paying the loan with money that has a higher "real" value.

These real interest rates apply to international trade and investment as well. If you are looking for a place to put some savings money or to make an investment, you are going to look for the places where the interest rates being paid are highest. In today's world of **open economies**—countries that freely trade most goods, services, and investments with few tariffs or other barriers—people, businesses, and governments can invest their money all over the world. And financial capital will always flow to the countries with the higher interest rates and out of countries with lower rates.

International Capital Flows

Because of how integrated the global economy has become, one country's economic status can affect other countries' economies. **International capital flows** are the movement of monetary funds and financial capital between open economies. This is money that is invested in interest-bearing accounts and other assets around the world (i.e. stocks, bonds, etc.). They are part of the financial investments that are calculated in a country's capital account, which makes up part of the balance of payments. This type of international investment directly relates to the flow of money into a country and out of an economy.

Capital Inflow When investors buy domestic assets from another country, that is called **capital inflow** (or inbound capital flow). The country that sold the asset has money added into its national economy. If Germany has a real interest rate of 6 percent, and the rate in the United States is 4 percent, foreign investors looking for places to put their money will choose to invest in Germany rather than the United States. This is because they can get a better yield on their funds as a result of the higher interest rate. This would cause an inflow of financial capital into Germany. Investors in the United States would also respond to the higher German interest rate by selling their domestic, U.S. assets and investing in German assets. Remember: higher interest rates attract the most investment.

There is a caveat to this rule, however. The risks involved in investing in one country rather than another play a significant role. For example, in 2018, the central Asian country of Kyrgyzstan had a real interest rate of about 18 percent. In the United States, rates were about 2 percent, but thanks to programs such as the FDIC and the overall strength of the U.S. economy, investments are considered safer in the United States than in Kyrgyzstan. So investors often chose to invest in the United States rather than Kyrgyzstan. The inflow of money from around the world helps keep U.S. interest rates low. Again, the theory is right: higher interest rates attract the most investment—all other things being equal. But they are not equal.

Capital inflow has a number of positive effects on an economy:

- the capital account balance grows (possibly to a surplus)
- the domestic money supply increases
- more loanable funds become available
- the currency value goes up on the forex

All of this can contribute to increased investments in the country and, ultimately, a higher GDP. The capital inflow will impact the domestic economy by increasing domestic investment and spending, which will boost aggregate demand (AD), increase prices and incomes, and lower unemployment as more supply is needed to meet the higher demand.

Real Interest Rates and International Capital Flows

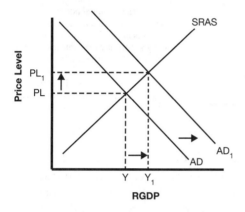

The increase in capital inflow positively affects a country's capital account balance, increases domestic money supply and available loanable funds, and raises the country's currency value on the forex. The result of this is an increase in aggregate demand (AD), higher prices, and most likely a drop in unemployment.

There is a trade-off that is negative that results from the positive effects of capital inflow.. A country's current account balance will usually drop because more consumers and businesses in the country can buy more imported goods from other countries. There will be inflationary pressure on the aggregate price level, which can mean the country's goods are more expensive to export (while imports remain cheaper) and can lead to a drop in net exports.

Capital Outflow When domestic investors invest their money in foreign assets, that is called **capital outflow** (or outbound capital flow) because money is moved out of the domestic economy. Using the Germany and United States example from above, the real interest rate of 4 percent in the United States, compared to Germany's 6-percent real rate, would cause U.S. investors to invest in Germany or other foreign countries offering higher rates. Capital outflow impacts an economy in some less-than-positive ways:

- the capital account balance drops (possibly toward a deficit)
- the domestic money supply falls
- loanable funds available decreases
- the value of the currency drops on the forex

Capital outflow also reduces domestic investment, and when combined with the effects listed above, it can all lead to a drop in GDP. A country's current account balance will usually increase because fewer consumers and businesses can buy imported goods from other countries. As domestic investment decreases, there will be a drop in aggregate demand (AD), which means producers have to adapt their supplies downward. Price levels will also decrease. The effects of capital outflow are lower consumption levels, higher unemployment, and reduced wages.

Effect of Capital Outflow on GDP

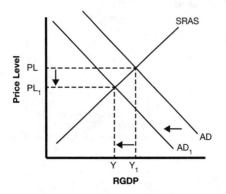

The increase in capital outflow negatively affects a country's capital account balance, decreases domestic money supply and available loanable funds, and lowers the country's currency value on the forex. The result of this is a decrease in aggregate demand (AD), lower prices, and most likely a rise in unemployment.

There are some positives that come with deflationary capital outflows. As mentioned, the aggregate price levels drop, exports to other countries are now cheaper, and the country's currency depreciates on the foreign market. This means imported goods into the country are more expensive, thus consumers buy fewer imported and more domestic goods. Net exports usually rise, which means the current account increases.

The Central Bank's Role One of the key roles of a country's central bank is maintaining economic stability. In the United States, the Federal Reserve serves as the central bank, and it engages in various efforts to meet that goal: oversight, enacting new federal monetary policies, production and distribution of U.S. currency, and providing the public with statistics and data about the economy are some of the Fed's responsibilities.

Central banks also influence capital flows through their reputation. Investors are more likely to invest their money in a county if they perceive the central bank as committed to well-established economic theories and independent of short-term political pressure.

Changes in real interest rates can play an important part in a country's capital inflow or outflow on the open market. If the central bank raises real interest rates, it can attract a lot of foreign investments. Conversely, if the central bank lowers real interest rates, foreign investors will look for higher rates elsewhere in the global market.

1. In one to three paragraphs, explain how differences in the real interest rate affect capital flows, foreign exchange markets, and loanable funds markets.

KEY TERMS

nominal interest rate
real interest rate
open economy

international capital flows
capital inflow
capital outflow

MULTIPLE-CHOICE QUESTIONS

1. Assume that the real interest rate in the United States is 3 percent and the real interest rate in Mexico is 1 percent. In which direction would capital flow move?

   (A) Capital flow would move from the United States to Mexico because Mexican investors would receive a better return on their investment.

   (B) Capital flow would move from Mexico to the United States because American investors would receive a better return on their investment.

   (C) Capital flow would move from the United States to Mexico because American investors would receive a better return on their investment.

   (D) Capital flow would move from Mexico to the United States because Mexican investors would receive a better return on their investment.

   (E) Capital flow would move from Mexico to the United States and create a trade surplus in Mexico.

2. Based on your answer to question 1, what would be the impact on the United States?

(A) Increasing the supply of loanable funds, increasing the real interest rate, and discouraging investment

(B) Increasing the supply of loanable funds, decreasing the real interest rate, and encouraging investment

(C) Increasing the supply of loanable funds, increasing the real interest rate, and encouraging investment

(D) Decreasing the supply of loanable funds, increasing the real interest rate, and discouraging investment

(E) Decreasing the supply of loanable funds, decreasing the real interest rate, and discouraging investment

3. What is the trade-off that results from an increase in capital flow?

(A) A decrease in net exports

(B) A decrease in aggregate supply

(C) A decrease in government expenditures

(D) A decrease in real gross domestic product

(E) A decrease in consumption

FREE-RESPONSE QUESTIONS

1. Use the following scenario to answer the free-response questions below.

A U.S. firm sells military planes to the government of Canada. Both have a 4 percent real interest rate at the time of the sale.

(a) In what way does the transaction affect Canada's aggregate demand? Explain.

(b) Assume that the real interest rate in the United States rises to 5 percent. Explain what effect this will have on the U.S. capital account?

(c) What is the effect of the change in real interest rate on the supply of the Canadian dollar?

(d) How will this change in the real interest rate affect the value of the Canadian dollar in the foreign exchange market?

(e) What is the effect of the sale of military airplanes on Canada's domestic investment?

THINK AS AN ECONOMIST: *DETERMINE THE EFFECTS OF CHANGES ON OTHER ECONOMIC MARKETS*

In trying to determine what economic policies to implement, government decision makers must consider the impact of policy changes on multiple markets. For example, they may consider an increase in tariffs with a trading partner in order to protect a particular industry. Those higher tariffs can have an impact on consumer spending, however. If the tariffs cover a wide range of products and are high enough, consumer spending could drop. That can have an impact on employment. Policy makers need to consider all possible ramifications of the policies they implement before moving forward.

Apply the Skill

The Federal Reserve has four tools to manage the money supply. In open-market operation, the Fed sells or buys government bonds. The second tool is to change the overnight interbank lending rate, which financial institutions use as the benchmark for their own interest rates. The Fed can change the reserve requirement for the nation's banking industry. Finally, the Fed can raise or lower the discount rate, the interest rate it charges for loans to banks.

Suppose that the nominal interest rate in the United States is 4.25 percent and the inflation rate is 3.7 percent. Investors are purchasing German and Japanese assets, as their real interest rate is 1.2 percent. Which tool or tools would the Fed use to attract more of those investors' funds to the U.S. dollar? What would be the effect of those actions on the following markets: (1) current account; (2) capital account; and (3) the foreign exchange market?

UNIT 6

Long Free-Response Question

1. The United States and Mexico are trading partners. Assume that both have a zero current account balance. The United States has low inflation, relative to that of Mexico, and is in a recession.

   (a) If real incomes in Mexico increase, indicate how each of the following would be affected:

      (i) The current account in the United States. Explain.

      (ii) The international value of the peso

   (b) Draw a correctly labeled foreign-exchange graph illustrating the change in the value of the U.S. dollar.

   (c) Now assume that to combat inflation, the central bank of Mexico sells bonds. What is the effect of the bond sales on each of the following:

      (i) Nominal interest rates in Mexico

      (ii) Mexico's capital account

   (d) Draw a correctly labeled aggregate demand and aggregate supply graph of the U.S. economy in its original state, then show the change you indicated in part (b). Label the long run Y_f and equilibrium price level and output PL_1 and Y_1 respectively. Then label the new equilibrium price level PL_2.

   (e) Now assume that the Mexican government engages in deficit spending. Using a correctly labeled graph of the loanable funds market, show the effect of the deficit spending.

   (f) Based on your answer in part (e), what is the effect on the business investment in Mexico?

   (g) Based on your answer in part (e), what is the effect on the international value of the peso relative to the U.S. dollar?

Practice Exam

1. When the Federal Reserve buys bonds on the open market, which of the following combinations occurs?

Money Supply	Aggregate Demand	Interest Rates
(A) Increase	Decrease	Decrease
(B) Increase	Increase	Decrease
(C) Decrease	Increase	Increase
(D) Decrease	Decrease	Remain the same
(E) Remain the same	Increase	Increase

2. Which is true of a bank's balance sheet?
   (A) Customers' deposits are listed as liabilities.
   (B) The total assets should exceed the total liabilities.
   (C) The bank's liabilities include loans and reserves.
   (D) A bank's balance sheet is used to keep track of outstanding loans.
   (E) Loans are listed as liabilities because they are money owed the bank.

3. Which of the following monetary policy tools would the Federal Reserve use to achieve a higher federal funds rate?
   (A) Increasing the excess reserves
   (B) Decreasing the required reserve ratio
   (C) Buying bonds on the open market
   (D) Selling bonds on the open market
   (E) Decreasing the discount rate

4. Sportz and Plai make tennis balls and golf clubs. With their resources, Plai can make 500 tennis rackets or 250 golf clubs and Sportz can make 150 tennis rackets and 50 golf clubs. If the terms of trade were such that 1 tennis racket could be traded for 4 golf clubs, who would specialize in making golf clubs and who would benefit from the terms of trade?

Specialize in Golf Clubs	Benefit from Terms of Trade
(A) Plai	Plai
(B) Plai	Sportz
(C) Sportz	Sportz
(D) Sportz	Both
(E) Sportz	Neither

5. Assume the United States is experiencing an inflationary gap. If no action is taken by the Federal Reserve or the government, what effect will the lack of policy change have on nominal wages and real output in the long run?

Nominal Wages	Real Output
(A) Increase	Decrease
(B) Increase	Increase
(C) Decrease	Stay the same
(D) Decrease	Increase
(E) Decrease	Decrease

6. Use the following table of economic figures below to calculate the gross domestic product of this country

Category	National Expenditures (in billions of dollars)
Personal Consumption	5,000
Government Expenditures	3,020
Gross Private Domestic Investment	2,200
Business taxes	635
Depreciation	400
Exports	150
Imports	-70

(A) $10,145   (D) $10,545

(B) $10,295   (E) $11,480

(C) $10,445

Use the graph below to answer questions 7–10.

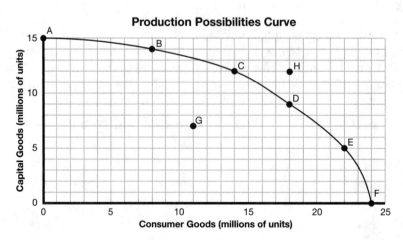

Production Possibilities Curve

Capital Goods (millions of units) vs Consumer Goods (millions of units)

7. Which of the following points on the graph represents the efficient use of a viable resource to produce both capital goods and consumer goods?
   (A) A
   (B) E
   (C) F
   (D) G
   (E) H

8. Which of the following points on the graph would be most likely to encourage long-term growth?
   (A) A
   (B) E
   (C) F
   (D) G
   (E) H

9. Assume the country's production possibilities curve shifted outward so that point H lies on the curve. This would most likely cause
   (A) an increase in aggregate demand
   (B) a decrease in aggregate demand
   (C) a decline in net exports
   (D) the long-run aggregate supply curve to shift to the right
   (E) the long run aggregate supply curve to shift to the left

10. What is the opportunity cost of moving production from point C to point D?
   (A) 2 million units of capital goods
   (B) 3 million units of capital goods
   (C) 5 million units of consumer goods
   (D) 7 million units of consumer goods
   (E) 7 million units of capital goods

11. If the nominal GDP in 2018 was $400 billion and the price index was 50, calculate the real gross domestic product.
   (A) $200 billion
   (B) $320 billion
   (C) $450 billion
   (D) $500 billion
   (E) $800 billion

12. Assume the United States and Australia are trading partners. The Federal Reserve, in trying to combat a recession, increases the money supply by purchasing bonds on the open market. How will this affect the price level in the United States and the value of the Australian dollar relative to the United States dollar?

U.S. Price Level	Australian Dollar
(A) Increase	Appreciate
(B) Increase	Depreciate
(C) Decrease	Appreciate
(D) Decrease	Depreciate
(E) Decrease	No change

13. Which fiscal policy is most likely to encourage spending by consumers and businesses?

    (A) Increasing the money supply
    (B) Lowering the discount rate
    (C) Cutting taxes
    (D) Raising the discount rate
    (E) Cutting government spending

14. Which of the following changes would most likely shift the short-run Phillips curve to the left?

    (A) A purchase of bonds on the open market
    (B) An increase in government expenditures
    (C) An increase in personal income taxes
    (D) A decrease in government business regulation
    (E) A decrease in the discount rate

15. Raising interest rates, an increasing the reserve requirement, and raising personal income taxes are all examples of

    (A) fiscal policy
    (B) monetary policy
    (C) policies to address a recessionary gap
    (D) policies to address an inflationary gap
    (E) price level stabilization policy

16. When the government operates in a budget deficit, what might be the effect on gross private domestic investment and the supply of loanable funds?

	Investment	Supply of Loanable Funds
(A)	Increase	Increase
(B)	Increase	Decrease
(C)	Decrease	Remain the same
(D)	Decrease	Increase
(E)	Decrease	Decrease

17. If a given loan has an interest rate of 10 percent and the inflation rate is 4 percent, what is the real interest rate?

(A) 10 percent

(B) 7 percent

(C) 6 percent

(D) 5 percent

(E) 4 percent

18. What effect would a decrease in business taxes have on real income and employment?

	Real Income	Employment
(A)	Decrease	Decrease
(B)	Decrease	Increase
(C)	No change	Increase
(D)	Increase	Decrease
(E)	Increase	Increase

19. Large numbers of foreign investors move their investment money from the United States to Britain because Britain is offering higher interest rates. Which of the following is most likely to result from this move?

(A) Real interest rates in the United States will fall.

(B) The value of the British pound will appreciate in relation to the United States dollar.

(C) The value of the United States dollar will appreciate in relation to the British pound.

(D) Britain's current account will increase.

(E) Britain's capital account balance will decrease.

20. Who of the following would be considered unemployed?
    (A) A glass blower who was laid off and has not applied for a job in three years
    (B) A computer consultant who left his job to begin a new business
    (C) A college student who just graduated from college and is looking for a position in their field
    (D) A person who lost their job due to the recent recession but has given up looking for a position
    (E) An older man who quit his job to care for his elderly parents

21. Aggregate demand would increase given which of the following Federal Reserve actions?
    (A) An increase in the discount rate
    (B) An increase in government spending
    (C) A decrease in taxes
    (D) A decrease in the reserve requirement
    (E) An increase in the sale of bonds

22. Which of the following monetary policy actions is designed to address an inflationary gap?
    (A) Buying securities
    (B) Lowering the discount rate
    (C) Lowering reserve requirements
    (D) Reducing the money multiplier
    (E) Increasing reserve requirements

23. The town of Jasper Springs spent $6 million on new tennis courts for its park district sports teams. If the marginal propensity to consume is 0.9, what will be the maximum change in GDP?
    (A) $60 million
    (B) $54 million
    (C) $40 million
    (D) $33 million
    (E) $25 million

24. Angel accepts a new job where he will make $5,000 more per month than at his previous job. His marginal propensity to consume is 0.8. How much of his new income will Angel save?

(A) $1,000

(B) $2,000

(C) $2,500

(D) $3,000

(E) $4,000

Use the balance sheet below of Southwestern Bank to answer questions 25 and 26.

SOUTHWESTERN BANK

ASSETS			LIABILITIES
Loans	$110,000	Demand Deposits	$150,000
Reserves	$130,000	Owners' Equity	$ 90,000

25. Assuming that Southwestern Bank has a reserve requirement of 20 percent, what is the maximum amount of new loans this bank can disperse?

(A) $6,000

(B) $30,000

(C) $50,000

(D) $100,000

(E) $110,000

26. Edgar deposits $4,000 into his bank account at Southwestern Bank. What is the maximum change in the money supply from his deposit?

(A) $4,000

(B) $5,000

(C) $10,000

(D) $16,000

(E) $20,000

27. What is meant by the velocity of money?

(A) It is the speed with which the value of money changes.

(B) It is the speed with which a person spends money.

(C) It is the speed with which currency wears out and needs to be replaced.

(D) It is the amount of money created by the money multiplier effect.

(E) It is the number of times a unit of currency is used within a specified period of time.

The table below shows the labor statistics for a given country. Use this table to answer questions 28 and 29.

Population	95,000
Employed	81,000
Unemployed	9,000
Not in Labor Force	5,000

28. Given the information above, what is this country's unemployment rate?
   (A) 1.8 percent
   (B) 10.0 percent
   (C) 11.0 percent
   (D) 17.0 percent
   (E) 18.0 percent

29. Given the information in the table, what is the size of the labor force?
   (A) 5,000
   (B) 9,000
   (C) 81,000
   (D) 90,000
   (E) 95,000

30. What monetary policy is most likely to discourage interest-sensitive spending?
   (A) Increasing the money supply
   (B) Decreasing the discount rate
   (C) Increasing the discount rate
   (D) Decreasing taxes
   (E) Decreasing government spending

31. What effect will a decrease in government spending and an increase in taxes have on price level and employment?

	Price Level	Employment
(A)	Increase	Increase
(B)	Increase	No change
(C)	Increase	Decrease
(D)	Decrease	Increase
(E)	Decrease	Decrease

32. Which of the following can cause cost-push inflation?

 (A) An increase in raw material costs

 (B) A decrease in wages and salaries

 (C) A sharp drop in natural resource prices

 (D) Federal incentive programs for eco-friendly goods

 (E) A relaxation in federal regulations

33. Inflationary expectations would most likely decrease if there was

 (A) an increase in the costs of raw materials

 (B) an increase in the money supply

 (C) an increase in consumption

 (D) a decrease in imports

 (E) a decrease in the money supply

34. The table below shows the nominal GDP and the price index of an economy between 2018 and 2019. Given the information, indicate what change, if any, there was to real GDP.

	Nominal GDP	Price Index
2018	$60,000	200
2019	$69,000	230

 (A) Real GDP increased by 30 percent.

 (B) Real GDP decreased by 30 percent.

 (C) Real GDP increased by 1.15 percent.

 (D) Real GDP decreased by 1.15 percent.

 (E) There was no change to real GDP.

35. Country A has a nominal GDP of $1,800 and the money supply is $600. Calculate the velocity of money.

 (A) 10.0

 (B) 5.0

 (C) 3.0

 (D) 2.5

 (E) 0.3

36. If nominal wages decrease, which of the following would occur to the price level and unemployment in the long run?

Price Level	Unemployment
(A) Increase	Increase
(B) Increase	Stay the same
(C) Decrease	Increase
(D) Decrease	Decrease
(E) Stay the same	Increase

37. Which of the following is an example of structural unemployment?

(A) A candy worker is laid off due to new taffy-pulling machines.

(B) A teacher retires.

(C) A doctor sells his practice and moves to another state.

(D) A college student is out looking for her first job.

(E) A lifeguard's pool closes during the fall.

38. Assume the United States is experiencing a recessionary gap of $24 billion, and the marginal propensity to consume is 0.75. The government decides it is prudent to cut taxes. What is the minimum amount taxes should be cut to close the recessionary gap?

(A) $24 billion

(B) $20 billion

(C) $15 billion

(D) $8 billion

(E) $6 billion

39. Which of the following is an example of a contractionary fiscal policy?

(A) Selling bonds on the open market

(B) Increasing the reserve requirement

(C) Increasing personal taxes

(D) Increasing government spending

(E) Increasing the discount rate

40. Assume the exchange rate between the United States dollar (USD) and the Lebanese pound (LBP) began at 4 USD to 1 LBP. Later, it changed to 3 USD to 1 LBP. As a result of this change, if prices in both countries stayed the same,

(A) imports from Lebanon it would be 4 times cheaper to purchase

(B) imports from Lebanon would become more expensive as the United States dollar depreciates

(C) imports from Lebanon would become cheaper as the United States dollar depreciates

(D) imports from Lebanon would become more expensive as the United States dollar appreciates

(E) imports from Lebanon would become cheaper as the United States dollar appreciates

41. Contractionary monetary policy actions affect interest rates and business investment in which of the following ways?

	Interest Rates	Business Investment
(A)	Stay the same	Increase
(B)	Increase	Increase
(C)	Increase	Decrease
(D)	Decrease	Stay the same
(E)	Decrease	Increase

42. Country A and Country B can produce cars and computers with their given resources. Country A can produce 50 cars or 10 computers and Country B can produce 80 cars or 20 computers. Before specialization and trade, what is the domestic opportunity cost of producing 1 unit of cars in each country?

	Country A	Country B
(A)	1/5 computers	1/4 computers
(B)	1/5 computers	5 computers
(C)	1/5 computers	4 computers
(D)	1/4 computers	4 computers
(E)	1/4 computers	1/5 computers

43. Assume the United States decides to increase government spending by borrowing. What is the budget deficit's effect on the international value of U.S. dollar and on the U.S. balance of trade?

Value of the Dollar	Balance of Trade
(A) Depreciate	No change
(B) Depreciate	Toward deficit
(C) Depreciate	Toward surplus
(D) Appreciate	Toward deficit
(E) Appreciate	Toward surplus

44. The following table includes data for the country of Fredonia:

Year	Real Gross Domestic Product (in dollars)	Nominal Gross Domestic Product (in dollars)
2016	150 billion	43 billion
2017	180 billion	120 billion
2018	190 billion	190 billion
2019	200 billion	220 billion

Which of the following can be concluded from the data in the table?

(A) The economy was producing higher quality goods and services in 2019.

(B) The base year for the price index was 2016.

(C) The base year for the price index was 2017.

(D) The base year for the price index was 2018.

(E) The economy was experiencing deflation during all 4 years.

45. What results would reducing the income tax paid on interest earned from savings accounts have on the loanable funds market?

(A) It would increase the supply of loanable funds by raising the interest rate, which would discourage borrowers.

(B) It would increase the supply of loanable funds, lowering the interest rate and stimulating investment.

(C) It would decrease the supply of loanable funds, raising the interest rate, and discouraging borrowers.

(D) It would decrease the supply of loanable funds by lowering the interest rate and stimulating investment.

(E) It is impossible to determine the effect based on the information provided.

46. Which of the following would shift the aggregate demand curve to the right?

(A) An increase in personal taxes

(B) A decrease in government spending

(C) An increase in exports

(D) A decrease in consumption

(E) A decrease in the money supply

47. The GDP deflator differs from the consumer price index (CPI) in which of the following ways?

(A) The GDP deflator measures a market basket of goods and services over a year, and the CPI measures inflation.

(B) The CPI measures the price of goods purchased by consumers, and the GDP deflator measures the price of all goods and services in an economy.

(C) The CPI only measures inflation, while the GDP deflator measures inflation, deflation, and the cost of a market basket of goods.

(D) The GDP deflator only measures deflation, while the CPI measures inflation and deflation.

(E) The GDP deflator measures government expenditures, while the CPI measures exports and imports.

Use the graph to answer questions 48 and 49.

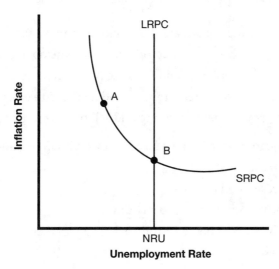

48. Which of the following would cause movement from point A to point B?
    (A) An increase in the price of oil
    (B) An increase in the discount rate
    (C) An increase in government spending
    (D) A decrease in personal taxes
    (E) An increase in the money supply

49. Which of the following would cause the SRPC to shift to the right?
    (A) An increase in the price of oil
    (B) An increase in the discount rate
    (C) An increase in government spending
    (D) A decrease in personal taxes
    (E) An increase in the money supply

50. Which of the following would increase the demand for money?
    (A) Lower inflation rate
    (B) Lower transfer costs
    (C) Higher incomes
    (D) Higher interest rate
    (E) Expectation of an increase in bond prices

51. Which of the following fiscal and monetary policies combined would most likely help bring a country out of a recession while keeping prices stable?
    (A) Increase business taxes and the discount rate.
    (B) Decrease business taxes and buy bonds on the open market.
    (C) Increase business taxes and increase personal taxes.
    (D) Increase the reserve requirement and decrease the discount rate.
    (E) Increase government spending and sell bonds on the open market.

52. Which of the following is considered a negative supply shock?
    (A) An increase in imports
    (B) A decrease in oil prices
    (C) An influx of immigrants to a country
    (D) A new hybrid car being introduced to the market
    (E) A drought

Use the graph to answer question 53–55.

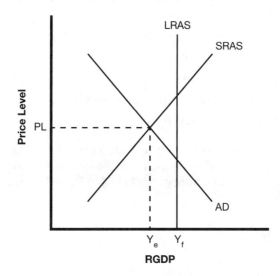

53. Which of the following solutions would likely close the ouput gap for the economy above?

(A) Decreasing the federal funds rate

(B) Increasing business taxes

(C) Increasing the reserve requirement

(D) Increasing sales of government bonds

(E) Increasing the discount rate

54. Assume the economy above has a gap of $400 billion and the marginal propensity to consume is 0.75. What is the minimum amount that the government should spend in order to close the gap?

(A) $100 billion

(B) $120 billion

(C) $150 billion

(D) $200 billion

(E) $400 billion

55. Given the output gap indicated in the graph, assume that no fiscal nor monetary policy is changed. What would happen in the long run?

(A) SRAS would shift to the right.

(B) SRAS would shift to the left.

(C) LRAS would shift to the right.

(D) AD would shift to the right.

(E) AD would shift to the left.

56. Which of the following monetary policies would encourage investment and increase output?

(A) An increase in the discount rate

(B) A decrease in personal income taxes

(C) A decrease in government spending

(D) A purchase of bonds on the open market

(E) An increase in the reserve requirement

57. Lee deposits $400 in his checking account at Southwestern Bank and there is a reserve requirement set by the Federal Reserve of 20 percent. As a result of his deposit, the money supply will increase by a maximum of

(A) $1,200

(B) $1,600

(C) $2,000

(D) $4,000

(E) $8,000

58. The United States and Britain are trading partners. Assume the Federal Reserve purchases bonds on the open market. What is the effect of this purchase on the nominal interest rate and on the value of the United States dollar relative to the British pound?

	Nominal Interest Rate	U.S. Dollar Value
(A)	Increase	Appreciate
(B)	Increase	Depreciate
(C)	Decrease	Appreciate
(D)	Decrease	Depreciate
(E)	No change	Appreciate

59. Assume that income levels in the United States increase. What effect would this have on money demand and bond prices?

	Money Demand	Bond Prices
(A)	Increase	Increase
(B)	Increase	Decrease
(C)	Increase	No change
(D)	Decrease	Decrease
(E)	Decrease	Increase

60. Which of the following will cause a decrease in output in the short run?

(A) An increase in government expenditures

(B) An increase in consumption

(C) An increase in wages

(D) An increase in productivity

(E) An increase in net exports

FREE RESPONSE QUESTIONS

1. Assume the United States economy is currently operating at above full employment with a real interest rate of 4 percent, an unemployment rate of 3 percent, and an inflation rate of 8 percent.

   (a) Draw a correctly labeled aggregate supply and aggregate demand graph and include each of the following:

      (i) Long-run aggregate supply labeled Y_f

      (ii) Equilibrium price level and output labeled PL_e and Y_e respectively

   (b) Draw a correctly labeled Phillips curve showing both the long-run and short-run Phillips curves utilizing the data given above to label the data point A.

   (c) Assume the output gap is $300 billion and marginal propensity to consume is 0.75. If the government decides to close the output gap using its ability to tax, by how much and in what direction would it change taxes? Show your work.

   (d) On your graph from part (a), show the effect of the change you indicated in part (c), labeling the new price level PL_1.

   (e) On your graph in part (b), show the effect of the change if no monetary nor fiscal policy action was taken and label this point B.

   (f) Instead of the government changing its fiscal policy, assume that the Federal Reserve steps in and takes action by attempting to alter interest rates. Identify an open market operation that would assist in eliminating the output gap. Explain your answer.

   (g) Uruguay, a trading partner of the United States, has a real interest rate of 4 percent and an inflation rate of 10 percent. Explain the effect of the Federal Reserve action on the following:

      (i) The demand for the U.S. dollar

      (ii) The value of the Uruguayan peso relative to the U.S. dollar

2. Assume the economy of Brazil, a longtime trading partner with the United States, is in long-run equilibrium with a zero current account balance. Brazil can produce 40 units of coffee or 10 units of cars with its given resources.

(a) Assuming a constant opportunity cost, draw a correctly labeled production possibilities curve depicting Brazil's economic trade-offs placing cars on the horizontal axis and computers on the vertical axis.

(b) Calculate the opportunity cost of 1 unit of coffee in Brazil.

(c) Assume there is an increase in exports of coffee to the United States from Brazil. Draw a correctly labeled aggregate supply and aggregate demand graph and include each of the following:

(i) Brazil's economy at its original point. Label the original price level PL_1 and output as Y_1.

(ii) The effect of the exports on its economy. Label the new equilibrium price level and output PL_2 and Y_2 respectively.

(d) What is the effect of the exports on Brazil's current account?

3. Use the following balance sheet to answer the questions below

First Hamilton Bank

Assets		Liabilities	
Required Reserves	$ 10,000	Demand Deposits	$100,000
Excess Reserves	$85,000	Owners Equity	$ 15,000
Loans	$20,000		

(a) Based on First Hamilton Bank's balance sheet, calculate the reserve requirement. Show your work.

(b) Assume the Federal Reserve purchases $4,000 worth of bonds from First Hamilton Bank. What is the dollar value of loans that this bank can now make?

(c) When this transaction occurs, what is the effect of the nominal interest rate and price of bonds on the open market?

(d) Cliff deposits $1,000 into his bank account at First Hamilton Bank. Calculate the maximum amount the money supply will change as a result of his deposit. Show your work.

(e) Assuming the excess reserves have not been lent out, what is the effect of Cliff's deposit on the real interest rate?

Index

Purchases of assets, 286

Q

Quality of life, 63
Quantity theory of money (QTM), 245

R

Rate of return, 174
Reaganomics, 277
Real exchange rate, 308
Real GDP, 86–87, 266
Real GDP per capita, 266
Real interest rate, 181
    calculation of, 321
    capital inflow, 322
    capital outflow, 323
    international capital flows and, 322–324
    open economies, 322
    role of central bank, 324
Real vs. Nominal GDP, 86
Recession
    budget deficits, 251–252
    COVID-19 pandemic financial crisis, 225
    definition, 91
    deflation, 178
    economic growth and, 267
    expansionary fiscal policy during, 154–155
    Great Recession of 2007–2009, 48
    gross domestic product and, 51
    Medicaid funds, 163
    negative demand shock during, 161
    phase in business cycle, 92
    reduction in reserve ratio, 209
Recessionary gap. *See also* Recession
    definition, 132, 145
    expansionary policy, 230–231
    Phillips curve and, 236
Recovery, 92
Rediscount rate, 209
Relative incomes, 296
Relative inflation, 296
Relative interest rates, 297
Representative money, 185
Required reserves, 195
Research and development, 275
Reserve account, 194
Reserve ratio, 195, 208–209
Reserve requirement, 195
Resource market, 53
Retaliatory policy, 310
Return on investment (ROI), 172
Ricardo, David, 8, 22

S

Salary, 184
Samuelson, Paul, 33
Savings and loan associations (S&Ls), 192
Scarcity, 3–7
    and choice, 4–5
Seasonal unemployment, 68
Securities, 172, 194, 229
Sell securities, 211
Services, 5
Shortage, 41
Short-run aggregate supply curve, 116
    changes in pricing, 117–118
    long-run curve shifts and, 125–126
    long-run macroeconomic equilibrium
        and, 132
    nominal wages, 117
    shifts in, 118–120
    sticky wages, 117
Short-run aggregate supply (SRAS), 115–120
    vs. long-run, 115–116
Short-run equilibrium aggregate output, 131
Short-run equilibrium aggregate price level, 131
Short-run macroeconomic equilibrium, 131
Short-run Phillips curve (SRPC), 238
Smith, Adam, 22, 27, 100
Smoot-Hawley Act (1930), 310
Social insurance programs, 151
Solar panels, 5
Soros, George, 40
Specialization, 22
Speculative demand for money, 200
Speculative motive, 200
Speculative risk, 173
Spending multiplier, 110
Stagflation, 138
Sticky wages, 117
Stocks, 172
Store of value, 185
Structural unemployment, 67
Supplemental Nutrition Assistance
    Program (SNAP), 162
Supply, 33
    change in technology, 34
    determinants, 33–35
    equilibrium price, 40
    government policies, 35
    in the loanable funds market, 217–218
    law of, 33
    market imbalances, 41
    number of producers, 34
    price of resources, 34
    prices of related goods or services, 34